Bridge Conventions Complete

AMALYA KEARSE

HART PUBLISHING COMPANY, INC.

NEW YORK CITY

COPYRIGHT © 1975

HART PUBLISHING COMPANY, INC., NEW YORK, N.Y. 10012
ISBN NO. 08055-1134-2 (paperback 08055-0191-6)
LIBRARY OF CONGRESS CATALOG CARD NO. 74-79940

MANUFACTURED IN THE UNITED STATES OF AMERICA

Contents

Chapter II

RESPONSES AND REBIDS AFTER NATURAL OPENING BIDS IN A SUIT

4

Chapter III

FORCING OPENING BIDS AND RESPONSES

Chapter IV 283

MAKING INQUIRIES

Chapter V 403

COMPETITIVE BIDDING

Chapter VI   513

TWO- AND THREE-SUITED OPENING BIDS

Chapter VII   545

OFFENSIVE PREEMPTIVE CONVENTIONS

Chapter VIII 555

CONVENTIONS FOR THE DEFENDERS

CLASSIFICATION OF CONVENTIONS

Effective April, 1974

ACBL regulations relating to systems, conventions, treatments and alerts apply (are mandatory) only to tournaments as opposed to club or Unit club-type games. The following games held in clubs are subject to regulations:

Districtwide games and Unitwide games—Restrictions apply when master points are awarded overall for more than one location.

Events for which these Classifications are optional—Rating point games, Club tournaments, Club Charity events, Continentwide events, Unit championships, Unit charity events, District charity events, Membership games.

CLASS A

(Must be allowed in all local or higher-rated events except as noted above.)

Blackwood, and conventions to handle interference with Blackwood.
Gerber over NT.
Grand Slam Force.
Stayman Club response to NT.
Lightner Double.
Takeout Double.
Unusual Notrump (by an unpassed hand must be at two-level or higher).
SOS Redouble.
Cue-bid for strong takeout.

Two club opening, forcing, strong and artificial.
Two diamond negative response to forcing two club opening.
Two NT negative response to strong two opening bid.
Negative Doubles.

CLASS B

(Must be allowed in championship events with sectional or higher rating.)

Four NT slam conventions (Blackwood variations, San Francisco, etc.).
Four Club slam conventions (Gerber over suits, other variations, etc.).
Two NT over opponent's takeout double as a conventional raise.
Stayman diamond response to NT.
Takeout bids over opponent's pre-empts.
Transfers (Jacoby & Texas).
Gambling three NT (maximum one side stopper).
Over opponent's one NT opening: two clubs for majors; two clubs for minors, two diamonds for majors; better minor for major suit takeout.
One NT response to major forcing.
Defenses after opponents' conventional calls.
One club forcing.
One diamond artificial negative response to one club opening.
Two diamond artificial response to natural two club opening.
Second negative response after artificial forcing opening bid.

CLASS C

(Must be allowed in regional or higher-rated events.)

Asking bids (suit control and trump quality asking).

Flint (three diamonds or three clubs).
Jump to two NT or three NT as forcing raise.
Jump and double-jump shift to show forcing raise.
Cue-bid for light takeout or two-suit takeout.
Responsive doubles.
Conventional responses and rebids after weak two-bids.
Conventional responses to natural strong two-bids.
Checkback or delayed Stayman.
Astro.
Brozel.
Calls which by agreement reveal a psych.
Drury.
Flannery two diamond opening.
Impossible negative.

CLASS D

(Must be allowed in national championship events.)

Strong ace asking other than four clubs or four NT.
Other artificial responses and rebids after natural NT.
Two diamond openings: Roman, Schenken, Precision, Stayman, Mexican.
Flannery two hearts.
Double of three NT for lead of specified suit.
Negative Slam Double.
Opening two NT or higher for minors.
One NT overcall for takeout.
Balancing two clubs for takeout.
Competitive doubles.
Opening four clubs and four diamonds transfers.
Artificial and step responses to forcing opening bids.

Roman two suit jump overcalls.

Two club or two diamond opening (three suiter) at or near minimum opening.

CLASS E

(May be used only if approved in advance on Form 505 or approved by the Tournament Committee for extended team play.)

Herbert responses to takeout doubles and one bids.

Strong artificial one diamond opening bid.

Dynamic one NT openings.

TAM II two diamonds.

Two suit non-forcing two club opening.

CLASS F

(May not be authorized for use in other than extended team play —matches of 16 boards or more.)

Big Diamond System, Pro System, Lea System, Roman System.

Introduction

This is THE book about bridge conventions. I could have guaranteed that statement before I ever read it, because I know Amalya Kearse and the way she works. But more about her later.

What are bridge conventions and who needs to know about them? Duplicate tournament players, of course. But rubber bridge players, too, whether you play in clubs or only socially. It is a great mistake, and it could be an embarrassing one, to say "Oh, we only play a few conventions like Blackwood and Stayman, and I know those."

Do you really know them? If partner answers a 4 NT bid with 5 ♣, how many aces does he have? Did you know he might have all four? Or if partner bids a Stayman 2 ♣ over your opening bid of 1 NT, must you show any four-card major, even one like 5-4-3-2? And if you have two majors, which one should you bid first? And if you deny a major by rebidding 2 ♢, if partner then bids 2 ♡ or 2 ♠ are you required to bid again? Even the most widely used of all conventions may be booby-trapped unless you really understand them.

Blackwood, for example, has such variations as "Key-card" and "Baby Blackwood." "Stayman" is played both "forcing" and "non-forcing." Any time you play with a new partner, or against unfamiliar opponents, you will be at a disadvantage unless you know the answer to questions you might be too embarrassed even to ask.

Some commonly used conventions should be thoroughly understood by you so that you don't suddenly come up against an idea you haven't had time to become familiar with and have no idea how to play against. Some less common conventions are so useful that, if you aren't playing them, you should consider doing so.

More and more players are using 1 ♣ and 2 ♣ openings as their only forcing bids. More and more players are using weak two-bids—which aren't really so weak. Jump bids, which always used to be strong, are not always treated so today. Sometimes the original meaning of a bid has so changed that you would be playing a "convention" if you didn't use it in the new sense. Consider a takeout double as an extreme example. Originally, if you said "Double" it meant that you didn't think the opponent was going to be able to make his contract and therefore you were increasing the penalty he would have to pay if he fell short. Today, however, a takeout double, asking partner to make some bid, is much more common than a penalty double. The original meaning of the bid has become so changed that it has become unconventional and therefore its use is in itself a convention. You would have to announce it as a convention, for example, if you played all doubles for penalties.

These are some of the reasons why what Amalya Kearse has done in this book can be so valuable to you. Also, the way she has done it.

If you haven't already heard of Amalya Kearse, you soon will—either as a brilliant bridge player or a brilliant lawyer. Or both. She is the first black and the second woman ever to become a partner in a major Wall Street law firm—quite an achievement for a young woman in her early thirties. Her bridge career in the tournaments of both the American Contract Bridge League and the American Bridge Association has already been crowned with impressive victories and national titles, even though she is a relative newcomer to big-time bridge.

Thus, this book combines penetrating thought, clarity of

expression and the thoroughness of the kind of research that goes into the preparation of a difficult legal case. It is stripped of non-essentials. You won't find it cluttered with subjects like the "Stripe-tailed Ape" double. There is such a bid, but it isn't a convention, and even if it were you'd have little occasion to want to know more about it.

So, if an opponent says, "I play the XYZ convention" and you can't find it here, tell him to forget it. It doesn't matter if he claims he can explain it in a single sentence—like, "When I bid one heart it means I have exactly seven spades." If it isn't here, it isn't legal.

This book is a must for tournament players and a gold mine for players of all kinds. It is intelligently arranged; you can see what's available to meet situations you may be having trouble with, even if you don't already know the name of the convention you are looking for. And of course it is indexed so that you can find everything you need to know about conventions, both in bidding and in play. Turning a thorough reference work into a fascinating book is quite an accomplishment. Amalya has brought it off.

RICHARD L. FREY

Foreword

In bridge, bidding is a language used to help the partnership to determine where it is going on any given hand. Part of the language may be perfectly straightforward signposts, involving natural bids. Thus, "natural call" is defined by the American Contract Bridge League (ACBL) as a call that suggests itself as the final contract, without giving partner any additional information on the basis of which further action is to be taken. Notrump opening bids, non-forcing raises of partner's suit, and penalty doubles are all examples of natural calls.

Some of the bridge language carries nuances that are not apparent on the face of the words used, although the nuances are related to the call made. Thus, the ACBL defines as "treatments" calls that either indicate a desire to play in the denomination named, or promise or request values in the denomination named, but that also, by agreement, give or request information on which further action can be based. Forcing bids, for example, are treatments. Cue-bids that show or ask about length or high cards in the suit named are treatments.

Conventions, unlike natural calls and treatments, are coded messages. The ACBL defines conventions as calls that, by agreement rather than by logical inference, give or request information unrelated to the denomination named. Transfer bids, for example, are conventions. When decoded they convey a message about a suit other than the one named. Cue-bids that show length in suits other than the one named, are conventions.

Since conventions are largely artificial bids, their use is like asking for or giving directions in a foreign language. If both partners are not speaking the same language, the partnership is not likely to arrive at the right place. They may on occasion end up at a very pleasant spot, but more often than not they will miss their target.

Moreover, the language used by the partnership cannot be a secret language. The opponents are entitled to know the content of each message. They are entitled to know whether a bid contains a coded message; and they may ask the partner of the bidder whether a bid has certain nuances. If the explanation given is not the correct one, the opponents may be awarded redress. Or if the explanation was correct but the player who made the bid had misused the convention and was able to take advantage of the explanation to adjust for his misuse, the partnership may be penalized.

Thus it is essential that the partnership agree on what conventions it will use. And both members of the partnership must understand and remember exactly how the conventions operate, in order to arrive at their proper destination, and in order not to mislead their opponents en route.

The organization of this book is intended to be functional. The conventions described are grouped principally according to the types of hands they describe, or the types of information they seek, or the situations in which they may be used.

Some of the conventions described are more valuable than others. Certain of them may be used with great frequency. Some, such as Stayman and Jacoby Transfers, may be combined and coordinated to great advantage. Some others are extremely complex and highly artificial. If the appropriate circumstances for their use occur infrequently, the agreement to use them may be a bit like learning an entire foreign dialect for a region to be visited once every five years: they may well tax the memory to an extent not warranted by the benefits they produce.

I

Responses to Notrump Opening Bids

Most conventions used in response to opening bids in notrump seek to get the partnership out of notrump and into a suit contract. These conventions fall principally into two categories: first, those by which the responder asks the notrump opener to clarify the distribution of his hand, and second, those by which the responder describes his own hand and at the same time attempts to ensure that the notrump opener will be declarer.

STAYMAN

One of the most widely used conventions in the world is the Stayman convention. It is based on the premise dating back to the days of auction bridge, that after the bidding has been opened in notrump, if the opener and the responder each hold four cards in the same major suit, the hand is likely to fare better in that suit than in notrump.

Fundamentally, therefore, the Stayman convention is designed to allow the partnership to discover whether or not it has an eight-card major suit fit, and if so to escape from notrump into that suit. There are a number of variations and extensions of the Stayman convention designed for other purposes, such as making inquiries about the opener's stoppers for play in notrump, and probing for slam.

Some versions of Stayman, called "Two-Way Stayman," use both a two club response and a two diamond response to a one notrump opening as artificial bids, asking the opener for information about his major suit holdings. It should be recognized that any of these conventions deprives the partnership of the use of the two diamond bid in its natural sense, and blocks potential partnership escape from one notrump at the two level when the responder has a poor hand with a long diamond suit. In addition, use of the two diamond bid as a branch of the Stayman convention precludes its use as any other convention.

See NON-FORCING STAYMAN, FORCING STAYMAN, DOUBLE-BARRELED STAYMAN, SLAM TRY STAYMAN, STAYMAN FOR STOPPERS, STAYMAN OVER A TWO NOTRUMP OPENING, STAYMAN OVER A THREE NOTRUMP OPENING, SHARPLES, MURRAY, AUGUST, FLINT TWO DIAMONDS, WEISSBERGER. *See also* DELAYED STAYMAN, STAYMAN AFTER NOTRUMP OVERCALLS, STAYMAN OVER OPPONENT'S NOTRUMP OVERCALL, JACOBY TRANSFERS and FLINT.

NON-FORCING STAYMAN

In its simplest form the Stayman convention consists of a two club response to an opening bid of one notrump. If the responder holds four hearts or four spades, or four of each, and has enough high cards to invite a game, he bids two clubs. This two club bid asks the opener to bid a four card major suit if he has one, and to bid two diamonds if he has no four card major.

There is a division of opinion as to whether the opener should bid two hearts or two spades when he holds four cards in each major suit. There seems to be little on which to base a preference between the two bids. No matter which major suit opener rebids first, he will always have a chance to show his other major if his first bid did not uncover a fit.

The description of any form of the Stayman convention as "non-forcing" is somewhat misleading. Since the two-club bid has nothing to do with responder's club suit, that bid is always forcing on the opening bidder. The non-forcing aspect of this version of the Stayman convention refers to the fact that if, after the opener answers the two-club bid, the responder bids a new suit on the two level, the opener is not required to bid further.

Thus, using non-forcing Stayman, the following auction is permissible:

Opener	Responder
1 Notrump	2 ♣
2 ♡	2 ♠
Pass	

After the opener has answered the responder's Stayman inquiry, the responder has a variety of bids available to describe his hand. If he has bid two clubs with less than 8 points and a hand such as

♠ Q x x x　♡ J x x x　◇ J x x x　♣ x

he can, of course, pass opener's rebid. Responder can also invite game, force to game, or suggest slam.

Inviting Game

After opener's bid in response to two clubs, if responder makes any bid at the two level, his bid is not forcing, but invites game. For example, opposite a 16 to 18 point one notrump opening responder might hold either of the following hands:

[A]　♠ A J x x　♡ x x　◇ Q J x x　♣ x x x
[B]　♠ K Q x x x　♡ Q x x　◇ x x　♣ x x x

With Hand A, if the opener has bid either two diamonds or two hearts in response to the two club Stayman call, responder would rebid two notrump. This bid invites the opener to bid three notrump if he has a maximum hand. The strength that responder needs for this sequence is the same strength he would have needed to raise the one notrump opening directly to two notrump, i.e., 8 or 9 high card points.

If the responder held Hand B, he would rebid two spades over his partner's two diamond or two heart bid:

Opener	*Responder*
1 Notrump	2 ♣
2 ◇ or 2 ♡	2 ♠

By using this sequence the responder shows a stronger hand than he would if he had simply bid two spades directly over the one notrump opening.

The opener is invited to raise spades if he has support for the suit, and a maximum notrump opening. With a hand such as

♠ A x x   ♡ Q J x x   ◇ A K x x   ♣ K x

the opener would raise to three spades, allowing the responder to continue to game unless his previous bids were made with less than an 8-point hand.

If, in response to the two club bid, the opener has bid either two hearts or two spades, and the responder holds four or more cards in the suit bid by opener, responder can make his game try by raising opener's suit:

Opener	*Responder*
1 Notrump	2 ♣
2 ♡	3 ♡

Responder might hold a hand such as:

♠ x x x   ♡ A Q x x   ◇ Q x x x   ♣ x x

Forcing to Game

If the responder has a hand worth from 10 to about 14 points he is entitled to force the hand to game. If the opener's bid over two clubs has revealed that the partnership has an eight-card, or longer, major suit fit, the responder may raise to game in that major.

For example, if responder held:

♠ K Q x   ♡ A Q x x   ◇ x x   ♣ J x x x

he would raise a two heart bid by the opener to four hearts. If the opener has bid two diamonds or two spades instead of two hearts, responder would bid three notrump.

After the responder has started a Non-Forcing Stayman sequence with two clubs, if he bids a new major suit on the three level, his bid is forcing to game. Thus, the following sequences are forcing to game:

(A) *Opener*   *Responder*
     1 Notrump   2 ♣
     2 ◇   3 ♡

(B) *Opener*   *Responder*
     1 Notrump   2 ♣
     2 ♠   3 ♡

The three heart bid made by the responder in each of the above examples promises a five-card heart suit and sufficient values for game. Responder might have a hand such as:

♠ K x   ♡ A J x x x   ◇ Q x x   ♣ J x x

In the following auction, the meaning of the three club bid must be agreed upon:

(C) *Opener*   *Responder*
     1 Notrump   2 ♣
     2 ♡   3 ♣ (or 3 ◇)

Some partnerships treat the bid of three of a minor suit in such an auction as weak, and some treat it as strong. If the partnership is using the jumps to three of a minor suit directly in response to the notrump opening as weak bids the three club bid in example (C) should be considered to be forcing to game, and to carry some slam implications. Responder might have one of the following hands:

(D) ♠ x x   ♡ A x x   ◇ K x   ♣ A Q x x x x

(E) ♠ A x x   ♡ K J x x   ◇ x x   ♣ A Q x x

With Hand D the responder would bid three clubs as in auction (C), to make a mild slam try in clubs. With Hand E the responder would bid three clubs en route to showing his support for opener's heart suit, showing interest in a heart slam.

When the Opponents Interfere over the Notrump Opening

If an opponent has doubled the one notrump opening, a two club bid by the responder is not the Stayman convention. In this situation the two club bid, like any other bid at the two level, is an attempt to escape from a penalty, and shows a desire to play in the suit named. (*See* CONVENTIONS USED OVER AN OPPONENT'S DOUBLE OF A ONE NOTRUMP OPENING.)

If an opponent has overcalled over one notrump, the responder obviously cannot use two clubs as Stayman. He has several choices of action, depending on the nature of his hand. If responder has a weak hand, even with two four-card major suits, he will pass (just as he usually would have done had there been no interference).

If the responder has a hand with 7 or 8 points with a five-card major suit that can be shown at the two level over the overcall, he should bid it. Using standard methods, responder's bid on the two level is not forcing. However, a bid of a new suit on the three level would be forcing. Therefore, if the overcall prevents responder from bidding his suit at the two level, he must either pass or bid two notrump with his 7 or 8 point hand. For example, suppose responder has a hand such as:

♠ x x   ♡ K Q x x x   ♢ x x x   ♣ Q x x

If the notrump opening has been overcalled with two clubs or two diamonds, responder should bid two hearts. However, if the overcall was two spades, responder cannot bid three hearts because his hand is not strong enough; over the two spade overcall responder should bid two notrump. (*See also* LEBENSOHL CONVENTION.)

The two notrump bid by responder is also used when responder has any balanced hand with which he would have invited game without interference. The opener may rebid three notrump if he has a maximum notrump opening and a strong stopper in the suit of the overcall. Opener may, with a maximum, try out a four-card major suit on his way to game in notrump, in case responder has a hand such as:

♠ K J x x   ♡ Q 10 x x   ♢ 10 x   ♣ Q x x

If responder has a hand worth 9 points or better and has one or both four card major suits, he should cue-bid the suit of the overcall. This cue-bid takes the place of the Stayman two club convention, and opener is expected to show a four card major if he has one. For example, suppose North opens one notrump and East overcalls two hearts, and the North and South hands are:

(North) ♠ A K x x   ♡ Q x   ◇ A J x x   ♣ K x x

(South) ♠ Q x x x   ♡ 10 x x   ◇ K x   ♣ A x x x

The bidding should go:

North	East	South	West
1 Notrump	2 ♡	3 ♡	Pass
3 ♠	Pass	4 ♠	

The cue-bid of the overcall is forcing to game, since its use to search for a suit fit does not leave the partnership enough room to make a game try.

Bidding over Doubles of the Stayman Bid

If an opponent should double a Stayman bid for a club lead, the opener should bid normally unless he has reason to believe that the double has given the partnership an opportunity to extract a profitable penalty. For example, holding

[A] ♠ A Q x x   ♡ K x x   ◇ A Q 10 x   ♣ Q x

in the auction

North	East	South	West
1 Notrump	Pass	2 ♣	Double

the opener should make his normal rebid of two spades.

However, if his club and diamond holdings were reversed, and his hand were

[B] ♠ A Q x x   ♡ K x x   ◇ Q x   ♣ A Q 10 x

opener should redouble. The redouble conveys the message to

the responder that opener has a good four card club suit, and if responder is willing, he should play two clubs redoubled. Responder might hold one of the following hands:

[C] ♠ K x x x   ♡ Q J x x x   ◊ A x   ♣ x x

[D] ♠ K x x x   ♡ A x   ◊ x x x x   ♣ J x x

With Hand C responder would jump to three hearts over his partner's redouble, showing his interest in game and his disinclination to play in two clubs redoubled. With Hand D, responder would pass the redouble of two clubs. Two clubs redoubled might be the partnership's only makeable game.

If, over the double of two clubs, the opener has only three clubs, he should pass the double around to his partner. For example, if North held

[E] ♠ A Q x x   ♡ Q x   ◊ A Q x x   ♣ K x x

the bidding could start:

North	East	South	West
1 Notrump	Pass	2 ♣	Double
Pass			

If responder has a reasonably strong hand with four clubs, he can redouble for penalties and North can pass. If South has fewer than four clubs, he can bid a suit, over which North will reveal his own four card major suit. For example, South might hold either of the following hands:

[F] ♠ K x   ♡ A x x x x   ◊ J x   ♣ Q 10 x x

[G] ♠ K x x x   ♡ A x x x x   ◊ J x   ♣ x x

If responder held Hand F opposite opener's Hand E, the bidding could go:

North	East	South	West
1 Notrump	Pass	2 ♣	Double
Pass	Pass	Redouble	Pass
Pass	Pass		

If responder held Hand G, the bidding could go:

North	East	South	West
1 Notrump	Pass	2 ♣	Double
Pass	Pass	2 ♡	Pass
2 ♠	Pass	3 ♠	Pass
4 ♠	Pass	Pass	Pass

If responder has no five card suit to bid, he may bid two diamonds to repeat his request that opener show a four card major suit.

FORCING STAYMAN

Like Non-Forcing Stayman, Forcing Stayman is a two club bid in response to a one notrump opening which requests the notrump opener to bid a four-card major suit if he has one. If the opener has no four-card major he must bid two diamonds.

The mechanical difference between Forcing and Non-Forcing Stayman is that, using Forcing Stayman, the opening bidder is not allowed to let the bidding die below the two notrump level. Thus, using forcing Stayman, if the auction starts

Opener	Responder
1 Notrump	2 ♣
2 ♡	2 ♠

the responder's two spade bid is forcing, and the opening bidder is required to bid again. Holding three or four spades the opener would raise spades. Holding only two spades, the opener would bid notrump.

As is the case with Non-Forcing Stayman, the label "Forcing" Stayman is slightly misleading, because the responder is not forced to bid again over the opener's rebid in answer to two clubs. For example, suppose the responder held the following hand:

(A) ♠ x x x x   ♡ Q x x x   ◇ x x x x   ♣ x

If his partner opened the bidding one notrump, responder would bid two clubs, planning to pass whatever the opener rebid, two diamonds, two hearts, or two spades.

The advantage said to result from using Forcing Stayman is that it permits the partnership to explore game and slam possibilities at a low level without the risk that the bidding will die prematurely. Most experts, however, prefer Non-Forcing Stayman, on the theory that they would rather do their exploring at the three level with their good hands, in exchange for being able to rest in peace at the two level with poor hands.

The effect that an agreement to play Forcing Stayman has on the responder is that he must have either a hand such as (A) above, in which he has four cards in each suit that opener could rebid, or a hand worth eight or more points. Thus facing a one notrump opening with a hand such as

(B)　♠ A 10 x x x　♡ x x　♢ Q x x x　♣ x x

the responder should simply bid two spades. If he were to bid two clubs and the opener rebid either two diamonds or two hearts, responder would be too weak to bid two spades, because the opener is forced to bid again over two spades. The partnership could well be overboard in two notrump if the opener's hand were

♠ Q x　♡ K J x　♢ A x x　♣ A Q x x x

or overboard in three spades if opener's hand were

♠ K Q x　♡ Q J x x　♢ A J x　♣ K x x

The agreement to play forcing Stayman places a concealed responsibility on the notrump opener. While it is obvious that when the auction proceeds

Opener	Responder
1 Notrump	2 ♣
2 ♢ (or 2 ♡)	2 ♠

the opener must bid again, what is less apparent is that if the opener has a maximum for his one notrump opening, he must now either bid game or make a forcing bid. The reason is simply that responder may have only an 8-point hand. If he does, he will pass opener's bid of two notrump or three spades. Therefore, if opener has a hand strong enough for game opposite eight points, he must show it by bidding more than he is forced to bid.

Other game invitations and game forcing bids by the responder have the same meanings using Forcing Stayman as they have using Non-Forcing Stayman.

With respect to opponent interference, *see discussion under* NON-FORCING STAYMAN.

DOUBLE-BARRELED STAYMAN

The most prevalent form of Two-Way Stayman, known as Double-Barreled Stayman, is a combination of non-forcing Stayman and game-forcing Stayman. The two club response is used as non-forcing Stayman, and the two diamond response is used as game-forcing Stayman. Both bids start a search for a 4-4 major suit fit.

Using this modification of the Stayman convention the responder would simply bid two clubs with a hand containing one or both four card major suits, and fewer than ten high card points. For example, responder might hold:

♠ K x x x   ♡ K J x x   ◇ x x   ♣ x x x

The rebids by the opener and the responder after the two club call have the same meanings as they would in a Non-Forcing Stayman sequence, with the exception that all of responder's rebids are at best invitational. Responder, having started with a two club bid, has no bids available with which to force the opener to bid a game.

Holding a hand worth ten points or more, the responder will usually bid two diamonds over his partner's one notrump opening, although he is not required to do so.

For tactical reasons, the responder might elect to bid two clubs even with ten or more points, planning to jump to game at his next turn. For example, if responder held

♠ A J x x   ♡ x x x   ◇ x x   ♣ K Q x x

bidding two diamonds would give the responder's left-hand opponent the opportunity to double that bid, asking for a diamond lead. Since responder will be able to place the final contract over whatever his partner rebids, it is to his tactical advantage to start with two clubs rather than two diamonds.

The two diamond response commits the partnership irrevocably to game. Over two diamonds, the opener bids a four card major suit if he has one; he normally bids two notrump if he has no four card major suit. However, opener is allowed to bid three clubs or three diamonds over responder's two diamond bid, if he has a five card suit.

Since the partnership is forced to game when responder bids two diamonds, slam possibilities may be explored at the two- and three-levels; and opener should therefore view any jump by responder to game as denying slam interest.

SLAM-TRY STAYMAN

The Slam-Try version of Two-Way Stayman, like Double-Barreled Stayman, uses both the two club and two diamond responses to ask the opener whether or not he has a four card major suit. The principal difference is that the two diamond response immediately indicates that the responder has slam aspirations. A second difference is that the responder may start with the two club response, and later make a game-forcing bid, just as he can playing simple Forcing or Non-Forcing Stayman.

The use of the two diamond bid as an immediate slam try is intended to alleviate the responder's problems when he has a hand with which the partnership may have a slam if opener's hand is suitable, but with which the partnership may get too high over a standard slam try if the opener's hand is not suitable. The two diamond slam-try allows the partnership to explore slam possibilities at a level which does not put it in jeopardy.

In answer to the two diamond bid, the opener chooses one of a series of bids to describe his hand, specifying how many four card major suits he has, and if he has no four card major, whether he has a minimum or maximum hand.

The complete schedule of responses is as follows:

2 ♡ = Four hearts, fewer than four spades.

2 ♠ = Four spades, fewer than four hearts.

2 NT = No four card major, minimum strength.

3 ♣ = Four hearts and four spades.

3 ♢ = No four card major, maximum strength.

3 ♡ = Five card heart suit.

3 ♠ = Five card spade suit.

For example, suppose responder held the following hand:

[A]   ♠ A Q x x   ♡ K x   ◇ Q J x x x   ♣ K x

If the partnership were not using Slam-Try Stayman he would make his normal Stayman bid (two clubs with one-way Stayman, or two diamonds with Double-Barreled Stayman), and would then want to make a slam try either in spades or in notrump. If opener did not show a four card spade suit, the responder would want to jump to four notrump:

Opener	Responder
1 Notrump	2 ♣
2 ◇	4 Notrump

Responder's bid of four notrump invites the opener to bid a slam with a maximum one notrump opening. If the opener has a hand such as

[B]   ♠ K J x   ♡ Q x x   ◇ K x x   ♣ A Q J x

he would pass the four notrump bid, but the partnership will be in jeopardy at the four level if a heart is led.

Using Slam-Try Stayman, however, the responder need not jump to four notrump because he will already have made his slam try by bidding two diamonds. With Hand B, opener would rebid two notrump in answer to the responder's two diamond bid, showing no four card major suit, and a minimum one no-trump opening. Responder can settle into three notrump secure in the knowledge that he has already made his slam try, and that his partner knows it:

Opener	Responder
1 Notrump	2 ◇
2 Notrump	3 Notrump

Even if the opener's rebid does not reveal his point count, the partnership can avoid going beyond game. For instance:

(C)	Opener	Responder
	1 Notrump	2 ◇
	2 ♡	2 Notrump

(D)	Opener	Responder
	1 Notrump	2 ◇
	2 ♠	3 ♠

The responder's bid of two notrump in auction (C), and his bid of three spades in auction (D), show the equivalent strength of the standard jump to four notrump over a one notrump opening.

If responder held a hand such as

[E] ♠ A Q x x   ♡ K x   ◇ A J x x x   ♣ J x

and the auction proceeded as in (D) above, the partnership could do most of its cue bidding below the game level. If opener had a hand such as

[F] ♠ K x x x   ♡ A J x   ◇ Q x x   ♣ A Q x

opposite Hand E, the auction might proceed as follows:

Opener	Responder
1 Notrump	2 ◇
2 ♠	3 ♠
4 ♣	4 ◇
4 ♡	5 ♡
6 ♠

STAYMAN FOR STOPPERS

Two-Way Stayman may also be used in a way in which only the two club bid searches for a 4—4 major suit fit. The two diamond bid would then be used to discover whether the partnership has all of the suits sufficiently well stopped to play in notrump.

Using this variation of Two-Way Stayman, the responder would normally reserve his two diamond bid for a hand containing a singleton or a void, such as

[A]   ♠ x   ♡ A x x   ◇ K Q x x x   ♣ Q x x x

Responder's two diamond bid asks the notrump opener to bid whichever major suit he has guarded. Suits containing four cards headed by the queen, or three headed by the queen and ten, would be considered minimum sufficient stoppers. If the opener has both major suits guarded he should bid two notrump.

If the opener's rebid in answer to two diamonds is in responder's short suit, responder can settle for game in notrump if his hand is not in the slam range. If the opener does not have the responder's short suit stopped, responder can explore other game, or slam, possibilities.

Indeed, the opener's weakness opposite the responder's short suit strengthens the partnership's slam potential. Opener might have one of the following hands:

[B]   ♠ A Q x x   ♡ K J x   ◇ J x x   ♣ A J x

or

[C]   ♠ J x x   ♡ K Q x x   ◇ A x x x   ♣ A K

When the opener has Hand B opposite a hand in which the responder is short in spades, such as Hand A, there is probably

41

too much duplication of values to make slam a good proposition. However, when the opener has a hand such as that in [C] with few of its values wasted in the spade suit opposite the responder's singleton, the hands mesh well for slam, even with a total of only 28 high-card points.

When the partnership is using two diamonds to ask for stoppers, the two club Stayman bid can be used as it is used in either Forcing Stayman or Non-Forcing Stayman. In either event, unlike in Double-Barreled Stayman, the responder is able to create game forcing sequences after he has started with a two club response.

STAYMAN OVER A TWO NOTRUMP OPENING

The Stayman convention may be used over an opening bid of two notrump just as easily as it is over an opening bid of one notrump. In simple form, the Stayman bid over a two notrump opening is three clubs, and the responder should have a strong enough hand to play in three notrump if a major suit fit is not found.

In addition, there is at least one two-way variation of Stayman over two notrump openings that uses both the three club response and the three diamond response to ask the opener to bid a four card major suit if he has one. The difference between the three club bid and the three diamond bid is that the latter shows slam interest.*

For example, suppose the responder holds one of the following hands:

[A] ♠ Q x x x   ♡ K x x x   ◇ x x x   ♣ x x

[B] ♠ K Q x x   ♡ x   ◇ x x x x   ♣ A x x x

With Hand A the responder would bid three clubs, planning to raise a major suit rebid by the opener to four, or to bid three notrump if the opener denies holding a four card major. With Hand B, the responder can envision a possible slam if the opener has some holding such as:

---

*Some partnerships agree to reverse the meanings of the three club and three diamond bids. They prefer to reserve the three club bid as the bid which suggests slam interest, to give the partnership more room to explore when such interest exists.

[C] ♠ A 10 x x   ♡ A x x   ◇ A K x   ♣ K Q x

Therefore, with Hand B, if the partnership has agreed to use this version of Stayman, the responder would bid three diamonds in response to two notrump. Since this bid itself indicates responder's slam interest, responder has no need to make slam tries above the game level which could get the partnership overboard. Using this convention, the following auctions all carry slam implications because responder has started by bidding three diamonds:

(E)	*Opener*	*Responder*
	2 Notrump	3 ◇
	3 ♡	3 Notrump

(F)	*Opener*	*Responder*
	2 Notrump	3 ◇
	3 ♠	4 ♠

(G)	*Opener*	*Responder*
	2 Notrump	3 ◇
	3 ♡	3 ♠

After his first response of three diamonds, any rebid by the responder above the game level shows a hand stronger than that shown in (B) above. Such a bid would invite the opener to bid a slam even with a minimum in high cards, if it is a minimum that is likely to mesh well with responder's hand. For example, responder might hold a hand such as:

[H] ♠ A x x x   ♡ K Q x x   ◇ x x   ♣ Q x x

With Hand H, responder would respond three diamonds to his

partner's two notrump opening, and raise opener's rebid, whatever it might be, one level beyond game. For example, either of the following auctions would be possible:

(J)	*Opener*	*Responder*
2 Notrump	3 ◊
3 ♠	5 ♠

(K)	*Opener*	*Responder*
2 Notrump	3 ◊
3 Notrump	4 Notrump

Suppose the opener held one of the following hands opposite his partner's slam try in auction (J):

[L]　♠ K Q x x　♡ A x x　◊ A Q x x　♣ A J

[M]　♠ Q J x x　♡ A x x　◊ K Q x　♣ A K J

Hands L and M both contain 20 high-card points. With Hand L, opener would carry on to six spades, on the theory that he could not possibly have a more suitable minimum hand. He has a good trump holding, he has aces, which are invaluable for a slam, and he has tenaces and a ruffing value.

Hand M, however, is not as good. Allowing for the responder to have a good 11-point hand, slam in spades might well be no better than on a finesse, and could be hopeless.

If the opener held one of the following hands opposite the responder's slam try in auction (K), he might drive on to slam in notrump:

[N]　♠ K Q x　♡ A J x　◊ A J 10 x　♣ A J x

[O]　♠ K x　♡ A J x　◊ A Q J x x　♣ A J 10

With either Hand N or Hand O, the opener would bid six notrump. Hand N will supply fillers for whichever major suit the responder holds. Hand O has a source of tricks of its own.

The agreement to use two-way Stayman over two notrump opening bids requires the partnership to give up the natural use of the three diamond response or other artificial uses of that bid, such as Flint and Jacoby Transfers. Both the Flint and the Jacoby Transfer conventions allow the partnership to rest in three of a major suit after the bidding has been opened with two notrump. To compensate for the loss of the use of these conventions, it is possible to treat the responder's immediate bid of three of a major suit as not forcing:

Opener	Responder
2 Notrump	3 ♡ or 3 ♠
	(not forcing)

This treatment, in turn, may prevent the responder from showing a five card major suit with a game-going hand, and thus from giving the opener a choice of whether to bid game in a major suit rather than in notrump.

For example, suppose responder holds:

[P]　♠ x x　　♡ Q 10 9 x x　　◇ K 10 x x　　♣ x x

If the partnership has agreed that an immediate bid of three hearts is not forcing, the responder must bid three clubs in response to the two notrump opening. If the opener rebids three spades, responder will be forced to sign off in three notrump, with no way to determine whether or not four hearts would be a better contract.

46

STAYMAN OVER A THREE NOTRUMP OPENING

The Stayman convention may also be used over opening bids of three notrump. The partnership should take care, however, to discuss whether the bid of four clubs in response to a three notrump opening is Stayman, or is instead the Gerber convention, asking for aces.

There is a great deal to be said for reserving the four club response to three notrump for use as Gerber, and using a response of four diamonds as Stayman. Use of the four diamond bid as Stayman does not in any way impair the opener's ability to respond in a four card major suit. The one drawback to using the four diamond bid as Stayman is that if the opener has no four card major suit, his response will be four notrump. If the responder has a five card heart suit and a poor hand he will not be able to show his suit over this rebid, whereas he might have been able to bid it if he had started with a four club Stayman bid. Of course, if the opener should rebid four spades, the heart suit would have been shut out no matter which suit was used as Stayman.

On balance, it is probably more valuable to use the four club bid as Gerber, giving the opener full room to show his aces, and to use four diamonds as Stayman.

SHARPLES

Responding to a one notrump opening with a hand containing one four card major suit and one or both four card minor suits may present responder with a problem. The Sharples convention is an extension of the Stayman convention that allows the responder to explore first the possibility of a four-four major suit fit, and then the possibility of a four-four minor suit fit.

The responder starts by responding two clubs, Stayman, to his partner's one notrump opening. If the opener does not rebid in responder's four card major suit, responder uses the Sharples convention by leaping to four of his minor suit. If the responder has both four card minors, he jumps to four clubs. The jump to the four level shows a hand at least strong enough to play in four notrump.

In the following sequence:

Opener	Responder
1 Notrump	2 ♣
2 ♡	4 ♣ or 4 ◇

responder might have a hand such as:

[A] ♠ K Q x x ♡ x ◇ A Q x x ♣ K J x x

or

[B] ♠ K Q x x ♡ x x ◇ A Q x x ♣ K J x

Responder would jump to four clubs on Hand A, and to four diamonds on Hand B. His four diamond bid denies a four card club suit.

The opening bidder is expected to raise the responder's suit if he has four card support. The opener may raise to the five level or to the six level, depending on the strength of his hand and the location of his high cards. A concentration of the opener's strength in the responder's suits would make his hand more attractive for a jump to slam.

If the opener lacks four card support for the suit that responder has bid at the four-level, opener should bid a new four card suit, if one remains in which responder has not yet denied holding four cards. Lacking such a suit, the opener rebids four notrump with a minimum hand, or five notrump with a maximum.

MURRAY TWO DIAMONDS

The Murray Two Diamond convention is a two diamond response to a one notrump opening that asks the opener to bid his longer major suit. The convention is designed to facilitate responder's bidding of weak, unbalanced hands containing 5—5 or 4—4 in the major suits. Responder might hold a hand such as:

♠ Q x x x x   ♥ J 10 x x x   ♦ x x   ♣ x

The opener is required to rebid his longer major. If he has equal length, he rebids two hearts. If he has no four card major suit, he bids a three card suit.

After the opener has bid two hearts or two spades, the responder will pass if he has a weak hand such as the one above. However, responder may have a strong hand such as:

♠ K J x x   ♥ A x x x   ♦ A J x x   ♣ x

In this event, he may bid two notrump, which requires the opener to bid three of his lowest ranking four card suit. This sequence allows the partnership to determine whether it has a four-four fit in any suit.

AUGUST TWO DIAMONDS

The August Two Diamond convention is similar to the Murray Two Diamond convention, but it is designed to help the responder bid a weak hand containing a four card major suit and a five card minor suit opposite a one notrump opening. The responder might hold a hand such as the following:

♠ Q x x x   ♡ x   ◇ x x x   ♣ K J x x x

As with the Murray convention, the August Two Diamond bid in response to a one notrump opening requires the opening bidder to rebid his longer major suit, or to rebid two hearts with major suits of equal length. If the opener's rebid is not in the major suit held by the responder, the latter will bid his five card minor suit. The minor suit bid is not encouraging, and the opener is required to pass.

If the partnership is using the August convention, the responder may show a hand containing two weak five card minor suits by bidding two clubs (Stayman, in theory) over one notrump, and then bidding three clubs over whatever the opener has rebid to two clubs. The opener will bid three diamonds if he has longer diamonds than clubs, otherwise he will pass.

This use of the two club bid does not impair the partnership's ability to use two clubs to locate its four-four major suit fits. However, it does preclude a strength-showing use of the three-club rebid by the responder.

FLINT TWO DIAMONDS

The Flint Two Diamond convention was designed primarily for use with weak notrump openings. This convention is forcing to three notrump or four of a minor suit, and on the way it searches out stoppers for notrump play.

The responder uses the Flint Two Diamond bid with one of two types of hands. He may have a hand containing a long solid minor suit, such as:

[A] ♠ x x   ♡ x x x   ◇ A K Q x x x   ♣ K x

Or he may have an unbalanced hand with at least four cards in each minor suit, such as:

[B] ♠ K Q x   ♡ x   ◇ A x x x x   ♣ Q x x x

Over the responder's Flint Two Diamond bid, the notrump opener rebids a four card major suit if he has one; otherwise he rebids two notrump. The responder then clarifies which type of hand he has, and at the same time probes for stoppers. If the responder's rebid is three of a minor suit, he shows a hand containing a solid minor suit, although not necessarily the suit he has just bid.

If the responder's solid suit is clubs, he will rebid three clubs; if his solid suit is diamonds, he would still bid three clubs if he had a hand such as [A] above, in which he had a club stopper. A three diamond bid by the responder, therefore, would show a solid diamond suit, and would deny a club stopper. With Hand A the auction would commence as follows:

Opener	Responder
1 Notrump	2 ♢
2 ♡, 2 ♠ or	
2 Notrump	3 ♣

After the responder has made a rebid that shows that he has a solid minor suit, the opener is required to bid three notrump if he has stoppers in all of the unbid suits. If he cannot stop the unbid suits he bids the lowest ranking unbid suit in which he has a stopper. Over opener's bid of a stopper, the responder can either bid three notrump if he now knows that the partnership has all suits stopped, or bid another stopper himself if he has one. If he is unable to do either, the responder must rebid his minor suit. Since this convention is not forcing past four of a minor, the responder should take care not to rebid just four of his suit if he has a game-going hand.

If the responder had a hand with both minor suits, such as Hand B above, he would bid three of a major suit over whatever the opener has bid in response to two clubs. Responder would bid the major suit in which he had the greater concentration of values. Thus with Hand B, the auction would be:

Opener	Responder
1 Notrump	2 ♢
2 ♡, 2 ♠ or	
2 Notrump	3 ♠

The opener now knows that he must have hearts well stopped in order to bid three notrump.

WEISSBERGER

A convention of little utility in the United States, the Weissberger convention was designed to complement a British-style
treatment of the Stayman convention, in which the responder's
jump rebid to three of a major suit is not forcing. In the United
States, the following auction would be forcing:

(A) *Opener*   *Responder*
     1 Notrump   2 ♣
     2 ◇   3 ♡ or 3 ♠

unless the partnership was using DOUBLE-BARRELED STAYMAN, in
which a two-diamond bid, forcing to game, also would ask the
opener to rebid a four card major suit if he had one.

When the sequence in (A) is not forcing, the Weissberger
convention helps the responder to bid hands worth about 10 to
14 points that contain either five spades and five hearts, or five
spades and four hearts, and hands worth 8 or 9 points that contain five spades and five hearts. The following would be typical
hands with which this convention would be used:

[B] ♠ K x x x x   ♡ A J x x   ◇ Q x   ♣ Q x

[C] ♠ A Q x x x   ♡ K Q x x x   ◇ x   ♣ x x

[D] ♠ K J x x x   ♡ Q x x x x   ◇ x x   ♣ x

The Weissberger convention is used after the responder has
tried a two club Stayman bid, and the opener has denied holding
a four card major suit. Weissberger is the three diamond bid in
the following auction:

(E) *Opener*   *Responder*
    1 Notrump   2 ♣
    2 ♦   3 ♦

The responder's three diamond bid promises a five card spade suit, and either four or five hearts. If the responder has only four hearts, he must have a hand worth ten or more points. Over three diamonds, the opener is expected to bid spades if he has three cards in that suit. If he has a maximum for his one notrump opening, he bids four spades. If he has only a minimum he bids just three spades, which the responder will raise to four if he has a game-going hand such as [B] or [C] above.

If the opener has only two spades with a minimum hand, he will bid his three card heart suit. If he has two spades, with a maximum, he bids three no trump. If the opener has bid three notrump over the Weissberger three diamond bid, the responder will correct to four hearts if he has either Hand C or Hand D above. If the opener has bid three hearts, however, showing a minimum notrump opening, the responder would bid three no-trump with Hand A, would bid four hearts with Hand B, and would pass with Hand C.

JACOBY TRANSFERS

Over the years, partnerships have learned that when one partner opens the bidding with one notrump, it is usually advantageous to have him be the declarer at whatever contract the partnership eventually reaches. The notrump bidder almost always has the stronger of the two hands. It is therefore better to have the opening lead come up to his high cards and tenaces, rather than through them. In addition, having the stronger hand concealed sometimes makes it more difficult for the opponents to defend accurately.

One convention designed to make the notrump opener the declarer as often as possible in responder's long major suit is the Jacoby Transfer Bid. (*See also* TEXAS TRANSFERS.)

When one partner opens the bidding with one notrump and the responder has five or more cards in a major suit he may make a Jacoby Transfer by making an artificial bid of two of the suit below the suit he actually holds. This bid requires the notrump bidder to bid the next suit—the suit actually held by the responder.

For example, opposite his partner's one notrump opening bid, the responder might hold:

    [A] ♠ K x   ♡ A 10 9 x x   ◊ A x x   ♣ x x x

or

    [B] ♠ Q J x x x   ♡ x x   ◊ x x x x   ♣ x x

Using a Jacoby Transfer, in [A] responder would bid two diamonds to show at least a five card heart suit and to ask the opener to bid two hearts. In [B], responder would bid two hearts to show at least a five card spade suit and to ask opener to bid two spades. The responder's bid of two diamonds in [A] says nothing about his diamond suit, and his bid of two hearts in [B] says nothing about his hearts.

After using the Jacoby transfer over the opener's one no-trump bid, the responder has a variety of options available to him depending on the strength and balance of his hand. If he has a very poor hand, such as that in [B], he may simply pass the opener's acceptance of the transfer. If responder has more than seven high card points, assuming that the opening notrump has shown 16 to 18 points, responder can invite game or force to game.

Inviting Game

If North has a middling hand of eight or nine points he may make a bid that invites the notrump bidder to bid a game. If the responder's hand is unbalanced, as, for example:

[A] ♠ x x   ♡ A 10 x x x   ◊ A x x x   ♣ x x

or

[B] ♠ x   ♡ A 10 x x x   ◊ A x x   ♣ x x x x

he should try for game by making a simple raise of his suit:

Opener	Responder
1 Notrump	2 ◊
2 ♡	3 ♡

By this sequence of bidding the responder has shown at least a five card heart suit, a singleton or two doubetons on the side, and eight or nine high card points. The opener is invited to bid game if he has a maximum one notrump opening of 17 or 18 points.

If the responder has eight or nine points, but his hand is

well balanced, that is 5-3-3-2, he can make his game try by bidding two notrump. This invites the notrump opener to bid four hearts with a maximum holding (17 or 18 points) and three or more hearts, or to bid three notrump with a maximum and a doubleton heart. The opener may decline the invitation by bidding three hearts or by passing two notrump.

Notice that whether the opener accepts or rejects the invitation, in either hearts or notrump, he will always be the declarer.

Forcing to Game

When the responder's hand is worth ten or more points he may force the hand to game. If he has a six-card suit he may simply bid game after his partner has accepted the transfer.

If the responder has a five card suit and either a singleton or two doubletons, and therefore a side suit of four or more cards, he may give the opener a choice of games by bidding his second suit. Thus, in the following auction:

Opener	Responder
1 Notrump	2 ♢
2 ♡	3 ♢

responder has shown at least five hearts and at least four diamonds. He gives the opener a choice of games in hearts, in diamonds, or in notrump.

The responder's three diamond bid should be treated as game forcing, so if the opener now bids just three hearts, the responder must bid again. Probably the responder should bid three notrump unless his hand is more unbalanced than he has indicated. If he has six hearts, he would bid four hearts; if he has five diamonds, he would bid four diamonds.

If the responder's ten point (or stronger) hand is balanced —5-3-3-2—he should make his game force by bidding three notrump. This gives the opener the option of passing if he has just two hearts, or of bidding four hearts if he has more than two.

Opener's Options

When the responder has made a transfer bid, the opener has an obligation to bid his partner's suit. On the great majority of hands, he will simply accept the transfer by bidding that suit at the two level. However, recognizing that with fewer than eight points the responder will pass the opener's acceptance of the transfer, opener may, if he has an especially good hand with a fit for his partner's suit, make his own game invitation.

Suppose the opener held:

♠ K J x x   ♡ A x   ◊ K Q x x   ♣ A x x

If responder transfers to spades over the one notrump opening, the opener should invite game on his own by jumping to three spades. Then the responder, with a hand such as:

♠ Q x x x x   ♡ x x x   ◊ A x x   ♣ x x

—a hand which would not have been strong enough to invite game—can bid the laydown four spade game over the opener's jump to three spades.

When the Opponents Interfere

Jacoby Transfers usually are not used after interference by an opponent. Therefore, if an opponent overcalls over the one notrump opening, any suit bid by the responder is a natural bid. For example, if the responder holds

♠ x x   ♡ Q J x x x   ◇ A x x   ♣ x x x

he would have bid two diamonds to transfer to hearts if there had been no interference. However, if his right hand opponent overcalls, the transfer may no longer be used, and responder should simply bid two hearts. Thus the auction might be:

North	East	South	West
1 Notrump	2 ♣	2 ♡	

While Jacoby Transfer bids are normally not used over doubles of one notrump, there are conventions that use transfers as well as other escapes over doubles. *See* CONVENTIONS OVER OPPONENT'S DOUBLE OF ONE NOTRUMP.

If an opponent has overcalled or doubled after the transfer has been made, for example:

North	East	South	West
1 Notrump	Pass	2 ◇	Double

the opener should not immediately accept the transfer unless he has at least three cards in his partner's suit. Opener may redouble if he has a reasonably good four-card holding in the suit doubled.

JACOBY OVER 2 NOTRUMP OPENINGS

Jacoby Transfers may also be used over opening bids of two notrump. The mechanism is the same, except, of course, that the transfer occurs at the three level rather than at the two level.

Opposite a two notrump opening showing 20 to 22 points, for example, the responder might hold any of the following hands:

[A] ♠ Q x x   ♡ K J x x x   ◇ x x   ♣ x x x

[B] ♠ Q x x   ♡ K J x x x x   ◇ x   ♣ x x x

[C] ♠ Q x x x x x   ♡ x x   ◇ x x x   ♣ x x

With Hand A, responder would bid three diamonds, transferring to three hearts. He would follow with a bid of three notrump, giving the opener a choice of games in notrump and hearts. With Hand B, the responder would bid three diamonds and raise the opener's bid of three hearts to four. With Hand C, the responder would bid three hearts, transferring to spades, and would pass his partner's three spade bid.

COORDINATING JACOBY TRANSFERS
WITH STAYMAN

An agreement to use Jacoby Transfers has a hidden benefit, because the transfers mesh quite well with the non-forcing Stayman convention. Use of this combination of conventions facilitates the responder's description of hands containing five cards in one major suit, and four or five cards in the other major suit.

Using Jacoby Transfers, the responder can transfer into his five card major suit and then either pass, invite game, or force to game. As a consequence, sequences in which the responder starts with a Stayman bid of two clubs and then rebids a major suit are no longer needed simply to show five cards in the major suit bid.

When Jacoby Transfers and Stayman are both in use, therefore, the auction

Opener	Responder
1 Notrump	2 ♣
2 ◇	2 ♡ or 2 ♠

can be used to show five cards in the major suit bid by responder, and four cards in the other major suit. The rebid of two of either major suit, as in the above sequence, is not forcing.

Likewise in the sequence

Opener	Responder
1 Notrump	2 ♣
2 ◇	3 ♡ or 3 ♠

the responder shows five cards in the major suit he bids, and four cards in the other major. The three-level bid of a major suit is forcing to game.

If the one notrump opener has three cards in his partner's bid suit, the hand should be played in that suit. If, instead, he has only two cards in the responder's bid suit, he will have three cards in the other major, in which the responder has four. The opener will then have to decide whether the hand should be played in the partnership's 5-2 fit, in its 4-3 fit, or in notrump.

Since the partnership is able to show five-four major suit distributions by starting with the two club Stayman bid, the responder can show that he has five cards in each major suit by transferring into one major and then bidding the other. For example:

(A) *Opener*   *Responder*
  1 Notrump   2 ♢ (transfer)
  2 ♡   2 ♠

By bidding two diamonds the responder has shown a five card heart suit. By next bidding two spades, he has shown, in addition, a five card spade suit. Similarly by using the sequence

(B) *Opener*   *Responder*
  1 Notrump   2 ♡ (transfer)
  2 ♠   3 ♡

the responder first shows a five card spade suit, and then a five card heart suit.

The choice between the sequences shown in (A) and (B) is determined by the strength of the responder's hand. If the responder has a hand that is poor in high cards, he chooses sequence (A), which permits the partnership to play in two spades if the opener has three spades. Sequence (B) shows a stronger hand since it commits the partnership to a higher level. Sequence (B) is forcing to game.

JACOBY FOR THE MINOR SUITS

There are a number of extensions of Jacoby Transfers that are designed to allow the responder to show a long minor suit holding. Two such extensions are described below.

Signing Off

When the responder hears his partner open the bidding with one notrump, and he holds a hand such as:

[A] ♠ x x   ♡ x x   ◇ Q x x   ♣ Q J x x x x

or

[B] ♠ K x x   ♡ x   ◇ J x x x x x x   ♣ x x

it is usually preferable to have the partnership play in three of responder's minor suit rather than in one notrump. To accomplish this it is possible to use a Jacoby-type transfer, in which a bid of two spades asks the opener to bid three clubs and a bid of three clubs asks him to bid three diamonds.

Using this Jacoby extension, the responder would bid two spades with Hand A:

(C)   *Opener*   *Responder*
       1 Notrump   2 ♠
       3 ♣   Pass

With Hand B, responder would bid three clubs:

(D)   *Opener*   *Responder*
       1 Notrump   3 ♣
       3 ◇   Pass

If in either auction (C) or auction (D), the responder had bid again rather than passing, he would have shown a much stronger hand than those set out in (A) and (B), and would have been indicating a mild interest in playing a slam in the suit into which he transferred.

Trying for Slam

An alternative use for the two spade bid is to make an immediate slam try in one or both minor suits. Using this type of variation of the Jacoby Transfer convention, which is also sometimes called minor-suit Stayman, the opener is asked to describe his hand. He is expected to bid a four card minor suit if he has one. If the opener has four cards in each minor suit, he may bid his better *major* suit over responder's two spade bid. Thus, in the auction

Opener	Responder
1 Notrump	2 ♠
3 ♡	

the opener might have a hand such as

[A]   ♠ J x   ♡ A Q x   ◇ K Q x x   ♣ A J x x

If the opening bidder has no four card minor suit he should bid notrump. A two notrump bid would encourage slam exploration, while a three notrump rebid would deny slam interest on opener's part.

One-Suited Slam Try

The factors to be considered in determining whether to encourage responder in exploring for slam, or to try to slow him down, depend on whether responder's two spade bid showed both minor suits or only one. If the partnership has agreed that responder may bid two spades on a hand containing just one long minor suit, rather than both, the opener should rebid two notrump with the maximum point count for his one notrump opening, and should bid three notrump with a minimum.

For example, the opener might hold either of the following hands:

[B] ♠ A K x x   ♡ 10 9 x   ◇ K J x   ♣ K Q x

[C] ♠ A K J   ♡ A K x x   ◇ K 9 x   ♣ 10 9 x

After the auction has begun with a two spade response to opener's one notrump bid, the opener would bid three notrump with Hand B, and would bid two notrump with Hand C. The responder's hand might be the following:

[D] ♠ x x   ♡ Q x   ◇ A Q x x x x   ♣ A x x

With responder holding Hand D opposite opener's Hand B, the auction would be:

Opener	Responder
1 Notrump	2 ♠
3 Notrump	Pass

If responder held Hand D opposite opener's Hand C, however, the auction could proceed as follows:

Opener	Responder
1 Notrump	2 ♠
2 Notrump	3 ♢ (slam try)
3 ♡ (cue bid)	3 Notrump
6 ♢	(not forcing)

Opener can reason that the responder must have the club suit well controlled, since he was willing to make a slam try without a solid diamond suit, and without the ace and king of hearts and without the ace and king of spades.

Two-Suited Slam Try

If the partnership has agreed that the two spade bid by responder promises at least five cards in one minor suit and at least four cards in the other minor, the opener's choice between the rebids of two notrump and three notrump, holding no four card minor suit, is determined by the location, rather than just the amount, of his high card strength. If his strength is concentrated in the major suits, he would bid three notrump, even with the maximum point count such as in Hand C above, to deny any interest in a slam. If the opener's high cards are instead concentrated in the minor suits, as in Hand B above, the opener should bid two notrump, leaving the partnership more room to probe for slam.

Over the opener's two notrump rebid, if the responder bids three hearts or three spades, he promises at most a singleton in the major suit he bids. If responder rebids four of the same major suit on the next round of the bidding, he shows a void in the suit he bids.

Responder's hand might be:

[E] ♠ x x   ♡ Q   ◇ A Q x x x   ♣ A x x x x

If responder holds Hand E opposite opener's Hand C,

[C] ♠ A K J   ♡ A K x x   ◇ K 9 x   ♣ 10 9 x

the auction would proceed:

Opener	Responder
1 Notrump	2 ♠
3 Notrump	Pass

If responder holds Hand E opposite opener's Hand B,

[B] ♠ A K x x   ♡ 10 9 x   ◇ K J x   ♣ K Q x

the partnership could well reach a slam by the following auction:

Opener	Responder
1 Notrump	2 ♠
2 Notrump	3 ♡ (singleton)
3 ♠ (cue bid)	4 ◇ (suit)
4 ♠ (cue bid)	6 ♣
6 ◇	

After bidding three hearts to show his singleton heart, responder proceeds to bid naturally. The responder knows from opener's two notrump bid that opener has several honor cards in the minor suits. From opener's three spade and four spade bids, respectively, responder knows that opener has the ace and king of spades. However, responder can infer that there is no point in

68

trying for a grand slam since opener apparently does not have the ace of hearts (because he would have bid four hearts to show that card in preference to bidding four spades to show the spade king), and if opener had the ace of hearts as well as the ace and king of spades, he could not have enough minor suit honors to solidify the responder's suits. Therefore, over the four spade cue bid by the opener, responder simply sets the level of the contract at six, and leaves it to opener to choose which minor suit to play in.

TWO NOTRUMP RESPONSE AS A RELAY TO THREE CLUBS

Some partnerships which use the two spade bid as a minor suit slam try use a bid of two notrump as a relay bid to enable the partnership to play in three of a minor suit. For these partnerships, a response of two notrump to a one notrump opening forces the opener to rebid three clubs. If the responder has a weak hand with a long club suit, he passes. If he has instead a weak hand with a long diamond suit, he bids three diamonds, which opener is required to pass.

Some partnerships also allow use of the relay when responder has a three-suited game-going hand with a singleton in one of the major suits. The responder shows this type of hand over opener's forced three club bid by bidding the suit of his singleton. For the auction

Opener	Responder
1 Notrump	2 Notrump
3 ♣	3 ♡

responder might hold, for example,

[A]   ♠ Q J x x   ♡ x   ◇ K x x x   ♣ A x x x

or

[B]   ♠ A Q x x   ♡ x   ◇ K x x   ♣ K Q x x x

The principal advantage of using the two notrump relay to permit escape into clubs or diamonds with weak hands is that it allows the partnership to use immediate jumps to three clubs or three diamonds directly over the one notrump opening as invitations to game. For a jump to three clubs, for example, responder might have

♠ x x   ♡ J x   ◇ x x x   ♣ A Q 10 x x x

The use of two notrump as a relay also means that the responder can no longer make a natural game invitation in notrump. Instead he must temporize with a two club Stayman bid, and then bid two notrump. Thus, the sequence

Opener	*Responder*
1 Notrump	2 ♣
2 ♡	2 Notrump

would not guarantee that responder had a four card spade suit, but only that he had enough high card points to try for game.

TEXAS TRANSFERS

Texas Transfers are designed to get the partnership to game in a major suit opposite a one notrump or two notrump opening bid, with the notrump bidder as declarer. The responder must have a major suit of six or more cards, and a hand suitable for game opposite the opening bid.

To make a Texas Transfer, the responder jumps to the four level in the suit below the suit he actually holds. Opposite opener's one notrump opening, for example, responder might hold:

[A] ♠ x   ♡ A Q J x x x x   ◇ x x   ♣ x x x
or
[B] ♠ K 10 9 x x x   ♡ K x x   ◇ x x x   ♣ x

Using a Texas Transfer with Hand A, responder would jump to four diamonds over one notrump, requiring his partner to bid four hearts. With Hand B, the responder would jump to four hearts, requiring the opener to bid four spades. The bid of four diamonds, as on Hand A, has nothing to do with the responder's diamond suit; and the bid of four hearts, as on Hand B, has nothing to do with his hearts.

When the Opponents Interfere

Some partnerships agree to use Texas Transfers even after interference by an opponent, provided the level of interference is not uncomfortably high. The simplest plan is to use Texas Transfers over overcalls through the three spade level, but to agree that if the overcall is made at the four level, all suit bids by the responder are natural.

For example, suppose the auction started as follows:

	North	East	South	West
(A)	*North*	*East*	*South*	*West*
	1 Notrump	2 ♢	4 ♡	

	North	East	South	West
(B)	*North*	*East*	*South*	*West*
	1 Notrump	4 ♣	4 ♡	

In Auction A, South's four heart bid would be a transfer to four spades. In Auction B, however, since the overcall was made at the four level, South's four heart bid would be natural.

COMBINING JACOBY TRANSFERS AND TEXAS TRANSFERS

The partnership's use of either Jacoby Transfers or Texas Transfers will enable the transfer of declarership to the strong hand. The value of agreeing to use both of these conventions is that the responder is given more leeway to describe his hand, and can create a variety of slam-going auctions.

When the partnership has agreed to use both Jacoby and Texas Transfers, the responder can use the four level transfer, Texas, to show a minimum game-going hand without slam interest. To show some slight slam interest the responder would transfer at the two level (Jacoby), and then jump to game.

For example, responder might hold either of the following hands facing a one notrump opening bid:

[A] ♠ x x   ♡ K J 10 x x x   ◇ A x x   ♣ x x

[B] ♠ K Q x x x x x   ♡ A J x   ◇ x x   ♣ x

With Hand A, responder wants to bid a game, but has no interest in slam. He would simply jump to four diamonds, requiring the opener to bid four hearts. Hand B, however, could produce a slam if the opener had a suitable hand such as

♠ A x x   ♡ K Q x x   ◇ K x   ♣ A x x x

To make a mild slam suggestion the responder can use the following sequence:

Opener	Responder
1 Notrump	2 ♡
2 ♠	4 ♠

Using this sequence to suggest slam interest has the additional benefit of keeping the level of the bidding low initially, so that the opener, if he had a maximum notrump opening and a good fit with responder's suit, could reveal this immediately by jumping to three spades over the two heart bid. It would then be the responder's responsibility not to content himself with a four spade bid, but to cue-bid towards slam.

Suppose now that the responder held one of the following hands opposite a one notrump opening bid:

[C] ♠ K Q J x x x x   ♡ x   ◇ K Q 10 x   ♣ x

[D] ♠ Q J x   ♡ K Q J x x x   ◇ A x   ♣ K x

With either Hand C or Hand D responder can visualize a slam if his partner has an appropriate hand. When he holds Hand C, responder simply wants to know how many aces his partner holds. When he holds Hand D, he wants to bid a slam if his partner has a maximum one notrump opening.

If the partnership is using both Jacoby and Texas Transfers, the responder will easily be able to find out whatever he needs to know after he transfers. Responder can use a bid of four notrump, after the Texas Transfer, as Blackwood, asking the notrump opener how many aces he has. If responder uses the Jacoby Transfer, he can follow with a bid of four notrump as a quantitative inquiry, rather than an ace-asking bid. Thus, in the auction

Opener	Responder
1 Notrump	4 ♡
4 ♠	4 Notrump

the 4 Notrump bid is Blackwood. This is the sequence that responder should adopt with Hand C. In the next auction,

Opener	Responder
1 Notrump	2 ◇
2 ♡	4 Notrump

the 4 Notrump bid simply asks the opener to bid six hearts with a 17 or 18 point notrump. This is the sequence that responder should use with Hand D.

If the partnership has agreed to use Jacoby Transfers, but not Texas Transfers, the responder will still have bids at his disposal enabling him to ask about the opener's aces, or to invite him to bid a slam with a maximum hand. The two level transfer followed by the jump to four notrump would still be responder's way of inviting the opener to bid slam with a maximum notrump. To ask about aces, responder would transfer at the two level and then jump to four clubs, which would be the Gerber convention.

The use of a Texas Transfer followed by the bid of four notrump is perhaps an improvement over the use of a Jacoby transfer followed by Gerber, for two reasons. First, if the opener has a good enough hand to jump in responder's suit, the four club bid will be ambiguous:

Opener	Responder
1 Notrump	2 ♡
3 ♠	4 ♣

In this sequence the four club bid could be either a cue bid or Gerber.

Second, even if the responder still has room to jump to four clubs, there may be more useful applications for that bid than just to ask for aces. If Texas is being used, for example, so that four clubs would not be needed to ask for aces, the jump to four clubs could be reserved to show a singleton club, as, for example, with Hand B above. *See* SPLINTER BIDS.

SOUTH AFRICAN TEXAS

There is a psychological danger in using the jump to four hearts as a Texas Transfer bid. The danger is that the notrump bidder will forget that the four heart bid is artificial, and will pass.

A modified version of the Texas Transfers that is designed to minimize this psychological danger is called South African Texas. The South African Texas convention uses a jump to four clubs to require the notrump opener to bid four hearts, and a jump to four diamonds to require the notrump opener to bid four spades.

Since neither jump to four of a minor suit is commonly used as a natural bid, South African Texas serves to jog the notrump opener's memory. The disadvantage of South African Texas is that it precludes the use of the jump to four clubs as the Gerber convention, to ask the notrump bidder how many aces he holds.

With respect to opponent interference, see discussion under TEXAS TRANSFERS.

FLINT

The Flint convention is designed to allow the partnership to play in three of a major suit after the bidding has been opened with two notrump. Unlike the Jacoby Transfer, which will also let the partnership play below the game level after a two notrump opening, the Flint convention does not always transfer declarership to the notrump opener.

Using the Flint convention as it is normally employed, the responder who has a long major suit bids three diamonds in response to his partner's two notrump opening. Over the three diamond bid, the opener is expected to bid three hearts. If the responder's long suit is hearts he will now simply pass; if instead he has a long spade suit, he will bid three spades over the opener's three heart bid. The opener is expected to pass responder's three spade rebid.

Getting to Game

Although the principal aim of the Flint convention is to provide the partnership with a means of stopping short of game, if the notrump opener has a suitable hand he may drive the hand to game anyway. To force to game, the opener should have a hand with which he can visualize a game opposite a hand little better than

> [A] ♠ x ♡ Q x x x x ◇ x x x ♣ x x x x
> or
> [B] ♠ J x x x x ♡ x x x ◇ x x ♣ x x x

Since the opener will not know at the time his partner bids three diamonds which major suit the responder holds, certain precautions may have to be taken to be sure the partnership arrives in game only when there is a good fit, and not when there is no fit. If the opener has the maximum for his two notrump bid and a good four card spade suit, it is safe for him to bid three hearts over three diamonds as he is expected to. If responder's suit is hearts, rather than spades, the partnership will have found its resting place. If responder's suit is spades, he will bid three spades over opener's three heart rebid; and with a hand such as

[C]   ♠ K Q x x   ♡ A x   ◇ A Q x x   ♣ A K x

opener will raise to four spades.

However, if the notrump opener has a maximum hand with a good four card heart suit, he cannot simply bid three hearts over three diamonds, for if this is responder's suit, responder will pass. Therefore, if opener has a hand such as

[D]   ♠ A x   ♡ A Q x x   ◇ K Q x   ♣ A K x x

he should bid three spades over responders' three diamond bid.

Thus, in the auction

Opener	*Responder*
2 Notrump	3 ◇
3 ♠	

opener's three spade bid shows a very fine hand containing four good hearts. If responder's suit is hearts, he will bid four hearts; if his suit is spades, he will pass.

If the opener has a maximum two notrump opening with four good hearts and four good spades, he is willing to play game in either major suit. To convey this message the generally prescribed bid is three notrump. Over the three notrump rebid the responder would simply bid four of his suit.

Strategically, however, the better bid to describe a maximum hand with four cards in each major suit is four hearts. If the responder is long in hearts he will pass; if his suit is spades he will bid four spades. The advantage of using the four heart rebid rather than the three notrump bid is that it will allow the stronger hand to be declarer fifty percent of the time.

Notice that except in the sequence just recommended, *i.e.*,

Opener	*Responder*
2 Notrump	3 ♢
4 ♡	Pass

whenever game is reached after the Flint three diamond bid has been used, the weaker hand becomes the declarer. This is the consequence of the original ambiguity of the three diamond bid, and of the maneuvering the opening bidder must do in order to ensure that game is reached if there is a fit, and avoided if there is no fit.

Showing Diamonds

Although the Flint convention deprives the three diamond bid of its potentially useful natural meaning, it is nevertheless possible for the responder to convey the information that he has a diamond suit. He does this by bidding three diamonds, and then making any rebid other than the minimum bid in a major suit. For example:

	Opener	*Responder*
(A)	2 Notrump	3 ♢
	3 ♡ or 3 ♠	3 Notrump

(B)   *Opener*   *Responder*
       2 Notrump   3 ♢
       3 ♡ or 3 ♠   4 ♣

In each of the above auctions the responder's three diamond bid has forced the opener to rebid a major suit, but the subsequent rebid by responder of three notrump in (A) and of four clubs in (B) deny long major suit holdings. These rebids show that responder instead has a genuine diamond suit, and suggests that he has interest in a slam.

FLINT THREE CLUBS

If the partners agree, it is also possible to use the Flint convention with three clubs, rather than three diamonds, as the conventional call. The three club bid requests the two notrump opener to bid three diamonds. This sequence allows the partnership to play in a contract of three diamonds, as well as three of a major suit.

If the responder has a long major suit, rather than diamonds, he simply bids three of his major suit over the opener's three diamond rebid. Thus any of the following auctions would be possible:

Opener	*Responder*
2 Notrump	3 ♣
3 ◇	Pass

Opener	*Responder*
2 Notrump	3 ♣
3 ◇	3 ♡ or 3 ♠
Pass	

Using the three club bid as the Flint convention means, of course, that the three club bid cannot be used as Stayman to ask the notrump opener if he has a four card major suit. To compensate, the bid of three diamonds would become the Stayman bid. Over this three diamond response, the notrump opener will bid his four card major suit if he has one, or will bid three notrump if he has no four card major.

GLADIATOR

The Gladiator convention is a system of responding to notrump opening bids that is designed to allow the partnership complete flexibility in exploring for slam, trying for game, or stopping at a low part score level. Gladiator is similar to the Flint three club convention, except that Gladiator may be used in response to one notrump, in which case two clubs is the conventional call.

Over the one notrump opening bid the responder's bid of two clubs requires the opener to bid two diamonds. Responder may pass if he has a long diamond suit and a poor hand. If responder bids the minimum number of any suit over opener's two diamond rebid, he shows a weak hand, and the opener should pass.

If the two club bid is used as Gladiator, a two diamond bid is used as a Stayman bid to inquire about the opener's major suit holdings. The two diamond response is forcing to game. The opener's rebids are two hearts with four hearts, two spades with four spades, two notrump with four of neither major suit, and three clubs with four of both.

A direct response of two of a major suit is forcing to game. Opener should raise responder's suit if he has three-card or better support, or bid two notrump without support.

Any jump by responder to the three level over one notrump invites a slam. Opener should raise or bid notrump depending on his fit and his slam interest.

CONOT TWO NOTRUMP

The Conot convention uses a response of two notrump to a one notrump opening bid to ask the opener to bid his longer minor suit. The convention is useful when the responder has a weak two-suiter in the minors, and wants to play in the partnership's better minor suit rather than in one notrump. In addition, the convention can help to uncover a duplication of values for slam purposes, or a duplication of weaknesses for notrump purposes.

The Conot Two Notrump response to one notrump requires the opener to bid three of his longer minor suit, or to bid three clubs if his minors are of equal length. If the responder has a weak hand, he will pass whatever the opener has rebid. Responder may also invite game in the partnership's minor suit by raising the opener's rebid to the four level.

If the responder rebids a major suit over the minor suit that the opener has rebid, he shows a singleton in that major suit. Suppose the opener has one of the following hands:

[A]   ♠ K Q J x   ♡ A x x   ◇ 10 x x   ♣ A Q x

[B]   ♠ K x x   ♡ K Q J x   ◇ Q x x   ♣ A Q x

[C]   ♠ A x x   ♡ A x   ◇ K J x x   ♣ K Q x x

In the auction

Opener	Responder
1 Notrump	2 Notrump
3 ♣	3 ♠

the responder has shown a singleton spade. With Hand A, the opener would bid three notrump, having sufficient spade strength

84

to play that contract opposite responder's singleton. With Hand B, the opener's spade stopper is more anaemic, and he would be better advised to bid four hearts, hoping to find his partner with a three-card heart suit. If responder had only two hearts, he could correct the contract by bidding five clubs. Responder might hold either of the following hands:

[D] ♠ x   ♡ A 10 x   ◇ K x x x x   ♣ K x x x

[E] ♠ x   ♡ A x   ◇ K J x x x   ♣ K x x x x

With Hand C above, the opener can envision a slam after responder has shown a singleton spade. His choice of bids is among (1) four diamonds, which is obviously forcing, but is slightly ambiguous as to whether it shows the ace of diamonds or a genuine suit; (2) four spades, cue bidding the ace; and (3) four notrump, Blackwood. Of the three possibilities, the four notrump bid is probably the least satisfactory on Hand C, since it becomes more difficult to explore for a grand slam.

When the Conot two Notrump response is being used, the partnership must find another way to invite game in notrump. The substitute most commonly employed is a non-forcing Stayman sequence:

Opener	Responder
1 Notrump	2 ♣
2 ◇, 2 ♡	
or 2 ♠	2 Notrump

This sequence would no longer promise a four card major suit in the responder's hand, but it would in any event invite game in notrump.

BOLAND

When the bidding proceeds

(A) *Opener*   *Responder*
    1 Notrump   4 Notrump
or

(B) *Opener*   *Responder*
    2 Notrump   4 Notrump

the responder's four notrump bid asks the opener to go on to slam if he has the top of his notrump bid. If the opener does not have the maximum number of high card points, he normally passes.

The Boland convention is used when the opener has better than a minimum notrump opening; it is a method of bidding designed to continue the slam exploration. If the opener has the middle of his notrump range—for example, 17 points using 16 to 18 notrumps, or 16 points using 15 to 17 point notrump openings, or 21 points using 20 to 22 point two notrump openings—the opener bids five of his lowest ranking biddable suit. If opener has no biddable suit he bids five notrump.

If opener has the maximum number of points for his notrump opening, he jumps to six of his lowest ranking biddable suit.

Over the Boland bid by the opener, the responder can raise if opener's bid has disclosed a fit for one of responder's suits, or responder can rebid a biddable four card suit of his own. The bidding of biddable suits up the line by both opener and responder allows the partnership to discover a fitting suit in which slam might be played, or discover that there is no such suit.

What is a "Biddable" Suit?

For the purpose of finding an appropriate trump suit in which to play a slam, a biddable suit is one not worse than four cards headed by the queen and jack. Bidding and raising only suits no worse than Q J x x insures the partnership against playing in a trump suit in which it is normally likely to lose more than one trick.

AUTOMATIC ACES

The Automatic Aces convention is one of the rare conventions in which the first artificial call is made by the notrump opener. The convention is used by the opener to indicate slam interest after a strength-showing three level response to an opening bid of one notrump or two notrump. For example:

(A) *Opener*   *Responder*
     1 Notrump   3 ♡

(B) *Opener*   *Responder*
     2 Notrump   3 ♠

If the opening bidder has no interest in slam, he simply raises his partner's suit to game if he has a fit, or rebids three notrump if there is no fit. If the opening bidder has a fit for the responder's suit and is interested in slam, he reveals this fit and interest by making a bid that tells the responder how many aces he holds. If the partnership is using strong notrumps, the opener must have at least two aces before he is allowed to show slam interest. If the partnership is using weak notrump openings, the opener needs only one ace in order to show slam interest.

The Automatic Aces convention requires the opener to show the number of aces he holds, in a series of steps excluding notrump, counting from the responder's bid as follows:

First suit step   = 2 aces
Second suit step = 3 aces
Third suit step   = 4 aces

Over a forcing jump to three clubs by the responder, for instance, a bid of three hearts, the second step, would show three aces. Over responder's jump to three hearts, the first step would be three spades, showing two aces, and the second step would be four clubs, showing three aces, etc. Since three notrump is the opener's proper rebid if he has no fit and no slam interest, that bid cannot be used as one of the steps to show aces.

Suppose the auction has started as in (A) above (1 Notrump—3 ♡), and the opener holds one of the following hands:

[C] ♠ K Q x x   ♡ K x x   ◇ A J x x   ♣ K x

[D] ♠ A x   ♡ Q x x x   ◇ A K x x   ♣ K x x

[E] ♠ A K Q x   ♡ A x x   ◇ Q J x   ♣ x x x

With Hand C the opener lacks the requisite two aces, and therefore rebids four hearts. With Hand D, opener would rebid three spades, showing his fit, his two aces, and his slam interest. With Hand E, the opener has a fit for responder's heart suit and has two aces, but he is not terribly interested in slam on account of his lack of control in two suits. With Hand E, therefore, opener would content himself with a four heart bid.

II

Responses and Rebids after a Natural Opening Bid in a Suit

A plurality of the conventions described in this Part fall into the category of strong trump raises. The fact that so many different ways have been devised to make strong trump raises is testimony to the difficulty of exchanging all of the information necessary for sound slam bidding.

The remainder of this Part is devoted to exploratory conventions that seek to solve a variety of problems, including how a responder who is a passed hand can show a fairly good hand without getting the partnership too high, how to show responding hands in the 17 to 18 point range that are normally difficult to describe, how to discover concealed 4-4 or 5-3 fits, and how to respond to weak two bids.

THREE NOTRUMP AS A STRONG MAJOR SUIT RAISE

In Standard American bidding the jump raise by the responder of his partner's opening bid is treated as a strong bid that is forcing to game. This raise normally shows at least four trumps and a hand worth 13 to 15 points.

When a partnership has agreed to treat the jump raise of a major suit opening bid as not forcing, it needs a replacement bid to show the type of hand on which the strong forcing raise would otherwise have been made. The most common replacement has been the response of three notrump. Using this convention and holding a hand such as

[A]　♠ K Q x x　♡ A x x　◇ K x x　♣ Q x x

the responder would bid three notrump in response to his partner's opening bid of one spade. The partnership is thus forced to game, and bids of other suits en route to four spades have the same meanings as they would have over a forcing raise to three spades.

Some partnerships have not adopted any bid to replace the forcing jump raise, but prefer to proceed by a series of forcing bids eventually ending in game. This procedure runs the risk of responder's misdescribing his hand to the opener. Holding Hand A opposite a one spade opening bid and having no immediate forcing trump raise available to him, the responder would be forced to make a temporizing bid on the two level before raising opener's suit. Certainly a two club response with Hand A does not reveal either responder's long suit or the location of his high card strength.

The use of the three notrump response as a strong raise

precludes the standard, natural use of this bid to show the equivalent of a notrump opening bid. The hands meriting a strong trump raise occur much more frequently, however, and on those rare occasions when the natural use of the three notrump call would have been made, the responder can instead make the temporizing bid on the two level before jumping to three notrump.

JACOBY TWO NOTRUMP

The Jacoby Two Notrump response to an opening bid of one of a major suit is a forcing raise, of unlimited strength. It does not indicate any desire on the responder's part to play the hand in notrump. Rather it supports the opener's suit and requests him to clarify the strength and distribution of his hand.

If the opener has a singleton, he is required to show it by bidding three of that suit. If the opener has a void, he bids four of his void suit. If the opener has no singletons or voids, he describes the strength of his hand. He bids four of his own suit if he has a minimum hand with no slam interest. He bids three of his suit if he has a strong hand, at least one king better than a minimum opening bid. He rebids three notrump if he has a sound opening bid of 14 or 15 points.

For example, the opener's and responder's hands might be:

(Opener)
♠ A x x x x   ♡ x   ◇ K Q x x   ♣ A x x

(Responder)
♠ K Q x x   ♡ x x x x   ◇ A J x   ♣ K x

Over a Jacoby Two Notrump response, the opener would bid three hearts, showing a singleton in that suit. Over three hearts it becomes safe for the responder to use Blackwood to check for aces. Discovering that the opener has two aces, responder reasons that the partnership is unlikely to be worse than a finesse away from slam. The complete auction might be:

Opener	Responder
1 ♠	2 Notrump
3 ♡	4 Notrump
5 ♡	6 ♠

If the responder is a passed hand, his jump to two notrump is not a Jacoby bid, but reverts to its standard meaning, i.e., a balanced notrump-type hand of just under opening strength.

SWISS

The Swiss convention, like the three notrump response as a forcing major suit raise, is used principally by partnerships which have agreed to use limit-jump major raises. Unlike the three notrump response, however, the Swiss convention also allows the responder to describe his hand more precisely in some respect agreed upon by the partnership.

The Swiss convention consists of a jump by responder to four clubs or four diamonds directly over a one heart or one spade opening bid. Both the four club bid and the four diamond bid show a balanced hand with 13 to 15 points and agree on the opener's suit as trumps. Neither bid has any meaning with respect to the responder's minor suit holdings.

The precise meaning of the jump to four clubs and the precise meaning of the jump to four diamonds depend on two factors: first, which ancillary feature (such as good trumps or good controls) the partnership has agreed that the Swiss bid will describe, and second, whether it is the four club bid or the four diamond bid that the partnership has agreed will promise the presence of that feature.

Some partnerships use the Swiss jumps to distinguish between raises made on sound trump suits and raises made on general values but mediocre trumps. Others use the convention to pinpoint hands rich in controls. Still others try to combine these two goals.

See TRUMP SWISS, CONTROL SWISS, TRUMP AND CONTROL SWISS and CONGLOMERATE MAJOR SUIT RAISES.

TRUMP SWISS

The Trump Swiss convention pays tribute to the need for a reasonably solid trump suit in order to make a slam. Holdings of A x x x opposite J x x x are fine for game contracts, but not good enough for slams.

When Trump Swiss is being used, the responder will jump to four clubs to show that his trumps are of high quality. Normally his four club bid will show at least four trumps headed by two of the top three honors, or five trumps headed by at least the ace or the king. For example, holding

♠ K x x   ♡ A Q x x   ◇ Q x x x   ♣ K x

the responder would raise opener's one heart bid to four clubs. With any hand worth a strong raise but not meeting these requirements in the trump suit, the responder would jump to four diamonds.

As hinted above, it is possible for the partnership to agree instead that the four diamond call will show the good trump holding and that the four club bid will show any other strong raise. In principle, however, it is normally more advantageous for the lower ranking response to show the stronger trump holding. This would give the partnership more room to explore slam where the responder's trump holding makes slam seem a more reasonable possibility.

CONTROL SWISS

It is also possible to use the jumps to four of a minor suit to distinguish between a responding hand that is rich in aces and kings and one that is filled with secondary values. When Control Swiss is being used, the responder will jump to four clubs whenever he holds three aces, or two aces and the king of the opener's suit. Lacking these controls as part of his strong raise, the responder will jump instead to four diamonds.

As is true with Trump Swiss, the partnership could agree instead to use the four diamond bid to show three controls, and the four club bid to show the general strength raise. Again, however, using the four club bid to show good controls allows the partnership more room for slam explorations when slam seems more likely.

The Control Swiss convention is most useful in arriving at slams that depend more on long suits and controls than on raw power. However, since there are other ways to determine what aces the partnership holds, Control Swiss seems less valuable than Trump Swiss.

TRUMP AND CONTROL SWISS

Some partnerships attempt to have the responder describe both the quality of his trumps and the possession of controls in a single bid. Using this version of the Swiss convention, a bid of four clubs would show good controls, and a bid of four diamonds would show strong trumps.

As might be expected of a compromise, however, neither the trump feature nor the control feature can be shown with as great accuracy as it can when both jumps to four of a minor are used to distinguish the quality of either feature alone. Thus, opposite a one heart opening bid, the Trump-and-Control Swiss convention is fine when the responder's hand is

[A] ♠ A Q x   ♡ K x x x   ◇ A x x x   ♣ x x
or
[B]   ♠ x x   ♡ K Q x x   ◇ K x x   ♣ A Q x x

With Hand A, the responder would bid four clubs, showing his three controls. With Hand B, he would bid four diamonds showing sound trumps. But the convention is less accurate if the responder holds

[C] ♠ A x x   ♡ K x x x   ◇ K Q x x   ♣ Q x
or
[D] ♠ A x x   ♡ K Q x x   ◇ A x x x   ♣ x x

With Hand C, neither four clubs nor four diamonds is appropriate, while Hand D is suitable for either bid.

SPLINTER RAISES

Splinter raises, like the Swiss convention, make use of bids that otherwise would be used only rarely. Rather than giving information about trump texture or side suit aces and kings, as in the Swiss convention, however, Splinter bids (also called "anti-fragment" bids) allow the responder to show a singleton or a void in a side suit while raising the opener's suit.

A splinter raise is any unusual jump, usually skipping two levels of bidding, into a singleton or void suit. It shows a strong raise in support of the opener's suit. For example, if responder held

[A] ♠ Q x x x   ♡ K J x x   ◇ A Q x x   ♣ x

he would jump to four clubs over his partner's opening bid of one heart or one spade. The opener might hold a hand such as

[B] ♠ A J   ♡ A Q x x x   ◇ K x   ♣ x x x x

Use of splinter bids makes it easier to reach a slam with Hands A and B. The auction might be

Opener	Responder
1 ♡	4 ♣
4 ♠	5 ◇
6 ♡	

The partnership should be sure to discuss whether in the auctions

(C) *Opener*   *Responder*
      1 ♠   4 ♡

and

(D) *Opener*   *Responder*
      1 ♡   3 ♠

the responder's bid shows a singleton in the major suit.

If the responder rebids the suit into which he has made the unusual jump, he shows a void in that suit. Thus, in the auction

Opener	*Responder*
1 ♠	4 ◇
4 ♡	5 ◇

the responder promises a 13 to 15 point hand, at least four card spade support, and a void in diamonds. In the bidding of Hands A and B above, therefore, the responder's bid of five diamonds over four spades showed the ace of diamonds but denied a club void, showing the opener that the partnership had a certain club loser.

Partnerships which do not use the Swiss convention can profitably use Splinter raises in combination with standard forcing raises, or with the three notrump response as a forcing raise. Use of these conventions in combination helps to distinguish responder's balanced raises from his distributional raises.

Delayed Splinter Raises

It is also feasible for the responder to use a splinter bid at a later stage in the auction, rather than in immediate response to the opening bid. However, if the unusual jump follows a change of suit by the opener, the responder will be showing support for the opener's second suit rather than his first suit.

For example, the responder might hold:

♠ K x x x ♡ x ◇ x x ♣ A Q J x x x

If his partner opens the bidding with one spade, responder will bid two clubs; responder should delay showing his singleton heart until he has bid his own long suit. If the opener now rebids two spades, responder can jump to four hearts, showing a singleton heart, at least five clubs, and attractive spade support. The auction would therefore proceed:

Opener	Responder
1 ♠	2 ♣
2 ♠	4 ♡

However, if, over the responder's two club response the opener had rebid two diamonds, responder could not jump to four hearts to show his singleton heart, because the jump in this sequence would show diamond support rather than spade support. For the auction

Opener	Responder
1 ♠	2 ♣
2 ◇	4 ♡

responder might have a hand such as

♠ Q x ♡ x ◇ K J x x ♣ A Q x x x x

Splinter Bids by the Opener

Since, as a purely mechanical matter, an unusual jump can be made by either member of the partnership, it is also possible for the opening bidder to make a splinter bid. The opener's splinter bid would be an unusual jump into a singleton and would show support for the suit bid by the responder.

The question of what jumps are unusual, however, is slightly more complex with respect to the opener's bids than it is for responder's bids. Any double jump into a new suit is still, of course, unusual; for example

(A) *Opener*   *Responder*
     1 ♦   1 ♠
     4 ♣ or 4 ♥

(B) *Opener*   *Responder*
     1 ♦   1 ♥
     3 ♠

In auction (A) opener's jump to four clubs or four hearts would show a singleton in the suit in which the jump is made, with a hand worth a game raise in spades. Opener might hold:

♠ K Q x x   ♥ A x x   ♦ A K Q x x   ♣ x

In auction (B), opener might have a hand such as

♠ x   ♥ A K x x   ♦ K Q J x x   ♣ A Q x

In addition to the obviously unusual jumps, when the opener jumps the bidding in a suit which in he could have made a strong forcing bid without jumping, the jump should be considered unusual, and therefore a splinter bid. For example:

(C)	Opener	Responder
	1 ♣	1 ♠
	2 ♡	

(D)	Opener	Responder
	1 ♠	2 ♢
	3 ♣	

In auction (C), opener has made a reverse bid which shows game possibilities. Although the reverse is not absolutely forcing, it is rarely passed. Therefore the auction

(E)	Opener	Responder
	1 ♣	1 ♠
	3 ♡	

is rarely used simply to force the responder to bid again. Auction (E) therefore, can be used by the opener to show a hand containing a singleton heart and good spade support.

Similarly, in auction (D), the opener's three level bid of a new suit virtually forces the partnership to game, since the responder has shown at least a ten point hand and the opener has shown better than a minimum opening bid. Therefore the auction

(F)	Opener	Responder
	1 ♠	2 ♢
	4 ♣	

can be used to show that the opener has a singleton club and a good diamond support. Opener might have a hand such as

♠ A Q x x x   ♡ A K x   ◇ K J x x   ♣ x

FRAGMENT BIDS

A Fragment Bid is an unusual jump rebid, either by the opener or by the responder, to show a fit with his partner and a singleton or void in the fourth suit. Using fragment bids, say opener opened one spade with a hand such as:

♠ A Q x x x   ♡ A K x   ◇ K J x x   ♣ x

If his partner responded two diamonds, the opener would jump to four hearts. Thus in the auction

Opener	*Responder*
1 ♠	2 ◇
4 ♡	

the opener's four heart bid would show some length in hearts, although not usually a biddable suit, a singleton in the unbid suit, clubs, and good support for his partner's diamond suit.

The responder also can make fragment rebids. Unlike splinter raises, however, fragment raises are not available to the responder at his first turn, because fragment bids require the naming of suits held rather than short suits.

Fragment bids by the responder may require detailed discussion by the partnership, because the responder's fragment bid may show shortness in one of the opener's suits. Consider the following two auctions:

(A)	*Opener*	*Responder*
	1 ◇	1 ♡
	1 ♠	4 ◇

(B) *Opener*   *Responder*

1 ♣   1 ♡

1 ♠   4 ◇

In auction (A), responder's jump to four diamonds promises shortness in the unbid suit, clubs. In auction (B), all four suits have been bid. Therefore, the jump to four diamonds promises support for opener's last bid suit, and a singleton in his other suit, clubs.

If the fragment bidder rebids the suit in which he has promised shortness, he shows a void. Thus, in the auction

Opener   *Responder*

1 ♣   1 ♡

1 ♠   4 ◇

4 ♠   5 ♣

the responder's five club bid would show that he is void in clubs.

CONGLOMERATE MAJOR SUIT RAISES

Recognizing that singletons, trump suit solidity, and extra high card values may all be crucial to slam potential, some partnerships have adopted a four-step scheme of strong major suit raises that allows each type of responding hand to be indicated with a single bid. These raises are entirely artificial, and start with the bid which is the next step above the single jump raise of opener's suit (the single jump being used as a limit raise). The complete schedule of responses is as follows:

	Response to 1 ♡ Opening	Response to 1 ♠ Opening	Type of Strong Raise
First Step	3 ♠	3 Notrump	singleton (not yet identified)
Second Step	3 Notrump	4 ♣	17 to 18 HCP
Third Step	4 ♣	4 ◇	Good trump suit (four cards with at least two of the top three honors, or five cards headed by the ace or king)
Fourth Step	4 ◇	4 ♡	General strong raise (not suitable for any of the above)

For example, suppose responder had one of the following hands opposite a one heart opening:

[A] ♠ x   ♥ A x x x   ♦ Q x x x   ♣ A Q x x

[B] ♠ K x   ♥ A J 10 x   ♦ K J x   ♣ A Q x x

[C] ♠ x x   ♥ A x x x x   ♦ K x x   ♣ A J x

[D] ♠ x x   ♥ A x x x   ♦ K x x x   ♣ K Q x

With Hand A, responder would use the first step, three spades, to show that he has a singleton somewhere, although it need not be in spades. With Hand B, responder would use the second step, three notrump, to show that he has an extremely strong hand in high cards. With Hand C, responder would bid the third step, four clubs, to show his excellent trump support. With Hand D, responder would bid the fourth step, showing a hand worth a game force, but one that is not suitable for any of the other special game raises.

There will, of course, be some hands that fit into more than one of the first three categories of hands, such as a hand with a singleton and extra strength, or a hand with very good trumps and extra strength. Such hands are best dealt with by responder's bidding the cheapest step that is applicable, and later making another move toward slam.

The use of the very first step to show that responder has a singleton somewhere in the hand is designed to allow enough room for opener to find out, below the game level, where the singleton is. Opener makes this inquiry, if he is interested, by bidding the next higher denomination over the singleton-showing response, e.g., by bidding three notrump over responder's three spade bid. Responder then bids the suit of his singleton if he can do so without going past four of the trump suit; otherwise he bids four of the trump suit. His singleton will be clearly identified.

For example, the auction might start

(E) Opener	Responder
1 ♡	3 ♠
3 Notrump	4 ◇

(F) Opener	Responder
1 ♡	3 ♠
3 Notrump	4 ♡

In auction (E), opener's three notrump bid, the cheapest bid he can make, asks where responder's singleton is; the four diamond bid shows that the singleton is in diamonds. In auction (F), responder's four heart rebid over three notrump shows that his singleton is in neither clubs nor diamonds, and is therefore in spades. Similarly, if the opening bid were one spade and responder had a hand worth a strong raise, with a singleton club, the bidding could start

Opener	Responder
1 ♠	3 Notrump
4 ♣	4 ♠

Here, opener's four club bid, the cheapest bid he could make over the singleton-indicating response, asks where the singleton is, and responder's rebid of four spades says the singleton is in the only suit he cannot actually mention without going past four of the trump suit: clubs.

JUMP SHIFT TO THREE CLUBS

One of the problems with using the Swiss convention, or Splinter bids, or three notrump as a forcing raise is that these conventions all take up a good deal of bidding room. The opener's next chance to bid comes at the four level. Indeed, if he has opened with a one heart bid and his partner jumps to four diamonds, if opener wants to make a slam try he must do so above the game level.

In order to keep the forcing raise at as low a level as possible, while reserving the jump to two notrump for notrump type hands, some partnerships use a jump shift to three clubs as a forcing major suit raise. The jump says nothing about the responder's clubs, and of course the partnerships using this convention cannot use this bid to show the very strong hand with a club suit.

Over the responder's jump to three clubs the opener is expected to rebid three diamonds if he has a singleton or a void anywhere in his hand. If he has no singleton or void, opener should rebid so as to describe his trump holding. His bids are as follows:

3 ♡ shows two of the top three trump honors

3 ♠ shows one of the top three trump honors

3 Notrump shows none of the top three trump honors

After the opener has bid three diamonds, showing that he has a singleton or a void somewhere in the hand, responder can show the quality of his trump support using the same schedule that opener would have used if he had had no singleton or void. After responder has shown how many of the top three trump honors he has, if opener is interested in slam he can identify his singleton, or bid Blackwood.

JUMP SHIFT SHOWING A SINGLETON

It is also possible to use a simple jump shift to show a strong raise of the opening bid, with a singleton in the suit in which the jump is made. This convention is similar to the Splinter bid, but uses a simple jump shift rather than an unusual jump. The use of this convention, which precludes the natural use of the jump shift, is not widespread.

BARON TWO NOTRUMP

Opposite an opening bid of one of a suit, a balanced hand of 17 or 18 points is difficult to describe. It is too strong for a natural three notrump response or rebid, and, being balanced, it does not lend itself well to repeated suit bids.

The Baron Two Notrump convention is a direct response of two notrump to an opening bid of one of a suit. The responder typically has a balanced hand with no singleton or five card suit, worth about 16 to 18 points. The opener is requested to rebid his hand naturally.

Suppose the opener and responder held the following hands:

(Opener)
♠ A Q x x x   ♡ K x x x   ◇ — — —   ♣ K Q x x

(Responder)
♠ K x   ♡ A x x   ◇ K Q x x   ♣ A J x x

Using Baron Two Notrump, the auction might start:

Opener	Responder
1 ♠	2 Notrump
3 ♡	3 Notrump

Opener infers that the responder has only two spades because he did not take a preference to three spades, as he would have with three card support. Nor did responder raise hearts as he would have with four-card heart support. Since responder would have bid a five card suit if he had one, he must have exactly two spades, three hearts, four diamonds and four clubs. Opener therefore can easily envision a slam in clubs if responder is not disproportionately laden with diamond values.

Since the Baron Two Notrump response is devoted to very strong hands, an immediate response of three notrump can be used to show a balanced hand of 13 to 15 points.

ONE NOTRUMP FORCING

When the partnership is using five card major suit openings, it may be useful to use the one notrump response as forcing on the opener for one round. The forcing notrump response can help to narrow the ranges of other bids by responder and help him out of otherwise difficult situations.

For example, normally in the auction

(A)   *Opener*   *Responder*
   1 ♠   2 ♠

the responder could have anywhere from five to ten points. Some partnerships use the sequence

(B)   *Opener*   *Responder*
   1 ♠   1 Notrump
   2 ◇   2 ♠

to show a weaker responding hand than the sequence shown in auction (A). Other partnerships use auction (B) to show a stronger hand than auction (A).

In addition, some partnerships which use five card major suit openings and limit jump raises, use the forcing notrump to start sequences in which the responder shows a hand of limit raise strength, about 10 to 12 points, but only three trumps. Thus in the auction

(C)   *Opener*   *Responder*
   1 ♡   1 Notrump
   2 ◇   3 ♡

the responder might have a hand such as

♠ x x　　♡ K J x　　♢ A Q x x　　♣ J x x x

This allows the partnership to reserve two-level responses in a new suit for stronger hands.

Use of the forcing one notrump response also enables the responder later to bid a long suit of his own without fear either of being passed in one notrump with an inappropriate hand, or of getting the partnership too high. For example, holding a hand such as

♠ x　　♡ x x　　♢ K J x x x x　　♣ x x x x

responder cannot bid two diamonds directly over an opening of one heart or one spade since this would show a considerably stronger hand, and he is loath to respond one notrump if his partner can pass.

Using the forcing notrump, however, responder could create either of the following non-forcing sequences:

(D) *Opener*　　　　　　　　*Responder*
　　1 ♠　　　　　　　　　　1 Notrump
　　2 ♣　　　　　　　　　　2 ♢

(E) *Opener*　　　　　　　　*Responder*
　　1 ♠　　　　　　　　　　1 Notrump
　　2 ♡　　　　　　　　　　3 ♢

The diamond bids by responder in auctions (D) and (E) are not forcing and not encouraging.

The forcing notrump response may also be useful if the partnership is using a combination of limit jump raises, with a three notrump response substituted as a strong major suit raise, and the Baron two notrump response. Using this combination of conventions leaves the responder no convenient way to respond to a major suit opening bid with a balanced 13 to 15 count and a doubleton in the opener's suit. For example, holding the following hand opposite a one heart opening bid:

♠ A J x   ♡ Q x   ♢ K J x x   ♣ Q J x x

Using standard bidding the responder would have jumped to two notrump over a one heart opening. If he has no other recourse he can temporize with a bid of two clubs, but this risks having the notrump contract played from the wrong side of the table if the opener should rebid notrump. However, if the partnership is using the one notrump response as forcing, the responder may bid one notrump and then jump to three notrump over whatever the opener rebids.

Opener's Rebids

Because forcing notrump responses are used only in conjunction with five card major suit openings, and because the one notrump response may be the start of an escape by responder into a long suit of his own, the opener is not allowed to rebid his suit unless it is at least six cards long. The opener should rebid a four card suit if he can do so consistently with the strength of his hand. If he has no four card suit he must bid a three card suit.

For example, the opener might have any of the following:

[A] ♠ A Q x x x   ♡ K x x x   ♢ x x   ♣ A x

[B] ♠ A Q x x x   ♡ K x   ♢ A J x   ♣ x x x

[C] ♠ A Q x x   ♡ K Q x x x   ♢ A Q   ♣ K x

[D] ♠ A Q x x   ♡ K Q x x x   ♢ x x   ♣ x x

With Hand A the opener has opened with one spade and makes his normal bid of two hearts. With Hand B, however, having no four card suit to rebid, the opener must bid his cheaper three card suit. Here opener rebids three clubs, even though his diamonds are considerably stronger. With Hands C and D opener has started with a one heart bid. Hand C is strong enough to reverse into his four card spade suit over the one notrump response, while with Hand D the opener simply has no adequate rebid. He may well end up playing a 5-1 heart fit.

LIMIT RAISES TO SHOW SINGLETONS

When the partnership is using one notrump as a forcing response to a five-card major suit opening, the responder is able to show a hand worth 10 to 12 points in support of his partner's major by first responding one notrump, and then bidding three of the suit opened. Some partnerships which use the forcing notrump response convention therefore reserve direct limit raise responses for hands containing a singleton in a side suit.

Knowing that the limit raise responder has a singleton somewhere in his hand, the opener may pass if he lacks the strength to bid a game, or he may bid game directly if he has no interest in slam, or he may explore for slam. If opener is interested in slam, he rebids three notrump to ask responder to identify his singleton. Responder normally does so by bidding the suit of the singleton. However, if hearts is the trump suit and responder has a singleton spade, he rebids four hearts over three notrump, to avoid going past four of the trump suit.

Suppose opener and responder have the following hands:

Opener:
♠ K   ♡ A K J x x   ◇ A J x x x   ♣ J x

Responder:
♠ A Q x x x x   ♡ Q 10 x x   ◇ Q x   ♣ x

Using this convention with these hands, one of the pairs on the team which won the 1974 Spingold championship bid a slam that their opponents at the other table did not reach:

119

Opener	Responder
1 ♡	3 ♡
3 Notrump	4 ♣
4 Notrump*	5 ◇
6 ♡	

---

*Blackwood

SHORT SUIT GAME TRIES

From time to time when the opening bidder's major suit has been raised to two by the responder, the opener wants to make a try for game. Since the partnership will rarely have any great surplus of values beyond the 25 to 26 points needed for game, it is useful to determine whether some of the values it has are likely to be wasted.

One convention designed to reveal such a wastage of values is the Short Suit Game Try. Using this convention, the opener's rebid of a new suit at the three level shows a short suit, usually a singleton, and asks the responder to bid a game if his values are principally outside that suit. For example, suppose the opener and responder held these hands:

(Opener)
♠ A K x x x   ♡ K Q x   ◇ x   ♣ K x x x

(Responder)
♠ Q x x   ♡ x x x   ◇ K Q x x   ♣ Q x x

The auction would proceed

Opener	Responder
1 ♠	2 ♠
3 ◇	3 ♠
Pass	

The three diamond rebid by the opener shows his singleton diamond. Since most of responder's values are concentrated in that suit, he signs off in three spades. If the opener had instead rebid three hearts, showing a singleton in that suit, responder would gladly have jumped to four spades.

The partnership should discuss whether or not a rebid of two spades in the auction

Opener	Responder
1 ♡	2 ♡
2 ♠	

shows a short suit. It is probably more useful to reserve this bid as a natural, strength showing bid, especially if the partnership is not using five card major suit openings.

Short Suit Game Tries can be extended to allow the responder to show his own short suit if, in response to the opener's short suit try, the responder still is not sure whether to bid game or settle for three. This gives the opener a chance to reassess his own strength. For example, the auction might start

Opener	Responder
1 ♠	2 ♠
3 ♣	3 ♡

Opener's and responder's hands might be:

(Opener)
♠ A Q x x x   ♡ K x x   ◇ A Q x x   ♣ x

(Responder)
♠ K J x x   ♡ x   ◇ J x x x   ♣ K x x x

With the hand shown, the opener would continue to four spades, not having a great deal of wasted heart values. If instead his diamond ace were the ace of hearts, he would settle for three spades.

The chief disadvantage of short suit game tries is that they are very revealing to the opponents. An opponent may be able to double a Short Suit Game Try to suggest an opening lead or to suggest a suit in which his side might sacrifice. And the early identification of the declarer's short suit may well aid the defenders throughout the hand.

TWO-WAY GAME TRIES

The opener who wants to make a try for game after his major suit opening bid has been raised by responder may have a hand with any of a number of distributions. He may have a singleton. Or he may have a side suit with no singleton but two doubletons. Or he may have neither a singleton nor a side suit.

With a singleton, opener often would like to make a short suit game try. With a side suit opener often would prefer to make a long suit game try. Using standard methods, a partnership must limit itself to one type of game try, for without some sort of converter the two types are largely incompatible.

Two-way game tries are a convention that gives the partnership the ability to make short suit game tries through a direct rebid of a new suit, and to make long suit game tries by way of a relay that converts the new suit rebid into a long suit bid. Using Two way game tries, a simple rebid of the trump suit by the opener is a power game try with neither short suit nor long suit.

Short Suit Tries

If the bidding has started 1 ♠ − 2 ♠, a rebid by the opener of three clubs, three diamonds, or three hearts shows a singleton in the suit bid. If the bidding has begun 1 ♡ − 2 ♡, a rebid of two notrump by the opener shows a singleton spade; a three club or three diamond rebid by opener shows a singleton.

For example, in the auction

Opener	Responder
1 ♡	2 ♡
2 Notrump	4 ♡

opener's two notrump rebid showed a singleton spade.

Responder's four heart bid showed that he had few wasted values in spades.

Long Suit Tries

In order to make a long suit game try, opener uses a relay. He makes the cheapest bid over the raise, forcing responder to bid the next suit. Over responder's forced bid, opener shows his long suit.

If the auction has started 1 ♠ − 2 ♠, opener relays by bidding two notrump, forcing responder to bid three clubs. Over responder's three club bid, opener bids three diamonds with a diamond suit, three hearts with a heart suit, or three spades with a club suit:

Responder	Opener
−	1 ♠
2 ♠	2 Notrump (relay)
3 ♣ (forced)	3 ◇ = diamond suit
	3 ♡ = heart suit
	3 ♠ = club suit

If the auction has started 1 ♡ − 2 ♡, two spades is the relay bid; over two spades responder must bid two notrump so that opener can show his long suit naturally:

Responder	Opener
−	1 ♡
2 ♡	2 ♠ (relay)
2 Notrump (forced)	3 ♣ = club suit
	3 ◇ = diamond suit
	3 ♡ = heart suit

DRURY

The responder who is a passed hand faces two special problems in describing his hand: first, a simple change of suit is no longer a forcing bid, so he cannot temporize. Second, his partner may well have opened the bidding on a sub-minimum hand, so that any jump response could get the partnership too high.

The Drury convention is a two club response to a third- or fourth-hand opening bid of one of a major suit. The two club response does not necessarily have anything to do with the responder's club suit; it merely asks the opener whether or not he has a full opening bid.

If the opener has a subminimal hand, he rebids two diamonds. If he has full values for his opening, he makes any other appropriate rebid. If opener has a full opening bid and his normal rebid would have been two diamonds, he can either jump to three diamonds, if his hand is very distributional, or he can temporize with a two diamond denial and later either bid diamonds naturally or rebid two notrump.

To use the Drury convention, the responder should have a ten to twelve point hand, and either a tolerance for the opener's suit, or a good six card club suit that he plans to rebid. For example, if the responder held

[A] ♠ K J x x   ♡ x x x   ◇ A Q x x   ♣ J x

opposite a third- or fourth-hand opening bid of one spade, he would bid two clubs, Drury. The opener might hold any of the following hands:

[B] ♠ A Q x x x   ♡ J x x   ◇ K J   ♣ x x x

126

[C] ♠ A Q x x x　♡ A J x x　◇ K x　♣ x x

[D] ♠ A 10 x x x　♡ A J　◇ K J x x　♣ K x

[E] ♠ A Q x x x　♡ x　◇ K J x x x　♣ A x

After the auction

Opener	Responder
—	Pass
1 ♠	2 ♣

the opener would bid two diamonds with Hand B, having less than a full opening bid. The responder would then sign off at two spades. With Hand C, the opener would make his natural rebid of two hearts. With Hand D he would rebid two diamonds, planning to rebid diamonds naturally at his next turn. With Hand E opener has uneven enough distribution to jump to three diamonds.

The responder might also hold a hand such as

[F] ♠ K x x　♡ K 10 x x　◇ A x x x　♣ Q x

With Hand F opposite Hand C above, the Drury convention makes it easier for the partnership to find his 4 − 4 heart fit. If Drury were not being used, responder would probably have contented himself with a jump raise to three spades.

If responder holds a hand such as

♠ x　♡ x x x　◇ A J x　♣ A J 10 x x x

he would bid two clubs over his partner's one spade opening, and rebid three clubs over whatever the opener rebid:

Responder	Opener
Pass	1 ♠
2 ♣	2 ◇, 2 ♡, 2 ♠
3 ♣	

SNAP (Strong notrump after passing)

The SNAP convention, an acronym for Strong Notrump After Passing, is designed to allow the partnership to play a low level contract when the responder as a passed hand has fair values, and the opener has a poor hand. Using the SNAP convention, the one notrump response by a passed hand shows a relatively balanced hand worth 9 to 12 points.

Unlike the Drury convention, which is used only over an opening bid in a major suit, SNAP may be used over any one-level bid in a suit by the third or fourth seat. The SNAP responder should not bypass a five card major suit in order to bid one notrump.

SNAP may create problems for weaker responding hands, especially when the opening bid has been one spade. The responder may be forced to pass six-point hands, and to bid eight-point hands at the two level in order to preserve the 9 to 12 point range for the one notrump response.

JUMP SHIFT BY PASSED HAND

Some partnerships agree to use jump shifts by passed hands to show support for the opener's suit, plus a long suit in the responder's hand. This convention may be used in conjunction with SNAP or DRURY. For example, the responder might hold:

♠ K x x x   ♡ x x   ◇ x   ♣ A Q J x x x

After passing in first or second seat, the responder would raise a one spade opening bid by his partner by jumping to three clubs. This bid promises spade support, and a long club suit.

The three club bid by responder is forcing on the opener for one round, but does not force the partnership to game. Rather it asks the opener to evaluate his hand in light of the responder's initial pass and subsequent bidding, and to bid a game if he can. In the above auction, if the opener held a hand such as

♠ A 10 x x x   ♡ K x x   ◇ K x x x   ♣ x

with no club fit, he would sign off in three spades.

DELAYED STAYMAN

When the bidding has been opened with one of a suit and the opener rebids in notrump, there is a convention designed to explore whether or not the partnership has an eight card major suit fit. This convention is described as "delayed" Stayman or "checkback" Stayman.

The delayed Stayman bid is a two club bid in response to the opener's one notrump rebid. The "delay", of course, has come in the bidding of notrump, not in the two club major suit probe. A typical auction would be

Opener	*Responder*
1 ◇	1 ♠
1 Notrump	2 ♣

Delayed Stayman can also be used after the opener has made a jump rebid of two notrump.

Using standard methods, the two club rebid by the responder would show a club suit and would not be forcing. Using delayed Stayman, in which the two club bid is artificial and forcing, the partnership can discover whether it has a 5 — 3 spade fit or a 4 — 4 heart fit. For example, in the auction shown above, the opener might have a hand such as

[A] ♠ x x x   ♡ Q J x x   ◇ K Q x x   ♣ A Q

or

[B] ♠ Q x   ♡ Q J x x   ◇ K Q x x   ♣ A x x

The opener's first obligation is to support the responder's spade suit with a three-card holding. With Hand A therefore, the opener should ignore his four card heart suit and bid two

131

spades. With Hand B, having only two spades, opener can show his four hearts. If opener had neither three spades nor four hearts, he would rebid diamonds or notrump.

Responder might have one of the following hands:

[C] ♠ K J 10 x x   ♡ K x x   ◇ A x x   ♣ x x

[D] ♠ K J 10 x x   ♡ A x x x   ◇ A x x   ♣ x

With Hand D, which is strong enough to force to game, the responder cannot take a chance on simply rebidding two hearts over the opener's one notrump rebid, since the two heart bid could be passed. Using standard methods the responder would jump to three hearts over the one notrump rebid.

The use of delayed Stayman allows him to reserve the jump to three hearts for a hand in which he has five spades and five hearts. Thus with Hand D, if the opener has supported spades, as he would with Hand A above, the responder can still show his four card heart suit by bidding three hearts over two spades. Opener can raise to four hearts, and the partnership will play in its 4 − 4 fit rather than its 5 − 3 fit. Playing in spades could be hazardous if one opponent has four spades and the responder is subjected to repeated club leads forcing him to ruff.

UNBID MINOR AS DELAYED STAYMAN

If the opener has started the auction by bidding one club and has rebid one notrump, and the partnership is using a two club rebid by responder as Delayed Stayman, the responder can no longer retreat from notrump into his partner's first suit, as he would like to do, for example, with

[A] ♠ x   ♡ x x x x   ◇ x x   ♣ x x x x

To preserve this escape route, some partnerships elect to "check back" by having the responder bid the unbid minor suit over the opener's notrump rebid. Their forcing auction would thus be

Opener	Responder
1 ♣	1 ♡
1 Notrump	2 ◇

While this solves the responder's problem on Hand A, it makes things more difficult for him when he holds length in the unbid minor suit and has a weak hand. For example

[B] ♠ x   ♡ A x x x x   ◇ Q 10 x x x   ♣ x x

Using the unbid minor suit as a force, the responder cannot rebid two diamonds over the one notrump rebid as in the above auction. However, it is valuable to have a checkback bid available, and it seems more valuable to allow responder to escape into a suit he knows his partner holds, than into one in which his partner may have a doubleton.

TWO CLUBS AS THE ONLY FORCE
AFTER A ONE NOTRUMP REBID

A very useful convention similar to Delayed Stayman in its initial stages uses a two club rebid by the responder as a forcing bid, and as the only forcing bid, after the opener has rebid one notrump. Like Delayed Stayman, the two club bid shows nothing about the responder's clubs. However, unlike Delayed Stayman, which seeks further information as to the opener's major suit holdings, the use of two clubs as the only forcing bid is designed principally to allow the responder to describe his hand with greater precision.

Use of two clubs as the responder's only forcing rebid means that all of his jump suit rebids are merely invitational. This further allows simple suit rebids to be recognized as sign offs. For example, in the auction

Opener	Responder
1 ◇	1 ♠
1 Notrump	

the responder might hold any of the following hands:

[A] ♠ K Q x x x x   ♡ Q x   ◇ x x   ♣ x x x

[B] ♠ A Q J x x x   ♡ x x   ◇ K x x   ♣ x x

[C] ♠ A K x x x x   ♡ Q x   ◇ x x   ♣ A x x

Using standard methods, responder must have a problem with either Hand B or Hand C, depending on whether the partnership has agreed to play responder's jump to three spades over one notrump in the above auction as forcing or only invitational. With Hand B responder wants to invite; with Hand C, he wants to bid a game, either in spades or in notrump.

Using the two club convention, responder can describe Hand C by first rebidding two clubs and then jumping to three spades. Using this sequence to show a forcing hand allows the responder to make an immediate jump rebid in his suit that is only invitational, the ideal rebid with Hand B.

Two-Suited Hands

After responder rebids two clubs over the one notrump rebid, if he bids a new suit or supports the opener's suit, his bid is forcing to game. This use of the two club rebid helps responder to distinguish between forcing and invitational two suited hands.

For example, suppose in the auction

Opener	Responder
1 ♣	1 ♠
1 Notrump	

responder had one of the following hands

[A] ♠ K x x x x   ♡ x   ◇ Q J x x x   ♣ x x

[B] ♠ K J x x x   ♡ x x   ◇ A Q x x x   ♣ x

[C] ♠ K Q x x x   ♡ Q x   ◇ A K x x x   ♣ x

With Hand A the responder would make the standard bid of two diamonds, which is neither forcing nor particularly encouraging. However, using standard methods he would be forced to make the same bid with Hand B, because a jump to three diamonds would be game forcing.

Using two clubs as the only forcing bid, the responder could jump to three diamonds on Hand B, to show a two suited hand with enough strength to invite a game but not enough to force. The auction might be

Opener	Responder
1 ♣	1 ♠
1 Notrump	3 ◇
Pass	

With Hand C, responder would start with the two club rebid and when he rebids his diamond suit the partnership will be forced to game.

Similarly, if the responder has a hand with which he would like to raise opener's suit in a way that forces to game, he rebids two clubs, followed by a bid in the opener's suit:

Opener	Responder
1 ◇	1 ♠
1 Notrump	2 ♣
2 ◇	3 ◇

The responder's three diamond bid in this auction is forcing to game. The availability of this sequence allows responder to invite game by simply jumping in the opener's suit:

Opener	Responder
1 ◇	1 ♠
1 Notrump	3 ◇

Responder might have a hand such as

♠ A x x x x   ♡ K x x   ◇ K x x x   ♣ x

Showing a Singleton

Since, after a two club rebid by the responder over the no-trump rebid, any new suit by responder would be forcing to game, the partnership could agree to use a jump in a new suit to show a singleton. For example:

Opener	Responder
1 ◇	1 ♠
1 Notrump	2 ♣
2 ◇	3 ♡

Since a two heart bid by the responder over two diamonds would have been forcing and shown a genuine heart suit, The jump to three hearts is not needed as a natural bid. Thus the responder shows a singleton heart in a hand such as

♠ K Q x x x   ♡ x   ◇ A J x x   ♣ K x x

or

♠ K Q x x   ♡ x   ◇ A J x x   ♣ K x x x

The opener can now assess his chances of playing in three no-trump opposite responder's known singleton.

Since the jump to three hearts in the auction above shows a singleton, the partnership may play that the jump to four hearts would show a void. Opener would then be able to determine whether the partnership has a duplication of values, or whether the hands mesh well for play in slam.

UNBID MINOR AS THE ONLY FORCE
AFTER A ONE NOTRUMP REBID

As is true with Delayed Stayman, if the opener has started the auction with one club, the responder cannot take a simple preference for clubs over the one notrump rebid if two clubs is a forcing bid. For this reason, some partnerships favoring the concept of using TWO CLUBS AS THE ONLY FORCE after a one notrump rebid, use instead the minor suit as the force.

When the responder has a weak hand and length in the unbid minor suit, he is forced to abandon the idea of giving his partner a chance to choose between this major suit and the unbid minor. For example, with a hand such as

♠ x   ♡ K Q x x x   ♢ Q x x x x   ♣ x x

in the auction

Opener	Responder
1 ♣	1 ♡
1 Notrump	

responder must simply rebid his heart suit.

TWO NOTRUMP FORCING RESPONSE
TO WEAK TWO BIDS

The weak two bid can be a valuable weapon, having both offensive and defensive potential. Its offensive potential is best realized when the bid is used with discipline, within well defined limits as to length and texture of suit, and as to high card strength. However, as a preemptive maneuver, one frequently cannot resist using the bid simply because it seems likely to embarrass the opponents.

The conflicting applications of the weak two bid leads to its use on a wide variety of hand. The response most commonly used to find out what sort of hand the opener has is two notrump.

Normally a two notrump response to an opening weak two bid is played as forcing for one round. The responder generally has a hand worth at least an opening bid with some fit for the opener's suit. The responder is usually not interested primarily in playing the hand in notrump. Rather he asks the opener to describe his hand further.

As to precisely what the opener's rebids promise, there are a variety of practices. Although some partnerships prefer to have the opener rebid three clubs on all minimum hands, the more popular method is to require the opener to rebid his suit with a minimum hand. With a maximum he would bid a side suit in which he had a high card, called a "feature".

For example, suppose opener holds:

[A] ♠ K Q J x x x   ♡ A x x   ◇ J x x   ♣ x

or

[B] ♠ x x x   ♡ x x   ◇ K Q J x x x   ♣ x x

Over a two notrump response, opener would rebid three hearts with Hand A, showing a maximum and a feature. He would simply rebid his suit with Hand B. With a solid suit, such as

[C] ♠ x x   ♡ A K Q J x x   ◇ x x   ♣ x x x

the opener would rebid three notrump.

For other methods of rebidding over a forcing two notrump response, see OGUST REBIDS, MC CABE ADJUNCT. For other uses of the two notrump response to weak two bids, see RELAYS OVER TWO BIDS, TWO RELAYS AND A TRANSFER.

OGUST REBIDS

The Ogust convention systematizes the opener's rebids over the forcing response of two notrump. Choosing one of four steps, the opener describes the strength of his hand and the quality of his suit:

$$3 \clubsuit = \text{weak hand, weak suit}$$
$$3 \diamondsuit = \text{good hand, weak suit}$$
$$3 \heartsuit = \text{weak hand, good suit}$$
$$3 \spadesuit = \text{good hand, good suit}$$

Some partnerships have agreed to reverse the meanings of the three diamond and three heart bids.

The responder might hold the following hand when his partner opens the bidding with two spades:

[A] ♠ K x x ♡ A x x x ◇ A Q x x ♣ x x

If the opener has a reasonable hand, such as either

[B] ♠ Q J x x x x ♡ K x ◇ x x ♣ A x x

or

[C] ♠ A Q J 9 x x ♡ Q x ◇ x x ♣ x x x

game would be a fair proposition.

Using Ogust rebids, opener would rebid three diamonds with Hand B, showing a good hand with a poor suit. Over this bid responder will bid four spades, since he can solidify the spade suit, and opener's side suit high cards may fit well with responder's hand.

With Hand C opener would rebid three hearts, showing a minimum hand in high cards, but a respectable suit. Opener's Hand C opposite responder's Hand A should produce a reasonable play for game.

However, if the opener has a hand such as

[D]   ♠ Q J x x x x   ♡ x x x   ◇ x   ♣ Q x x

game is out of the question. With Hand D opener would rebid three clubs, announcing a minimum hand with a ragged suit. Responder would sign off at three spades.

McCABE ADJUNCT

Normally after the opener has made a weak two bid, the responder's bid of a new suit is natural and forcing. If the responder has a weak hand and a long suit, he has no way to play in three of that suit using standard methods. The McCabe Adjunct is a convention that preserves the forcing nature of the change of suit, while giving the partnership a means of playing the hand in responder's long suit at the three level.

Using the McCabe Adjunct, a two notrump response requires the opener to rebid three clubs, whatever his hand may be. The responder may now play in his own long suit, either by passing three clubs if clubs is his suit, or by bidding three of his suit, which the opener must pass.

If the partnership is using a direct raise of the weak two bid suit as preemptive, the McCabe Adjunct may be used constructively. The responder first bids two notrump, forcing the opener to rebid three clubs, then responder retreats to three of the opener's suit. By this sequence of bids, responder invites opener to bid game with a hand containing general strength.

Using the McCabe Adjunct, the responder may get information from the opener by making a simple change of suit. This bid is forcing. With support for the responder's suit—three small cards or a doubleton honor should suffice—the opener should raise the responder's suit, so long as he does not have to go past three notrump to do so. Without support for responder's suit, opener is expected to rebid his suit if he has a minimum hand, or to show a feature with a good hand, or to rebid three notrump with a solid suit.

RELAYS OVER WEAK TWO BIDS

Another method of responding to weak two bids is to use the cheapest bid—either notrump if the opening bid was two spades, or the next higher suit—as a relay bid. A relay is a bid which has no meaning of its own, but simply asks one's partner to describe his hand.

The relay asks the opener to bid a stopper outside of his suit if he has one. If his stopper is in the relay suit, he rebids in notrump. Lacking any stopper, opener rebids his own suit. For example:

Opener	Responder
2 ♡	2 ♠ (relay)
2 Notrump	

The two notrump bid by the opener shows a spade stopper. This enables the responder to raise to three notrump with a hand such as

♠ x x   ♡ x x   ◇ A x   ♣ A K Q J x x x

or perhaps with a hand such as

♠ x x x   ♡ K Q x   ◇ A x x x   ♣ A x x

on which the partnership might make exactly nine tricks in whatever contract it plays.

Using this method, the relay bid is the responder's only forcing bid. All other bids by responder, including two notrump when this is not the relay bid, are sign offs. However, if the responder uses a relay and then rebids a new suit, his rebid is forcing.

TWO RELAYS AND A TRANSFER

Another system of responding to weak two bids uses two relays and a transfer. In this system, a single raise of the weak two bid is constructive, inviting the opener to bid game with a maximum hand. The two notrump response is natural and not forcing. Almost all other responses are artificial and forcing for at least one round.

The bid of the cheapest suit is a relay, forcing to game. This bid, i.e., two hearts over a two diamond opening, two spades over a two heart opening, or three clubs over a two spade opening, shows nothing about the suit bid by the responder. It merely asks the opener to bid his lowest ranking feature, whether it be an ace, a king, a singleton or a void. If the opener has a minimum hand and no feature, he rebids his suit.

Suppose opener's and responder's hands were as follows:

(Opener)
♠ A Q x x x x   ♡ x   ◇ Q x x   ♣ J x x

(Responder)
♠ K x x   ♡ J x x x x   ◇ A K x x   ♣ A

Using the game forcing relay, the auction could proceed:

Opener	Responder
2 ♠	3 ♣ (please show a feature)
3 ♡ (heart feature)	
4 ♠ (no interest)	4 ♣ (cue bid)
6 ♠ (interest awakened)	5 ◇ (cue bid)

Using this system of responses to weak two bids, the bid of

the second higher ranking suit, i.e., two spades over a two diamond opening, three clubs over a two heart opening, or three diamonds over a two spade opening, is forcing for one round, and is game invitational. Again the responder's bid is a relay, showing nothing about his holding in the suit he has named. This relay asks the opener to show his point count. With a minimum, i.e., 6 to 9 points, the opener rebids his suit. With a maximum, 10 to 12 points he makes the cheapest suit rebid. Thus the auction could go

Opener	Responder
2 ♠	3 ◇ (tell me your
3 ♡ (maximum)	point range)
	4 ♠

Since the simple direct raise of the opener's weak two bid is played as constructive, this system uses a transfer bid to make a preemptive raise. The bid of the suit just below the suit of the weak two bid forces the opener to rebid his suit. Thus with a hand such as

♠ x x x   ♡ Q J x x   ◇ K x   ♣ K Q x x

the responder would bid three diamonds in response to two hearts, forcing the opener to rebid three hearts.

The preemptive transfer raise can be used for jumps as well as simple raises. For example

Opener	Responder
2 ♡	4 ◇
4 ♡	

The responder might have a hand such as

♠ x   ♡ J x x x   ◇ K x x x x   ♣ Q x x

However, this extension of the transfer preempt concept has a twofold disadvantage. First, it informs the opponents that the responder is bidding four hearts preemptively and secondly, it allows them the opportunity to cue bid four hearts. The standard approach of raising directly to four on preemptive hands as well as on very strong hands is tactically much sounder, since it forces the opponents to guess, to their great sorrow if they guess wrongly, whether or not they are being talked out of their own game.

III

Forcing Opening Bids and Responses

Most bidding systems reserve at least one opening as a strong forcing bid, to be used with a hand of game-going or near-game-going strength. A variety of artificial forcing bids are described below, together with the conventional responses used with each. *See* ARTIFICIAL TWO CLUB OPENING, BLUE TEAM CLUB, SCHENKEN CLUB, PRECISION CLUB, ROMAN CLUB, LITTLE ROMAN CLUB, PRO SYSTEM, SCHENKEN TWO DIAMONDS, STAYMAN TWO CLUB AND TWO DIAMOND OPENINGS, MEXICAN TWO DIAMONDS, TAM II TWO CLUBS AND TWO DIAMONDS, BIG DIAMOND SYSTEM, DYNAMIC ONE NOTRUMP.

In standard bidding, opening two-bids are strong and forcing to game. There are a number of conventional methods of responding. *See* TWO NOTRUMP NEGATIVE, HERBERT NEGATIVE, ACE-SHOWING RESPONSES, ACE AND KING SHOWING RESPONSES.

TWO NOTRUMP AS A NEGATIVE RESPONSE

The traditional negative response to a strong opening two-bid is two notrump. This response shows a hand worth less than 7 or 8 points, counting high cards plus distribution. For his two notrump response to two hearts, for example, the responder might have either of the following hands:

[A] ♠ x x x   ♡ x x x x   ◇ x x x   ♣ x x x
or
[B] ♠ Q x x x x   ♡ x x   ◇ Q x x   ♣ Q x x

If the responder bids anything other than two notrump in response to the opening two-bid, his response is positive, showing at least 7 or 8 points and usually at least one quick trick (an ace, or two kings, or a king and queen in the same suit). Positive responses include a raise of the opener's suit, a jump in notrump, and the bid of any new suit. If the responder bids a new suit in response to a strong two-bid, he promises at least a five-card suit, headed by no worse than the king, or the queen and jack.

HERBERT NEGATIVE

The Herbert Negative response to a forcing two-bid is the bid of the cheapest suit over the opening bid, for example,

Opener	Responder
2 ♡	2 ♠

The responder's two spade bid shows nothing about his spade suit; it merely says that responder has less than 7 or 8 points in support of the opener's suit.

There are two purposes to using the Herbert negative response. One is that frequently after the bidding has been opened with a strong two-bid the hand will be played in notrump. The use of Herbert enables the strong hand to be declarer. The second purpose of the Herbert Negative is to save room when the bidding has been opened with a strong two-bid in a suit other than spades.

If the responder has a hand with which he would have made a positive response in the cheapest suit, he must jump in that suit to show length and strength. Thus with a hand such as

♠ A Q x x x   ♡ K x   ◇ x x x   ♣ x x x

responder would have to bid three spades in response to the two heart opening bid.

ACE-SHOWING RESPONSES

Ace-showing responses to strong forcing two-bids are designed to show the two-bidder immediately whether or not the responder has any aces, and if so, which ones.

If the responder has no aces he responds two notrump. If he has one ace, he responds in the suit of the ace. For example, suppose responder held one of the following hands in response to a two diamond opening bid:

[A] ♠ K Q x x x   ♡ Q x x   ◇ x x   ♣ x x x

[B] ♠ K x x x x   ♡ A x   ◇ x x x   ♣ x x x

Using ace-showing responses over the two diamond opening, responder would bid two notrump with Hand A, showing that he has no aces. He is not allowed at this point to bid his long strong spade suit, for that would show the ace of spades, and would show nothing else about the spade suit. With Hand B, responder would bid two hearts over the two diamond bid, showing the ace of hearts.

There are at least two methods of showing that the responder has two aces. Using one of these methods, the responder shows his aces one at a time, by first bidding the ace he can show most inexpensively over the opening two-bid, and bidding the second one later. Using this method, if responder held

♠ x x x   ♡ A x x x x   ◇ x x   ♣ A x x

in response to a two-diamond opening, his proper response would be two hearts. Over the opener's rebid, responder must then bid clubs. When responder runs out of aces to bid, he must rebid the minimum number of notrump.

Using an alternative method of showing two aces in the responding hand, the responder would jump to the suit of his lower ranking ace. For example, holding the aces of spades and diamonds, the responder would jump to three diamonds over a two club opening bid, or would jump to four diamonds if the opening bid had been two hearts.

ACE AND KING SHOWING RESPONSES

Some partnerships agree that the responder will show his aces and kings in response to an opening two bid. Some combinations can be shown in one bid; others require more rounds of bidding. With no aces and no kings, the responder bids two notrump; with one king and no aces, he first responds two notrump, and then if his partner makes a bid below the game level, he bids the suit in which he has the king.

If responder has one ace and no kings, he bids the suit in which he has the ace; if he has two kings and no aces, he jumps to three notrump; if he has two aces and no kings, he jumps to four notrump; if he has one ace and one king, he first bids the suit in which he has the ace, and later bids the suit in which he has the king. For example; opener's and responder's hands might be:

(Opener)
♠ K Q J 10 9 x x   ♡ —   ◇ A Q x   ♣ A K Q

(Responder)
♠ A x   ♡ Q x x x x   ◇ K x x   ♣ x x x

The bidding would proceed:

Opener	Responder
2 ♠	3 ♠
4 ♣	4 ◇
7 ♠	

Responder's three spade bid showed the ace of spades; his four diamond bid showed the king of diamonds.

155

The disadvantage of the responder's showing his aces, or his aces and honors, directly in response to the opening two-bid is that the partnership loses much of its ability to explore for suit fits at a low level of the auction. Since the responder does not get to bid his own suit naturally for the first round or two, hands that have been opened with a strong two-bid usually end up being played in the opener's suit. This is fine if opener's suit is the best place to play; however, sometimes responder's hand will provide a better trump suit.

ARTIFICIAL TWO CLUB OPENING

When the partnership is using strong opening two-bids, a two club bid to show such a hand with a club suit is not a convention. However, many partnerships use weak opening two-bids, and for most of these partnerships the two club bid is the only strong, forcing opening bid.

The strong, artificial two club opening may be made on any of three types of hand. It may be made on a hand worth a forcing strong two-bid in any suit, such as

♠ A K Q J x x   ♡ A K x   ◇ A K x   ♣ x

In many partnerships, the bidding may be opened with two clubs also on a hand that is almost, but not quite, worth a game forcing two-bid. For example, holding

♠ K x   ♡ A K Q x x x x   ◇ A Q x   ♣ x

the bidding could be opened with two clubs if the partnership did not treat that bid as forcing to game.

In addition, many partnerships today have lowered the trational range of the two notrump opening bid to 20 to 22 high card points. These partnerships use a two club opening bid, followed by a rebid of two notrump, to show a hand worth 23 to 24 high card points. The two club opener might have a hand such as

♠ K Q x   ♡ A Q x x   ◇ A Q J x   ♣ A J

To learn which of the above types of hands the opener has for his two club bid, the responder must wait until the opener rebids.

There are several types of responses to the forcing two club bid that can be adopted. Some are designed to show very weak responding hands, some are designed to show how many aces and kings the responder holds, and some are designed simply to help the opener describe his hand.

See TWO DIAMOND NEGATIVE, STEP RESPONSES, CHEAPER MINOR AS A SECOND NEGATIVE, AUTOMATIC TWO DIAMONDS, TWO DIAMONDS AS ONLY POSITIVE RESPONSE, TWO DIAMONDS NEGATIVE AND TWO HEARTS NEUTRAL, ACE-SHOWING RESPONSES, HERBERT SECOND NEGATIVE.

TWO DIAMOND NEGATIVE

Over a strong artificial two club opening bid, the negative response most commonly used is two diamonds. The two diamond response shows nothing with respect to the responder's diamond suit. It simply shows that he has a weak hand, less than about 8 points. The two diamond response to two clubs is the equivalent of the negative two notrump response to a natural strong two-bid.

After the negative two diamond response, many partnerships have agreed that the bidding may end below the game level. Thus either of the following auctions would be possible:

(A) *Opener*   *Responder*
    2 ♣   2 ◊
    2 Notrump   Pass

(B) *Opener*   *Responder*
    2 ♣   2 ◊
    2 ♠   2 Notrump
    3 ♠   Pass

If the responder has a genuine diamond suit and a hand strong enough for a positive response, he must show it by jumping to three diamonds. This could be a handicap if the opener's suit is clubs and he has the minimum for his two club bid.

HERBERT SECOND NEGATIVE

In response to a strong artificial two club opening bid, some partnerships attempt to have the responder distinguish between hands that are weak and hands that are in extremis. To achieve this, the responder first makes the negative two diamond response; then over the opener's rebid, he employs the Herbert convention by bidding the cheapest suit over the rebid.

For example, in the auction

Opener	Responder
2 ♣	2 ◇
2 ♡	2 ♠

the responder's two diamond bid was negative, showing 0 to 7 points. His two spade bid showed that he was rather closer to 0 than to 7. The two spade bid does not promise length or strength in spades.

This convention has the advantage of keeping the bidding low when the responder has a very weak hand and the opener has either a minimum or a two-suited hand. However, it has the disadvantage of preventing the responder from showing his suit cheaply if it happens to rank next above the opener's suit. For example, suppose responder holds:

♠ Q x x x x x   ♡ x   ◇ x x x   ♣ x x x

Over his partner's two club opening bid, responder is happy to bid two diamonds. But over a two heart rebid by opener, he would like to be able to bid two spades to show his long spade suit. Using the Herbert convention as a second negative, this responder would have to bid his spades on the three level, with-

160

out knowing whether or not the opener has a fit. The opener, for example, might hold either of these two hands:

[A] ♠ x   ♡ K Q J 10 x x   ◇ A K x   ♣ A K x

or

[B] ♠ K x x   ♡ A K Q x x x   ◇ A K x   ♣ x

If the opener held Hand A, the partnership could be too high once the responder showed his spade suit at the three level. With Hand B, however, the partnership has a probable game in spades.

CHEAPER MINOR AS A SECOND NEGATIVE

In order to facilitate the showing of a long major suit with a weak hand opposite a strong artificial two club opening bid some partnerships avoid using the Herbert convention as their second negative, and instead substitute a bid of the cheaper minor suit. Using the cheaper minor as a second negative, the responder has comfortable rebids with each of the following hands:

[A] ♠ Q x x x x x   ♡ x   ♢ x x   ♣ x x x x

[B] ♠ Q x x x   ♡ x x   ♢ x x x   ♣ x x x x

After the bidding has started

Opener	Responder
2 ♣	2 ♢
2 ♡	

responder would bid two spades with Hand A, a natural rebid showing a long spade suit. With Hand B responder would make an artificial rebid of three clubs. This bid says nothing about his club suit; it merely says that his weak hand is very weak, and that he did not have a long spade suit he could bid over two hearts.

Most partnerships carry their use of the cheaper minor as a second negative only through three diamonds. Thus, in the auction

Opener	Responder
2 ♣	2 ♢
3 ♣	3 ♢

responder's three diamond bid would be a second negative. But in the auction

Opener	Responder
2 ♣	2 ♦
3 ♦	

responder would have no second negative available.

If the partnership is not using a convention such as Herbert or cheaper minor as a second negative, the responder is forced to rebid two notrump with extremely weak hands. This has the undesirable effect of making the very weak hand the declarer in any notrump contract that might eventually be played.

AUTOMATIC TWO DIAMOND RESPONSE

Some partnerships use the two diamond response to a strong artificial two club opening bid as a waiting bid. When used in this way, the two diamond response neither shows length in the suit, nor gives any information about the strength or weakness of the responder's hand.

The purpose of using the two diamond bid as a relay-type bid is to allow the opening bidder to describe his hand further. The rationale is that after that rebid the responder will have a much better idea of what his hand is worth.

The use of the two diamond bid as a waiting bid also has the effect of making it easier for the opening bidder to complete a description of a two-suited hand if he has one. The drawback, of course, is that while the responder is waiting and relaying, he is not showing opener either the strength or the shape of his hand.

TWO DIAMONDS AS THE ONLY
POSITIVE RESPONSE

Some partnerships use the two diamond response to an artificial
strong two club opening as the only positive response available
to the responder. If the responder makes a bid in any other suit,
or if he bids notrump, he shows less than the 7 or so points
needed for a positive response.

Using this method, the two diamond response forces the
partnership to game. This convention has the advantage of allowing the partnership to explore for slam at the two level. A drawback, however, is that the responder once again makes a bid with
very limited meaning, and cannot begin to reveal the contours
of his hand until the next round of the bidding.

TWO DIAMONDS NEGATIVE, TWO HEARTS NEUTRAL

A few partnerships use the two diamond response to an artificial two club opening bid as an extreme negative response, and use a two heart response with a hand of any other strength. Any response other than two diamonds or two hearts would be positive and game-forcing.

Using these methods, the two diamond response would be made with about 0 to 3 points—the type of hand with which a HERBERT SECOND NEGATIVE or CHEAPER MINOR SECOND NEGATIVE response might be used. The two heart response is artificial, and shows at least 4 high card points. Two hearts may be bid with a hand not strong enough for a positive response, or with a hand worth a positive response, but with which the responder simply wants to hear opener's rebid before taking any positive action.

Suppose responder held one of the following hands:

[A] ♠ x x   ♥ x x x   ♦ Q x x x   ♣ J x x x

[B] ♠ x x   ♥ x x x   ♦ K Q x x   ♣ J x x x

[C] ♠ x x   ♥ K Q x   ♦ K Q x x   ♣ J x x x

[D] ♠ K x   ♥ K x x   ♦ K x x x   ♣ Q x x x

[E] ♠ K x   ♥ A x x x x   ♦ K x x   ♣ J x x

Using these methods, with Hand A responder would bid two diamonds over two clubs. With Hand B, responder has enough strength to bid two hearts, showing at least a modicum of values. With Hand C, which is worth a positive response, responder would also bid two hearts, temporizing to hear what opener will rebid. With Hand D, however, which has the same point count as Hand C, responder would bid two notrump in response to the two club opening, because if the hand is to be played in notrump, the partnership will surely be better off having the lead come toward responder's hand rather than through it. With Hand E, responder would bid two hearts even though this response does not show his heart suit. However, he does not want to use up a whole level of bidding by jumping to three hearts to make a positive response; therefore he temporizes with a two heart bid.

Over a two diamond response, using these methods, the partnership may agree that a minimum rebid by the opener is not forcing, and that in order to force the responder to bid again the opener must make a jump rebid. This agreement would allow the partnership to play at the two level if both opener and responder had the minimum allowed for their respective bidding. However, it would make it difficult for opener to describe a two-suited hand, since to be sure of having an opportunity to show his second suit he would have to make a jump rebid.

More profitably, the partnership could agree that a minimum rebid by the opener is forcing, and that the jump rebid of a major suit is invitational. This would allow the partnership to stop at the three level whether the opener had a one-suited hand or a two-suited hand. Under this agreement, the following auctions would be possible:

(A) | Opener | Responder |
|---|---|
| 2 ♣ | 2 ♦ |
| 2 ♡ | 3 ♡ |
| Pass | |

(B) | Opener | Responder |
|---|---|
| 2 ♣ | 2 ♦ |
| 3 ♡ | Pass |

In auction (A), opener's two heart rebid would show either a hand with which he was no longer interested in bidding game once he found out that responder had at most 3 points, or a two-suited hand. However, his pass of the raise to three hearts indicates that he has the former type of hand. With a two-suited hand opener would either bid game over a raise or show his second suit if responder did not raise.

In auction (B), opener's jump to three hearts shows that he is interested in game if responder has 3 points rather than none, or if responder has as little as a side singleton and three trumps.

If the responder has bid two hearts over the two club opening bid, the partnership will usually reach game. The one sequence by which the partnership can play below game is

Opener	Responder
2 ♣	2 ♡
2 ♠	2 Notrump
3 ♠	Pass

In the auction

Opener	Responder
2 ♣	2 ♡
3 ♡	

opener's three heart bid is forcing. Similarly, in the auction

Opener	Responder
2 ♣	2 ♡
2 Notrump	

opener's two notrump bid may not be passed. Opener has shown 23 to 24 points and responder has shown at least 4 to 7 points. The partnership therefore theoretically has the values to be in game.

ACE-SHOWING RESPONSES TO TWO CLUB OPENINGS

Ace showing responses may be used in conjunction with the strong artificial two club opening bid as well as with strong natural two-bids. Using this convention, the two diamond response is negative, showing no aces and less than 7 or 8 points; a response of two notrump would show a hand with no aces, but one that is worth a positive response.

A bid of two hearts, two spades, three clubs or three diamonds would show the ace of the suit bid. None of these responses promises any length in the suit bid.

There are several methods by which the partnership may choose to have the responder show a hand containing two aces. One method is to have the responder jump to three notrump with any two aces. The theory behind this agreement is that the opener will normally have two aces himself, and will therefore know which two aces the responder holds.

A second method is to jump to three hearts, or three spades or three notrump to show specific pairs of aces, as follows: A jump to three hearts would show aces that do not match either in rank or in color (either clubs and hearts, or diamonds and spades); a jump to three spades would show two aces of the same color (clubs and spades, or diamonds and hearts); a jump to three notrump would show two aces of the same rank (majors or minors).

A third method of showing aces uses the two notrump response as the only bid that says responder has no aces, and thus allows the bid of two diamonds to be made to show the ace of diamonds. All of the other single-ace showing bids described above remain the same. However, to show two aces, the responder would jump to the suit of his lower ranking ace. For these purposes, the spade suit would be deemed to rank below the club suit. Thus, with the aces of spades and clubs, the responder would bid three spades directly over the two club opening; with the aces of clubs and hearts, he would jump to four clubs; with the aces of hearts and spades, he would jump to three hearts, and so forth.

STEP RESPONSES TO TWO
CLUB OPENINGS

A convention devised to allow the responder to show both his aces and his kings in a single response to the two club opening is called Step Responses to Two Clubs. Counting each ace as two controls and each king as one control, the responses to the two club opening are as follows:

2 ♦ = 0 or 1 control

2 ♡ = 2 controls (one ace or two kings)

2 ♠ = 3 controls, consisting specifically of one ace and one king

2 Notrump = 3 controls, consisting specificially of three kings

3 ♣ = 4 controls (two aces, or four kings, or one ace and two kings)

3 ♦ = 5 controls (two aces and one king, or one ace and three kings)

The reason underlying the separation of the two types of hands containing three controls is that if the hand is to be played in notrump, the hand with three kings should be the declarer so that the lead will come up to him rather than through him.

Some partnerships use a variation of Step Responses designed to allow the responder show at once whether he has a very weak hand or just a moderately weak hand. Using this variation, a two diamond response to the two club opening would show 0 or 1 control with less than 6 points; a two heart response would show 0 or 1 control, with at least 6 high card points. The other responses would be as follows:

2 ♠ = 2 controls

2 Notrump = 3 kings (3 controls)

3 ♣ = one ace and one king (3 controls)

3 ◇ = 4 controls

BLUE TEAM CLUB

The Blue Team Club system is based on a forcing one club opening bid, with responses showing how many controls the responder has. Opening bids of one of a suit other than clubs are limited to less than a good 17 points. The opening bid style of Blue Team Club is canape, meaning that there is a tendency to bid short suits before long suits.

For example, in the auction

Opener	Responder
1 ♡	2 ♣
2 ◇	2 ♠

The opener's one heart bid could have been made on a four-card suit, and his diamonds are as long as or longer than his hearts. The responder tends to canape also. His two club bid may have been made on as few as three clubs, and his two spade rebid shows a spade suit that is probably longer than his club suit.

Using Blue Team Club, balanced hands worth 16 to 17 points are opened one notrump; balanced hands worth 21 to 22 points are opened two notrump. In addition, there is a bid to show strong three-suited hands: this is the NEAPOLITAN TWO DIAMOND opening, showing a hand containing three four card suits and 17 to 24 points. All other hands worth 17 or more points are opened with one club.

BLUE TEAM ONE CLUB OPENING

There are three types of hands that may be opened with a one club bid. First there are balanced hands that are outside the ranges assigned to the one notrump and two notrump openings. Thus balanced hands worth 18 to 20 points or worth 23 points and up should be opened with one club. The opener's rebid will be in notrump, as follows:

18 to 20 points: open one club and rebid the minimum number of notrump

23 to 24 points: open one club and jump rebid in notrump

25 to 26 points: open one club and jump to three notrump over a one diamond response

One club may be opened with unbalanced hands worth 17 or more points. These hands may have one or two long suits; or they may have three four card suits if they have more than 24 points. The first rebid with such a hand will be in a suit.

The third type of hand with which a one club opening may be made is a hand with eight or more playing tricks, even if it has less than 17 points. A hand such as

♠ A Q J x x x   ♡ x   ◇ x   ♣ A K J x x

would qualify for a one club opening.

Responses to One Club

The responder's first bid informs the opener how many controls responder has. Counting each ace as two controls and

174

each king as one, responder shows his strength as follows:

$1 \diamondsuit = 0$ to 2 controls, less than 6 points

$1 \heartsuit = 0$ to 2 controls, 6 or more points

$1 \spadesuit = 3$ controls

$1\,\text{NT} = 4$ controls

$2 \clubsuit = 5$ controls

$2 \diamondsuit = 6$ controls

$2\,\text{NT} = 7$ controls.

The two heart and two spade responses are used to show hands worth 0 to 5 points with a six-card suit headed by two honors. The maximum holding would be K J x x x x. The two heart and two spade responses are not forcing. If the opener has a balanced 18 count without a good fit for the responder's suit he is allowed to pass.

The one diamond response is negative. After the responder has bid one diamond, he is not required to bid again unless the opener makes a jump rebid in a suit.

Responder is, however, required to bid again after he has responded one heart. This response is semi-positive, and could in fact be quite strong in point count, for example:

♠ K Q x   ♡ Q J 10 x x   ♢ Q J x   ♣ K J

This hand contains 15 high card points, but is not worth a full positive response because it has so few controls.

The one heart response forces the partnership to at least two notrump. Responses that show three or more controls force the partnership to game.

When the Opponents Interfere

If an opponent doubles or overcalls over the one club opening bid, adjustments are made in the control showing responses. If the interference is a double, all of the regular responses of one heart and higher remain applicable. However, the double gives the responder two additional calls with which to clarify a negative response. A pass over the double will show 0 to 3 points; a redouble will show 3 to 5 points with values in the club suit; the one diamond bid will show 4 to 5 points with values outside the club suit.

If the opponent overcalls over the one club opening at the one level, the responder will pass with 0 to 5 points—a hand with which he would have responded one diamond had there been no overcall. Responder will double the overcall with six or more points and less than three controls—a hand with which he would have responded one heart had there been no overcall. To show three or more controls, responder bids up the line. The cheapest bid over the overcall shows three controls; the next bid shows four controls, and so forth. For example, if the bidding has gone

North	East	South	West
1 ♣	1 ♠		

and South has

♠ x x x   ♡ A K x x   ◇ x x x   ♣ x x x

he bids one notrump, the cheapest bid, to show that he has three controls.

In bidding up the line over the overcall, however, responses of two of an unbid major suit retain their original meanings. Thus in the auction above, if South bids two hearts over the one spade overcall he does not show six controls even though that is literally the fourth step over the overcall; instead he shows 0 to 5 points with a six-card heart suit headed by two honors. If South had a hand with six controls, his proper response over the one spade overcall would be two spades. If the opponent overcalls one notrump over the one club opening, the responder should pass or bid a long suit with a poor hand. He should double with any hand worth 6 points or more, regardless of the number of controls he holds. If the notrump overcaller retreats into a suit after being doubled, the responder can either pass with a minimum hand, or double for penalties, or bid a new suit, which is forcing. In addition he can show approximately how many controls he has. To show his controls, he bids two notrump with three or four controls, or cue-bids with five or more controls.

If the opponent overcalls over one club at the two level, the responder may double for penalties, or he may pass with a hand that has fewer than three controls, or he may bid a new suit, which is forcing. In addition he may bid two notrump with three or four controls.

SCHENKEN CLUB

The Schenken system is based on a forcing one club opening bid, with natural responses showing that the responder has high card strength. The one club opening normally shows 17 or more high card points, and may be made on one of three types of hands.

The Schenken one club opening may be made on a balanced hand containing 17 to 22 points. If opener has a balanced 16 to 18 point with all suits stopped, he would open with one notrump. However, with a balanced 17 or 18 points and one suit unstopped, the opener bids one club and rebids a suit.

If the opener has a balanced 19 to 20 points he opens one club and rebids one notrump. If he has a balanced 21 to 22 points, he rebids two notrump. If he has a balanced hand with more than 22 points, he opens a SCHENKEN TWO DIAMOND bid.

One club may also be opened with a slightly unbalanced, although not freakish, hand worth 17 or more high card points. With this type of hand the opener will rebid a suit. In addition, a hand may be opened with one club with less than 17 points if it has such great playing strength that game is likely if the responder has a moderately good fit and the right king or queen. For example, holding

♠ A K 10 x x   ♡ A Q J x x x   ◇ x   ♣ x

the opener would bid one club even though the hand contains only 14 high card points.

Using the Schenken system, freakish hands that may produce a slam opposite the right one or two cards in the responder's hand are opened with a SCHENKEN TWO DIAMOND bid.

Responses to One Club

In response to a one club opening, the negative response is one diamond. All other responses are positive and forcing to game. The responder must bid one diamond unless he has at least 9 high card points including at least 1½ quick tricks, i.e., an ace and a king, or an ace and queen in the same suit, or three kings, or a king and queen combination and another king. However, the responder is allowed to make a positive response with only 8 points if those 8 points consist of two aces.

After a one diamond response to the one club opening, a simple non-jump rebid by the opener is not forcing. Thus the auction could go.

Opener	Responder
1 ♣	1 ◇
1 ♠	Pass

If the opener wants to force the responder to bid again he must jump in a suit. Even this jump, however, is not forcing to game; if the opener later rebids his suit, the responder is allowed to pass.

Responses of one heart, one spade, one notrump, two clubs and two diamonds are all positive responses, showing 9 or more points (or possibly two bare aces). These responses are natural, showing the suit in which the responder bids, and are forcing to game.

An alternative treatment is to use the two club response as a semi-positive response, showing 7 or 8 points including one ace or one king. When this treatment is used, the responder promises to rebid over whatever the opener rebids.

Holding a solid or semi-solid six-card suit, with a hand worth a positive response, the responder jumps in his suit. A single jump shows a solid suit, i.e., no worse than A K Q 10 x x or A K Q x x x x. A double jump shows a semi-solid suit, i.e., a suit needing one of the top three honors to be solid. Thus in the auction

Opener	Responder
1 ♣	3 ♠

responder shows a semi-solid spade suit, and at least 1½ quick tricks. If responder had K Q 10 x x x in his suit and nothing outside, his proper response would be one diamond.

When the Opponents Interfere

If an opponent overcalls over the one club opening with any bid up to and including three diamonds, the only ways for the responder to show a positive response are to double or cue-bid. The double is not for penalties, and does not describe the shape of the responder's hand. It simply says he had the strength for a positive response. A cue-bid shows a positive response and first round control of the suit overcalled.

Any bid of a suit over the overcall shows a fair hand, but one not strong enough for a positive response. A notrump bid over the overcall shows two stoppers in the suit overcalled, and some values, but again less than the strength for a positive response.

Suppose North opens with one club and East overcalls one heart, and South has one of the following hands:

[A] ♠ K Q x x x ♡ x x ◇ J x x ♣ x x x

[B] ♠ Q J 10 x x x ♡ x x ◇ x x ♣ x x x

[C] ♠ x x ♡ K Q 10 x x ◇ A x x ♣ Q x x

[D] ♠ A Q x x ♡ x x ◇ K Q x x ♣ x x x

With Hand A, responder would bid one spade over the overcall; however, with Hand B, he should pass because his hand is so weak. With Hand C, responder should pass in the hopes that his partner will reopen with a takeout double which he can pass for penalties. With Hand D, responder should double to show a positive response.

PRECISION CLUB SYSTEM

The Precision Club system is a largely natural system of bidding that uses a forcing one club opening with hands worth 16 points or more, and natural positive responses. Using the Precision system, the bidding is opened with one club much more frequently than it can be in the Schenken or Blue Team club systems in which a minimum of 17 points are required to open one club.

Using the Precision system, all hands worth 16 or more high card points, with one exception, are opened one club. The exception is that balanced hands worth 23 to 24 points are opened two notrump. In addition, hands that are very strong in playing strength may be opened with one club even without 16 points.

Responses to One Club

A one diamond response to a one club opening is negative and shows fewer than 8 high card points. After a one diamond response, a minimum suit rebid by the opener is not forcing. If the opener wishes to force the responder to bid once again, he must jump in a suit.

Other minimum responses to the one club opening, i.e., one heart, one spade, one notrump, two clubs and two diamonds, are positive responses. Each shows 8 or more high card points, and five or more cards in the suit bid. In principle, these bids are forcing to game. However, if the later bidding shows a misfit, and each partner has an absolute minimum, the partnership may stop below game.

After a positive response, a jump shift by the opener shows a solid six-card or longer suit, and at least 19 points. The bid is forcing to game, and fixes the trump suit. Thereafter, bids by the opener or the responder, other than game in the established trump suit, are slam tries. For example, opener's and responder's hands might be:

(Opener)
♠ x x ♡ A K Q x x x x ◇ K x ♣ A K
(Responder)
♠ A K x ♡ J ◇ x x x ♣ Q J x x x x

The bidding could go

Opener	Responder
1 ♣	2 ♣
3 ♡	3 ♠
4 ♣	4 ♠
6 ♡	Pass

Responses in notrump show balanced distribution. The one notrump response shows 8 to 10 high card points; the two notrump response shows 11 to 13 high card points; a three notrump response shows 14 to 15 high card points. As an alternative, the partnership might agree to use the one notrump response to show either the minimum positive response or a response worth 15 or more points. This would enable the opener to describe his hand naturally at a low level; the responder would bid aggressively later in the auction if he had 15 or more points.

When the response to one club has been one notrump, a raise to two notrump by the opener is not forcing. Opener shows a minimum hand, and invites responder to bid game if he has closer to ten points than to eight.

Responses of two of a major suit may be used to show hands containing six-card suits with 4 to 7 high card points. Jumps to the three level by the responder over one club can be used to show seven card suits with four to seven points. (But see UN-USUAL POSITIVE, below.)

Since suit bids in response to a one club opening show at least five cards, and since notrump responses show balanced distribution, the Precision responder has a problem showing a hand worth a positive response if its distribution is 4-4-4-1. There are two alternative methods for dealing with these hands. See IMPOSSIBLE NEGATIVE; UNUSUAL POSITIVE.

When the Opponents Interfere

If the opponents overcall over the one club opening, a pass by the responder is the most negative possible bid, showing 0 to 4 points. The cue-bid is the only action that immediately reveals that the responder has the values for a positive response.

Between the negative pass and the immediately positive cue-bid, there are three avenues open to the responder. If he has a five-card suit and 5 to 8 points, he may bid his suit. If he has a six-card suit and 5 to 8 points, he may jump in his suit. If he has 5 to 8 points but no long suit, responder may double. This double is not for penalties; it simply tells the opener that responder has 5 to 8 points. In addition, some partnerships use the negative double, followed by responder's bid of a new suit as the equivalent of a positive response.

If the opponents make a takeout double rather than an overcall, there are essentially two alternative means of coping with the double. One method is to pass with 0 to 7 points and four or more clubs, or to bid one diamond with 0 to 7 points with fewer than four clubs. All other responses have the same meaning they would have had if there had been no double. A redouble would show 8 or more points with two four card major suits.

An alternative method allows the responder to show a five-card suit with less than the values needed for a positive response. Using this method, the responder will bid freely with a five-card suit and 5 to 8 points. With a hand worth a positive response, he will redouble.

IMPOSSIBLE NEGATIVE

The Impossible Negative is a convention used by a PRECISION CLUB responder to describe a hand worth 8 or more high card points with 4-4-4-1 distribution. Over the one club opening bid the responder bids one diamond, as if he had less than an 8 point hand. However, over the opener's rebid, the responder will jump in a new suit or in notrump to show that he did not really mean his first bid. Hence the term "impossible" negative.

There are two methods by which the singleton can be shown. The simpler is for the responder to jump at his second turn in the suit of his singleton. This shows that he has four cards in each of the other suits. If responder's singleton is in the suit that the opener has rebid, responder jumps in notrump, to avoid giving the impression that he is raising the opener's suit. For example, suppose the responder held the following hand opposite a one club opening:

♠ K x x x   ♡ x   ◇ A Q x x   ♣ Q x x x

The auction could start

	Opener	Responder
	1 ♣	1 ◇
	1 ♡	2 Notrump
or		
	Opener	Responder
	1 ♣	1 ◇
	1 ♠	3 ♡

After the responder's jump bid, opener should have a fair idea of

186

where the hand should play. Subsequent bidding will be more or less natural.

An alternative way to show the singleton is for responder to jump in the suit below the singleton. Again, however, a jump to three of the suit bid naturally by opener is a natural raise; a jump to three notrump would show the impossible negative with a singleton in opener's suit. A jump to the suit below openers' suit, therefore, is used to show a singleton in the suit above opener's suit. For example, responder holds one of the following hands:

[A] ♠ A x x x   ♡ x   ◇ J x x x   ♣ K Q x x

[B] ♠ x   ♡ A x x x   ◇ J x x x   ♣ K Q x x

[C] ♠ K Q x x   ♡ J x x x   ◇ A x x x   ♣ x

and the auctions starts as follows:

Opener	Responder
1 ♣	1 ◇
1 ♠	

With Hand A, responder jumps to three diamonds over one spade, showing a singleton heart and four cards in each of the other suits. With Hand B, responder jumps to three notrump, showing a singleton spade. With Hand C, responder jumps to three hearts, showing a singleton in the suit ranking above opener's suit, i.e., clubs.

The advantage of jumping to the suit below the singleton is that the opener can easily make an asking bid by cue-bidding the singleton, to find out how many controls the responder has. For the type of control-showing sequences that are available, *see* UNUSUAL POSITIVE.

Unusual Positive

An alternative to the IMPOSSIBLE NEGATIVE for handling game-going 4-4-4-1 responding hands in the PRECISION CLUB system is called the Unusual Positive. It consists of an immediate jump to two hearts, two spades, three clubs or three diamonds to show a hand worth 8 or more points, with a singleton.

As with the Impossible Negative, there are two ways in which the singleton can be pinpointed. The simpler is for the jump to be made in the suit of the singleton. Thus responder's jump to two hearts would show a singleton heart; his jump to three clubs would show a singleton club; etc.

The more sophisticated way of pinpointing the singleton is for responder to jump in the suit below the singleton. Thus, responder's jump to two hearts would show a singleton spade; his jump to three clubs would show a singleton diamond; etc.

Use of either form of the Unusual Positive is, of course, incompatible with the use of these jumps to show long suits with 4 to 7 points.

When the Unusual Positive is used with responder jumping in the suit below the singleton, it enables the opener cheaply to ask responder how many controls he has by bidding the suit of the singleton. Responder shows his controls (ace = two controls, king = one control) in steps. The first step shows 0, 1 or 2 controls; the second step shows 3 controls, and so forth. Thus, in the auction

Opener	Responder
1 ♣	3 ♢
3 ♡	4 ♣

responder's three diamond bid showed a positive response with a singleton heart, and four cards in each of the other suits. Opener's three heart bid asked about controls, and responder's four club response, the third step, showed four controls.

PRECISION TRUMP ASKING BIDS

In the Precision system, if the responder makes a positive response and the opener makes a single raise of responder's suit, opener's raise is an Asking Bid. It asks the responder how good his trump suit is. The responder replies in steps, as follows:

First step = none of top three honors, any length

Second step = one of top honors, five card suit

Third step = two of top three honors, five card suit

Fourth step = one of top three honors, six card suit

Fifth step = two of top three honors, six card suit

Sixth step = all three top honors, any length

Using this method, when opener uses the asking bid, and the responder has, for example, a six card spade suit headed by the ace and queen, the auction would start:

Opener	Responder
1 ♣	1 ♠
2 ♠	3 ♠

An alternative method is for the partnership to agree that responder will use a four-step series of responses, and will show only how many honors he has, not how long his suit is. Using this variation, the first step would show none of the top three honors; the second step would show one of the top three honors; the third step would show two of the top three honors; and the fourth step would show all three honors. If the opener is interested in how long responder's suit is, he can repeat the bid of responder's suit to ask that question. For example:

Opener	Responder
1 ♣	1 ♠
2 ♠	3 ♦
3 ♠	

Responder's three diamond bid shows two of the top three spade honors; opener's three spade rebid asks how long responder's suit is. Responder gives the answer in steps, using the first step to show five cards, the second step to show six cards, and so forth. An advantage of using this alternative method of responding to the trump asking bid is that often the opener is interested only in honor strength, not in length. This method simply uses less space, making it easier for the responder to get on to his next question.

PRECISION CONTROL ASKING BIDS

After the opener has made a trump asking bid, if he bids a new suit it asks the responder about his controls in the new suit. For example, in the auction

Opener	Responder
1 ♣	1 ♡
2 ♡	3 ♣
3 ♦	

opener has learned that responder has 8 or more points, with at least five hearts headed by two of the top three honors. Opener's three diamond rebid asks responder whether he has any sort of control of the diamond suit. Control could take the form of high cards or shortness. Responder answers in steps as follows:

First   step = no control (three or more small cards)

Second step = 3rd round control (queen or doubleton)

Third   step = 2nd round control (king or singleton)

Fourth step = 1st round control (ace or a void)

Fifth   step = 1st and 2nd round control (ace & king, or ace & queen)

With respect to opponent interference with Control Asking Bids, *see discussion under* PRECISION ACE ASKING BIDS.

PRECISION ACE-ASKING BIDS

Using standard Precision bidding, a jump shift by the opener after a positive response shows a solid suit with a 19 point hand. As a modification, the partnership could agree to use the jump shift by the opener as an ace-asking bid. To use this bid the opener will either have a solid suit, or a semi-solid suit, i.e., one that is missing one of the top three honors.

Using this method, the jump shift asks responder two questions: first, whether or not he has the missing trump honor, and second, whether or not he has any aces.

If the responder does not have the missing trump honor, and does not have an ace, he rebids the minimum number of notrump. If he has the missing trump honor but no side ace, he raises opener's suit. If he has one side ace, but not the missing trump honor, he makes a minimum bid in the suit in which he has the ace.

If the responder has two key cards, he must jump to show them, as follows. If he has the missing trump honor and a side suit ace, he jumps in the suit in which he has the ace. If he has two aces, but not the missing trump honor, he jumps in notrump. If he has the missing trump honor and two side aces, he jump raises the opener's suit.

For example, suppose the responder held

♠ A x x x x   ♡ J x x   ◇ x x   ♣ K x x

and the auction started

Opener	Responder
1 ♣	1 ♠
3 ♣	

responder's proper bid would be four spades, showing the ace of spades and the king of clubs.

Note that the opener may have a solid suit, and there may be no missing trump honor. In this event he will be seeking information only about the responder's aces, a fact that responder will not know until later.

After the responder has responded to the opener's ace-asking jump shift, if the opener rebids in a new suit he asks about responder's controls in that suit. Responder will show his controls in steps according to the same schedule used for CONTROL ASKING BIDS (see above).

When the Opponents Interfere

If the opponents overcall over an asking bid, the responder uses a double to show that he would have responded with the first step of the asking bid responses; he uses a pass to show that he would have responded with the second step. To show the third and subsequent steps the responder bids up the line, the cheapest suit over the overcall showing the third step, and so forth.

This method of coping with interference can be used over either the trump suit asking bids or the control asking bids. For example, suppose the bidding had gone

Opener	Responder
1 ♣	2 ♣
3 ♣	3 ♦
3 ♡	

and over the three heart control asking bid the opponent bids three spades. Responder would double with no heart control; he would pass with third round control; he would bid three no-trump with second round control, four clubs with first round control, and four diamonds with first and second round control.

In the above auction, if the opponent had overcalled three spades over the three club bid, which asked about responder's trumps, responder would have used the same method. He would double with none of the top three club honors, that being the first step he would have made without interference, or would pass with a five card suit headed by one of the top three honors. To show the third and succeeding steps, responder would bid up the line:

3 NT = a five card suit headed by two of the top three honors (3rd original step)

4 ♣ = a six card suit headed by one of the top three honors (4th original step)

4 ♢ = a six card suit headed by two of the top three honors (5th original step)

4 ♡ = all three top honors, any length (6th original step)

ROMAN CLUB

The Roman System is a system that attempts to define high card strength and overall distribution with almost every opening bid. There are opening bids that show balanced hands, opening bids that show hands containing long suits, opening bids that show specific two-suited hands, and opening bids that show three-suited hands.

Balanced hands, i.e., 4-4-3-2 or 4-3-3-3, are opened with either a forcing one club bid or with a notrump bid. The one notrump opening shows 17 to 20 points; the two notrump opening shows 23 to 24 points.

Three suited hands, i.e., 4-4-4-1 or 5-4-4-0, are opened with two of a minor suit. The two club opening shows 11 to 16 high card points. The two diamond opening shows 17 to 20 high card points. *See* ROMAN TWO CLUBS and ROMAN TWO DIAMONDS.

Hands with limited playing strength containing at least one long suit, i.e., five cards or more, are opened in a suit other than clubs. The openings of one diamond, one heart and one spade are natural *and forcing*. However, since the Roman system uses the canape style of bidding short suits before long suits, the opening bid of one diamond, one heart or one spade usually does not show the opener's long suit.

The high card strength of the opening one-bids other than one club is not limited nearly so much as it is in the Blue Team, Schenken and Precision Club systems. The one diamond, one heart and one spade openings may range from a meager 12 points to just under the strength of a forcing two bid. The opener's rebid serves to clarify the strength of his hand.

Negative Responses to One Diamond, One Heart or One Spade

The openings of one diamond, one heart and one spade are forcing on the responder for one round. The usual negative response is the bid of the next higher denomination. For example, a response of one heart to a one diamond opening, and a response of one notrump to a one spade opening are negative. In each instance the negative response shows less than 9 points and denies support for the suit the opener has bid.

If the opener rebids one notrump after the negative response, he shows 12 to 14 points with five or more cards in the "negative" suit. If the opener's long suit is the "negative" suit and he has 15 to 17 points, he bids two of that suit. If the opener has a long suit other than the "negative" suit, he bids the minimum number of his suit with 12 to 17 points, or jumps in it with 18 to 21 points.

In addition to the next-suit negative bid, the responder can also make a negative response by raising the opener's bid suit to the two level. The raise shows at least four-card trump support, a doubleton in a side suit, and less than 9 points.

Constructive Responses to One Diamond, One Heart or One Spade

Other responses fall into two categories: constructive responses and positive responses. With a hand worth 9 to 11 points, responder may make a constructive response by making a minimum bid in a suit other than the "negative" suit. If the responder's bid is to be at the two level, he must have at least 10 points. Constructive responses are forcing for one round, but are not forcing to game.

If the responder has 9 to 11 points and a one-suited hand,

he bids and rebids his long suit. With two suits, the responder's bids, like the opener's, are made in the canape style. Therefore, if the responder bids two suits, his second is usually longer than his first.

For example, if responder has the following hand opposite a one diamond opening

[A] ♠ K Q x x   ♡ A J x x x   ◇ x x   ♣ x x

he will respond one spade, showing, for the time being at least, a constructive response. After the opener's rebid, responder will show his heart suit at the minimum level. For example:

Opener	Responder
1 ◇	1 ♠
2 ◇	2 ♡

With a hand worth 9 to 11 points, the responder is not allowed to reverse, i.e., bid a higher ranking suit after bidding a lower ranking suit. Therefore, if instead of hand (A) above responder had

[B] ♠ K Q x x x   ♡ A J x x   ◇ x x   ♣ x x

he could not respond two hearts over one diamond and follow with a spade rebid. With hand (B), responder should simply bid and rebid spades:

Opener	Responder
1 ◇	1 ♠
2 ◇	2 ♠

As a general matter, the responder should be conservative

about making constructive responses. With hands that could create a rebid problem, he should tend to make an initial negative response, planning to bid aggressively at his next turn. For example, suppose opposite a one heart opening responder had

♠ K x x   ♡ A x x   ♢ Q x x x x   ♣ J x

If responder makes the constructive response of two diamonds and opener rebids three clubs (forcing for one round), the responder has no suitable rebid. If he rebids his straggly diamond suit, opener is likely to pass with a singleton; responder cannot take a preference to hearts, in which opener could well have just three cards; and a three notrump rebid could put the partnership on distinctly thin ice. Therefore, with such a hand responder does better to make a negative response first, and raise the opener or bid notrump later.

Positive Responses to One Diamond, One Heart or One Spade

If the responder has 12 or more points, he may make a positive response, forcing the partnership to game. Any notrump response, except one notrump over a one spade opening, is a positive response. One notrump in response to one diamond or one heart shows 12 to 15 points, with all unbid suits stopped. A two notrump response shows 16 to 18 points.

A jump raise of the opener's suit is also a positive response. Because of the canape style of bidding, the responder may not make a jump raise without at lease five cards in the suit opened.

Responder may also make a positive response by jump shifting into a long, strong suit of his own. With a hand worth a positive response but not suitable for notrump or a jump raise or a jump shift, the responder starts by bidding a new suit. He will make it clear at his next turn that this was not just a constructive response, by either reversing or jumping into a long suit. For example, with a hand such as

♠ K Q x x x   ♡ A Q x x   ◇ x x   ♣ Q x

in response to one diamond, responder would bid two hearts. At his next turn he would rebid spades:

Opener	Responder
1 ◇	2 ♡
3 ◇	3 ♠

Responder's three spade bid is a reverse, showing at least twelve points, and longer spades than hearts.

If responder's short suit outranks his long suit, his bidding first the short suit and then the long suit will not be a reverse. In these circumstances, to show a positive responder would make a jump rebid to show a positive response; responder jumps in his longer suit unless that would take him past three notrump, in which event he must jump to three notrump. With

♠ K Q x x   ♡ A Q x x x   ◇ Q x   ♣ x x

responder would respond one spade over the one diamond opening, and follow with a jump to three hearts:

Opener	Responder
1 ◇	1 ♠
2 ◇	3 ♡

After responder has made a constructive or positive response, opener's rebid will clarify the strength of his hand. If opener has 12 to 14 points and just one long suit, he will make the minimum rebid in that suit. This rebid is not forcing if responder has not made a positive response. If opener has 15 to 17 points with one long suit, he makes a jump rebid in his suit. If the responder has made a constructive response, the jump rebid is forcing to game.

If the opener rebids a second suit, that suit is at least five cards long, and his hand is worth 12 to 17 points. This bid of a second suit is forcing on the responder for one round.

Opening Bids of Two Hearts and Two Spades

Applying the canape principle, with two-suited hands, the Roman opener bids his shorter suit first. However, when his shorter suit is clubs, this method cannot be used. Therefore, the Roman system uses opening bids of two hearts and two spades to show 12 to 16 points with at least five cards in the major suit bid, together with a four- or five-card club suit. For example,

♠ A K x x x ♡ K x x ◇ x ♣ K J x x

In response to the opening of two hearts or two spades, the responder may pass, or take a preference to clubs. He may also bid a new suit; such a bid is forcing for one round, and shows either a six-card or longer suit, or a hand worth a slam try. If the responders' hand is of the slam-try variety, he will later jump in clubs or in the opener's major suit. Responder normally will not bid a new suit that is only five cards long, since he has a way to find out whether or not the opener has three-card support for his suit.

A two notrump response to a two heart or two spade opening bid is artificial, and asks the opener to clarify his distribution. If the opener bids three clubs, he shows four clubs, five cards in his major suit, and doubletons in the unbid suits. If opener bids a new suit other than clubs at the three level, he shows three cards in that suit, four clubs, and five cards in the major suit he opened. For example, in the auction

Opener	Responder
2 ♡	2 Notrump
3 ♠	

opener shows 3-5-1-4 distribution. If the opener rebids three notrump over two notrump, he shows five cards in clubs and five in his major suit, with a doubleton and a singleton in the unbid suits. If the opener has five clubs and five of his major suit and a void in one of the other suits, his proper rebids are (a) four clubs holding three cards in the unbid major suit, or (b) four diamonds holding three diamonds. For example, opener's and responder's hands might be

(Opener)
♠ A K x x x   ♡ J x x   ◇ —   ♣ K Q x x x

(Responder)
♠ x x   ♡ A K x x x   ◇ K x x   ♣ J x x

The auction would go

Opener	Responder
2 ♠	2 Notrump
4 ♣	4 ♡

Over the two notrump response, if the opener simply rebids the major suit he has opened, e.g.,

Opener	Responder
2 ♡	2 Notrump
3 ♡	

he shows a six card major suit. He may have four or five clubs; if he rebids clubs after having rebid his major suit he shows a five card club suit.

One Notrump Opening and Responses

The opening bid of one notrump in the Roman system shows a balanced hand with 17 to 20 high card points. With a weak balanced hand, i.e., 0 to 5 points, responder may pass. With a weak unbalanced hand, responder may use GLADIATOR-type responses at the two level.

Holding 0 to 5 points and a five-card or longer suit, responder may respond two clubs to the notrump opening. The two club bid is a relay, forcing opener to rebid two diamonds. Opener is expected to pass any rebid by responder over the forced two diamond bid, but he may raise if he has 20 points and no worse than three-card support for responder's suit, headed by two of the top three honors. If opener's and responder's hands were

(Opener)
♠ K J x   ♡ A K x x   ◇ K x x   ♣ A x x

(Responder)
♠ Q x x x x x   ♡ x x   ◇ x x x   ♣ x x

the auction would be

Opener	Responder
1 Notrump	2 ♣
2 ♢	2 ♠
Pass	

Because the two club bid is used as a relay, a two diamond response to the one notrump opening is used as Stayman, and is forcing to game. Opener rebids a four card major suit if he has one, or bids two notrump if he has none.

If responder has 6 or 7 points and a balanced hand he may invite game by raising to two notrump. If opener elects to accept the invitation, he may either bid three notrump directly, or he may bid three clubs to learn whether or not responder has a four card major suit. However, special responses to the three club inquiry are used in order to allow opener, with his much stronger hand, to be the declarer. If responder has no four-card major suit, he rebids three notrump. If he has a four-card major suit, he bids the suit *below* his four card major. If he has both four hearts and four spades, he rebids three diamonds. Thus the auction could go

Opener	Responder
1 Notrump	2 Notrump
3 ♣	3 ♡
4 ♠	Pass

Responder's three heart rebid promised a four card spade suit, but denied a four card heart suit. If responder had both four card major suits and opener had four spades, the auction could have gone

Opener	Responder
1 Notrump	2 Notrump
3 ♣	3 ◇
3 ♠	4 ♠

Opposite the one notrump opening, if responder has a six-card major suit headed by no better than the ace and jack, but no worse than the king and jack, he may jump to three of his suit. After this response bid opener may place the final contract, either by passing, or by raising responder's suit, or by bidding three notrump.

If responder has better than 7 points and has a five-card or longer suit, he may force to game by bidding two hearts, two spades, three clubs or three diamonds. Over these responses opener is required to show his strength and the quality of his support for responder's suit, by the following four steps:

First   step = minimum hand, poor support

Second step = minimum hand, good support

Third   step = maximum hand, poor support

Fourth step = maximum hand, good support

In this context, good support means no worse than four small cards or three cards headed by the queen.

After opener has shown his strength and his trump support, responder may sign off in three notrump or in game in his suit. Alternatively, responder may bid a new suit to ask about opener's support for that suit. Opener uses a two-step schedule of responses; the first step shows poor support; the second step shows good support. For example, in the auction

Opener	Responder
1 Notrump	2 ♠
3 ◇	3 ♡
3 ♠	3 Notrump

opener's three diamond bid showed a maximum one notrump opening, but poor support for responder's spade suit. Responder three heart bid asked about opener's heart holding; opener's three spade bid, the first step, showed that his support for hearts was also poor. Opener's and responder's hands might be

(Opener)
♠ A x   ♡ x x x   ◇ A K Q x   ♣ A K x x

(Responder)
♠ K Q x x x   ♡ K x x x x   ◇ J x   ♣ x

Jumps to four hearts or four spades by responder over the one notrump opening are normal sign offs, showing a long suit and no interest in slam.

If responder has interest in slam and no five-card suit to bid, he may elect to show opener his point count. Thus responder's jumps to four clubs, four diamonds, and to any bid from four notrump through five notrump show responder's exact number of high card points as follows:

$$4 ♣ = 14 \text{ points}$$

$$4 ◇ = 15 \text{ points}$$

$$4 \text{ NT} = 16 \text{ points}$$

$$5 ♣ = 17 \text{ points}$$

$$5 \diamondsuit = 18 \text{ points}$$

$$5 \heartsuit = 19 \text{ points}$$

$$5 \spadesuit = 20 \text{ points}$$

$$5 \text{ NT} = 21 \text{ points}$$

Over responder's point count showing response, opener may sign off with a minimum bid in notrump, or he may bid a slam. Alternatively, opener may bid his lower ranking four card suit, looking for a 4-4 fit in which to play slam. For example, if opener's and responder's hands were

(Opener)
♠ K J x   ♡ A Q x x   ◇ K Q x x   ♣ A J

(Responder)
♠ A Q x   ♡ K J x x   ◇ A x   ♣ K x x x

the bidding would go

Opener	Responder
1 Notrump	5 ♣
5 ◇	5 ♡
7 ♡	

Responder's five club response showed 17 high card points. Since opener had 20 points, he had visions of a grand slam, especially if a 4-4 fit could be found.

One Club Opening

A forcing opening bid of one club in the Roman system may be made with any of four types of hands. It may show 12 to 16 points with even distribution, specifically 4-3-3-3 or 4-4-3-2. If the opener has this hand he will usually rebid a major suit or no-trump; or, if responder has made a constructive response, opener may raise responder's suit if he has four card support.

One club may also be opened with a balanced hand worth 21 to 22 points or 25 to 26 points. If opener has one of these hands, his rebid will be a jump in notrump.

The one club opening may also be used with an unbalanced hand of game-forcing strength. If opener has this hand he will make a jump rebid, or other non-minimum rebid, in his suit. One club may also be opened with a two-suited hand that includes at least four clubs, with 17 to 20 points. If opener has this hand, he will rebid clubs.

A one diamond response to one club is negative. This response shows less than 8 high card points, although it may be made with more than 8 points when responder has no four-card major suit and no five-card minor suit.

Constructive Responses to One Club

With a hand worth 8 to 11 points, the responder may make a constructive response. Constructive responses are minimum responses in suits.

When deciding what suit to bid, the responder should prefer a four card major suit to a longer minor suit. For example, with

♠ K x x x   ♡ x   ◇ A J x x x   ♣ J x x

responder would bid one spade over a one club opening, planning to bid diamonds later—a canape series of bids.

If responder has two four card major suits, he should bid

one heart, leaving opener room to rebid one spade. If responder has two five-card major suits, he should bid hearts first and then bid spades. With five cards in each minor suit, responder should bid diamonds first and then bid clubs. With a five-card major suit and a five-card minor suit, responder should simply bid and rebid his major suit.

For example, if responder holds

♠ K Q x x x   ♡ x x   ◇ A x x x x   ♣ x

the bidding might go

Opener	Responder
1 ♣	1 ♠
1 Notrump	2 ♠

With the above hand, responder systemically has no way to show his diamond suit without distorting either his strength or his distribution. If he were to respond one spade and follow with a diamond rebid, he would show longer diamonds than spades; if he were to respond two diamonds and follow with a spade rebid, he would show a hand worth a positive response, i.e., more than 12 points.

If responder has no four-card major suit in which to respond to the one club opening, he may bid a minor suit if he has at least 9 points and at least five cards in his suit. Thus, with a hand such as

♠ K x x   ♡ J x x   ◇ x x x   ♣ A Q x x

responder is forced to temporize with a one diamond "negative" response. After the auction has started 1 ♣ — 2 ♣, or 1 ♣ — 2 ◇, therefore, opener can rely on responder to have either 9 points and five cards in the suit bid, or the values for a positive response.

Positive Responses to One Club

If responder has 12 points or more, he may make a positive response. The immediately positive responses are one notrump, two notrump, two hearts and two spades. The notrump responses show balanced or nearly balanced distribution (4-3-3-3, or 4-4-3-2 or 5-3-3-2). One notrump shows 12 to 15 points; two notrump shows 16 or more points.

The response of two hearts or two spades promises a five-card or longer suit; unless the response is followed by a bid of the other major suit, it promises two of the top three honors. For example, holding

♠ J x x   ♡ A Q x x x   ◇ K x x   ♣ A x

responder would jump to two hearts over the one club opening.

If responder has a hand worth a positive response with five cards in each major suit, he responds by jumping in the stronger major and then bidding the other major. For example, if responder has

♠ K x x x x   ♡ K Q x x x   ◇ x   ♣ A x

he will jump to two hearts over one club, and rebid his spade suit.

If responder has five cards in each minor suit, he bids clubs first and then rebids diamonds. Bidding clubs first and then diamonds is the reverse of what responder does with both five-card minor suits and a merely constructive hand.

If responder has a five-card major suit and a five-card minor suit, he bids the minor suit first and then bids his major suit. Initially this sequence is ambiguous because it can be used to show a longer major suit than minor suit; however, the extra minor suit card can be shown later.

If the responder has a five-card or longer suit and a four-card suit, he first responds in the short suit, and then rebids the longer suit. If this short suit ranks higher than his long suit, he will have to make a jump rebid in the long suit to show that his response was positive. Indeed, with respect to any positive response that begins other than with a notrump bid or a jump to two of a major suit, responder's first response is ambiguous; it could be either positive or constructive. Responder's rebid will clarify the strength of his hand. With a positive response, responder's rebid will be either a reverse bid or a jump.

Suppose responder has one of the following hands opposite the one club opening:

[A] ♠ K Q x x x   ♡ A x x   ◇ x   ♣ A x x x

[B] ♠ K Q x x x   ♡ A x   ◇ x   ♣ A x x x x

[C] ♠ K Q x x   ♡ A x x x x   ◇ A x x   ♣ x

With Hand A, responder would bid two clubs, his short suit, and then rebid spades, his long suit. The auction might start

Opener	Responder
1 ♣	2 ♣
2 ◇	2 ♠

Similarly with Hand B, responder would bid two clubs and then rebid his spade suit. In this case responder has an extra club, but his first two bids would be the same as with Hand A.

With Hand C, responder would start with a one spade bid, and then rebid hearts. However, since his short suit outranks his long suit, the non-jump rebid of hearts would show a constructive hand rather than a positive hand; therefore, responder must jump rebid hearts to show his strength. The auction might start

Opener	Responder
1 ♣	1 ♠
1 Notrump	3 ♡

Preemptive Responses to One Club

In addition to the routine negative, constructive and positive responses described above, the responder is allowed to make certain descriptive preemptive responses. These include unencouraging jumps to four of a major suit, weak jumps to three of a major suit or four of a minor suit, and somewhat constructive jumps to three of a minor suit.

If responder holds a six- or seven-card major suit headed by the ace and king, or the king, queen and jack, and has a modicum of outside values, he may jump to four of his suit. For example, holding

[A]   ♠ Q x   ♡ K Q J x x x x   ◇ x   ♣ x x x

responder would jump to four hearts over the one club opening.

If responder holds a six- or seven-card club or diamond suit headed by no worse than the ace, king and jack, he may jump to three of his suit. For example, with

[B]   ♠ x x   ♡ x x x   ◇ x x   ♣ A K Q x x x

responder would jump to three clubs over the one club opening. Opener would use his best judgment in setting the final contract.

If responder has a weaker hand and a weaker suit than those in (A) and (B) above, he may jump to three hearts, three spades, four clubs or four diamonds. For example, responder might hold

[C] ♠ K J x x x x x ♡ x ◇ x x ♣ x x x

or

[D] ♠ x ♡ J x x ◇ K Q 10 x x x x ♣ x x

With Hand C responder would jump to three spades over the one club opening. With Hand D responder would jump to four diamonds. If opener has a hand such as

♠ A x x ♡ A x x x ◇ x x ♣ A Q x x

he would bid four spades over responder's three spade bid (Hand C), but would pass responder's jump to four diamonds (Hand D).

Rebids When the One Club Opener Has a Minimum Hand Opposite a Negative Response

When the response to the one club opening has been the one diamond negative, opener's first aim with a minimum one club opening (12 to 16 points) is to find a safe home at the one level. Opener therefore bids a four-card major suit if he has one; if he has four cards in both major suits, he rebids one heart. If opener has no four card major suit, he rebids one heart if he has a three-card heart suit; only as a last resort does he rebid one notrump. Thus a one notrump rebid after a one diamond response shows specifically three spades, two hearts, four clubs and four diamonds.

After having made a negative response, responder may pass opener's rebid if he has a very poor hand; however, even with a poor hand, if he has a four-card spade suit that he can show at the one level, he should do so.

If responder has any significant values, he should bid as strongly as seems appropriate at his second turn, since opener is likely to pass any unencouraging sounding rebid. For example, if responder has a hand such as

♠ x   ♡ A 10 9 x x   ◇ Q x x   ♣ x x x x

and the bidding has started

Opener	Responder
1 ♣	1 ◇
1 ♡	

responder should show his maximum negative pointcount, and his good trump support and distribution by jumping to three hearts.

Rebids When the One Club Opener Has a Minimum Hand Opposite a Constructive Response

When opener has a 12 to 16 point balanced hand opposite a constructive response, his first rebid shows whether he has the top (15 to 16) or the bottom (12 to 14) of his range. The rebid may also show one of opener's four card suits. A 15 to 16 point rebid will force the partnership at least to the two notrump level, and frequently the partnership will reach game after such a rebid, either because the hands fit well, or because responder makes a rebid that reveals extra values.

If opener makes a simple raise of responder's suit, he shows

213

a 12 to 14 point hand. If responder's suit was a major, the raise promises four card support; if responder's suit is a minor, which normally promises a five card suit, opener may raise with three card support. If opener has support for responder's suit but has 15 to 16 points, he may not raise immediately, but must temporize with a non-minimum rebid before raising.

If opener rebids one notrump over the constructive response of one heart or one spade, he shows 12 to 14 points; however, if he rebids two notrump over a response of two clubs or two diamonds, he shows 15 to 16 points. If opener rebids a new suit, he shows 15 to 16 points if he has bypassed one notrump, but a minimum if he has not. For example,

(A) Opener   Responder
    1 ♣   1 ♠
    2 ♦

(B) Opener   Responder
    1 ♣   2 ♣
    2 ♦

In auction (A), opener's two diamond bid shows 15 to 16 points. Opener might have a hand such as

[C] ♠ Q x   ♡ A K x x   ◇ A Q x x   ♣ x x x
or
[D] ♠ A Q x x   ♡ x x   ◇ Q x x x   ♣ A K x

With Hand D, opener could not raise responder's spade suit because his hand is too strong; therefore he temporized with a two diamond bid, bypassing one notrump.

In auction (B), opener's two diamond bid showed a 12 to 14 point hand, since he did not bypass one notrump in making his rebid. In order to show a maximum hand in auction (B), opener would have had to rebid two notrump.

After opener has clarified his point count opposite a constructive response, the bidding proceeds naturally.

Rebids When the One Club Opener Has a Minimum Hand Opposite a Positive Response

There are three immediately positive types of responses: one notrump, showing a balanced 12 to 15 point hand; two notrump, showing a balanced hand worth more than 15 points; and a jump to two of a major suit, showing a five-card or longer suit headed by two of the top three honors. Opener has a special set of rebids for each of these responses.

After a one notrump response, opener should raise to two notrump with a maximum (15 to 16 points), or rebid a four card suit, preferably a major suit, with a minimum hand. If opener has bid a suit to show 12 to 14 points, responder may rebid two notrump if he has 12 points, giving opener the opportunity to pass if he too has only 12 points. This is the only rebid by responder that can be passed.

If opener has shown a maximum hand by raising to two notrump, responder may bid three clubs as a Stayman-type inquiry for a major suit fit, or he may bid a five-card suit at the three level. For example, in the auction

Opener	Responder
1 ♣	1 Notrump
2 Notrump	3 ♠
4 ♠	

opener has shown 15 to 16 points with his two notrump rebid.

Responder's three spade bid showed a five-card spade suit, and opener's raise to game showed three- or four-card support. Opener might have a hand such as

♠ K x x   ♡ A J x x   ◇ x x   ♣ A K x x

If responder's positive response to the one club opening was two notrump, opener must rebid to show his point count as follows:

$$3 \clubsuit = 12 \text{ to } 13 \text{ points}$$
$$3 \diamondsuit = 14 \text{ points}$$
$$3 \heartsuit = 15 \text{ points}$$
$$3 \spadesuit = 16 \text{ points}$$

After learning opener's point count, responder may sign off in three notrump. Over a three club or three diamond bid by opener, responder may bid three hearts or three spades in search of a major suit fit. Or, over any of opener's point count showing rebids, responder may bid four clubs, a bid that shows slam interest, and asks opener to bid his lower ranking four card suit. Opener and responder thus bid their suits up the line in search of a 4-4 fit.

If opener's and responder's hands were, for example, as follows

(Opener)
♠ A Q   ♡ K x x x   ◇ Q J x   ♣ K x x x

(Responder)

♠ J x   ♡ A Q x x   ◇ A 10 x x   ♣ A Q x

the bidding could go

Opener	Responder
1 ♣	2 Notrump
3 ♡	4 ♣
4 ♡	6 ♡

Opener's three heart rebid showed precisely 15 points; responder, with his good controls, was interested in slam if a 4-4 fit could be found, despite having only 17 points. When opener showed a four-card heart suit, responder bid the slam.

If the positive response to the one club opening was a jump to two hearts or two spades, opener is required to rebid in steps to show his range and the quality of his support for responder's suit as follows:

First   step = minimum hand, poor support

Second step = minimum hand, good support

Third   step = maximum hand, poor support

Fourth step = maximum hand, good support

Over opener's rebid, responder should be able to set the final contract. For example, if opener's and responder's hands were

(Opener)

♠ K x x   ♡ K J x x   ◇ x x x   ♣ A Q x

(Responder)

♠ A Q x x x   ♡ A x   ◇ K Q x   ♣ J x x

the bidding could go

Opener	Responder
1 ♣	2 ♠
3 ♣	4 ♠

Opener's three club rebid, the second step, showed a minimum hand with good spade support. Responder gave up his hopes of a slam on account of opener's minimum, and bid the game in spades rather than notrump based on opener's announced good trump support.

Rebids When the One Club Opener Has a Strong Balanced Hand

When opener has bid one club with a balanced hand worth 21 to 22 or 25 to 26 points, he must jump in notrump over his partner's response. If responder has bid a negative one diamond in response to the one club opening, opener jumps to two notrump with 21 to 22 high card points, or jumps to three notrump with 25 to 26 high card points.

After opener's jump to two notrump over one diamond, if responder has 0 to 3 points, he should pass if he has a balanced hand, or bid three diamonds, three hearts or three spades if he has length in one of those suits. Such a bid by responder is not forcing, but opener may raise if he has a maximum hand and strong support for the suit. A three club bid by responder is a Stayman inquiry for the major suits. It promises 4 to 8 points, and is forcing to game.

218

After opener's jump to three notrump over one diamond, showing 25 to 26 points, responder may bid game in a long major suit if he has one, or he may bid four clubs as Stayman. Or, if responder has 7 to 8 points, he may try for slam by raising to four notrump. This bid asks opener to bid his lower ranking four card suit, following which the partnership bids its four-card suits up the line in search of a 4-4 fit in which to play a slam.

If the response to the one club opening was constructive, and opener has the strong balanced hand, he makes a single jump in notrump, regardless of whether he has 21 to 22 points, or 25 to 26 points. Thus, over the constructive response of one heart or one spade, opener will rebid two notrump—the partnership is of course forced to game. Over the constructive response of two clubs or two diamonds, opener will jump to three notrump.

After opener's jump rebid in notrump following the constructive response, responder is expected to bid his long suit—whether it be the suit of his initial response or another suit. Over any suit bid by responder, opener must clarify his strength and show his support for the suit responder has just bid. Opener rebids in steps as follows:

First   step = minimum hand (21 to 22), poor support

Second step = minimum hand, good support

Third   step = maximum hand (25 to 26), poor support

Fourth step = maximum hand, good support

If responder thereafter bids a new suit, opener uses a two-step schedule of replies to describe his support for responder's new suit.

Opener and responder might have the following hands:

(Opener)

♠ K Q x   ♡ A K Q x   ◇ A K x x   ♣ A x

(Responder)

♠ A x x x   ♡ x x   ◇ x x   ♣ K Q x x x

The bidding might proceed as follows:

Opener	Responder
1 ♣	1 ♠
2 Notrump	3 ♣
3 ♠	4 ♠
5 ♣	6 ♠
6 Notrump	

With his constructive hand, responder starts by bidding his four-card major suit in response to one club, and over the two no-trump rebid he shows his long suit to find out opener's point count and his club support. Opener's three spade rebid, the third step, showed a maximum point count and poor club support. Hoping to find opener with a four card spade suit, responder bid four spades; opener's five club bid, the second step, showed good spade support. Responder could then jump to six spades, knowing that he had shown only a four-card spade suit by bidding first spades and then clubs. If opener had had four spades he would have passed six spades; as it was, he corrected to six notrump.

Rebids When the One Club Opener Has a Strong Unbalanced Hand

To show a strong unbalanced hand after opening one club, opener must rebid a suit; after a constructive or positive response, he must jump in his suit to show such a hand; after a negative response, any suit rebid at the two level shows such a hand. For example:

(A) *Opener*   *Responder*
   1 ♣   1 ♠
   3 ♡

(B) *Opener*   *Responder*
   1 ♣   1 ♡
   2 ♠

(C) *Opener*   *Responder*
   1 ♣   1 ◇
   2 ♠

(D) *Opener*   *Responder*
   1 ♣   1 ◇
   2 ◇

In auction (A), opener's jump to three hearts shows a hand similar to a traditional forcing two-bid. In auctions (B) and (C), opener's jumps to two spades show the same type of hand as in auction (A). In auction (D), even though opener did not jump, his two diamond bid shows the same type of strong hand, since with a 12 to 16 point type hand, opener is not allowed to go to the two level over a one diamond response.

After a strong suit rebid by opener over any type of response, responder is required to show his support for opener's suit in a series of nine steps, as follows:

First step = void or small singleton

Second step = two or three small cards

221

Third   step = singleton ace, king or queen

Fourth   step = two or three cards headed by the
                    ace, king or queen

Fifth   step = four small cards

Sixth   step = four cards headed by the ace, king
                    or queen

Seventh   step = three cards headed by two of the
                    top three honors

Eighth   step = four cards headed by two of the
                    top three honors

Ninth   step = ace, king and queen

For these purposes the jack is considered a small card. In the auction

Opener	*Responder*
1 ♣	1 ♡
2 ♠	3 ♠

responder's three spade bid shows that he has four small spades. His hand might be

 ♠ J 10 x x ♡ A Q x x ◇ Q x ♣ x x x

After responder has shown his support for opener's first bid suit, opener may make either of two further asking bids, depending on whether he bids a higher or lower ranking suit. If he rebids a second suit that ranks higher than his first suit, opener asks responder to show his support for the second suit in the same nine-step series just used. If opener instead bids a second suit that ranks lower than his first suit, he asks responder to show what control he has of the new suit, using a five-step schedule as follows:

First   step = no first or second round control

Second step = singleton

Third   step = void

Fourth step = king

Fifth   step = ace

If opener has two long suits and he wants to know whether or not responder has support for either of them, he must take care to bid his lower suit first. If he bids the higher suit first, his rebid of the lower suit will get him information about responder's control of the suit rather than his support for it.

Consider the following auctions:

(E) *Opener*   *Responder*
    1 ♣   1 ♡
    2 ♠   3 ♡
    4 ♢

(F) *Opener*   *Responder*
    1 ♣   1 ♡
    3 ♣   3 ♢
    3 ♠

In auction (E), opener's two spade rebid forces responder to show his spade support; responder's three heart bid shows the ace, king or queen of spades, doubleton or tripleton. Opener's rebid of four diamonds, a lower ranking suit than his first suit,

223

asks about responder's control of diamonds. Opener might have a hand such as

♠ A K 10 x x x x   ♡ A K Q x   ◇ A x   ♣ —

In auction (F), opener's three club bid asked about responder's club support, and responder's three diamond bid showed a singleton or void in clubs. Opener's rebid of three spades asked about spade support. Opener might have a hand such as

♠ A K Q 10 x x   ♡ A K   ◇ —   ♣ K Q J x x

If responder bids three notrump, showing a singleton or void in spades, opener will sign off in four spades.

When the Opponents Interfere

If an opponent makes a takeout double over the one club opening, responder has two ways to show that he would have made a negative response. With less than 8 points and three or more clubs, the responder passes; if the next hand also passes, opener will pass if he has a four-card club suit. If opener has fewer than four clubs, he will seek another resting place, by redoubling with a minimum hand, or by bidding one diamond with a maximum. If the responder has less than 8 points and fewer than three clubs, he will redouble the double, asking the opener to find another suit.

Over the double, a response of one diamond now becomes a constructive response. All other minimum suit responses are constructive, as they would have been without the double. After interference, the constructive response is not forcing, and any rebid by the opener shows a maximum.

With a hand worth a positive response, responder may bid one notrump, two notrump, two hearts or two spades if that is what he would have done had there been no double. In addition, responder may make a positive response by jumping to two diamonds if he has at least a five-card diamond suit headed by two of the top three honors.

With a hand worth a positive response that does not fit any of these specialized responses, the responder must pass, planning to bid later, or to double the opponents for penalties.

If the opponent overcalls over one club instead of doubling, responder's pass is the only negative call. Responder may make any constructive bid at the one or two level, but he should not go to the three level without a strong hand. For example

South's three diamond bid shows a positive response, not a constructive one. As when the interference has been a double, the opener may pass a constructive response if he has a minimum.

When responder has a strong enough hand to make a positive response he has four choices. If he has four good cards in the suit of the overcall, he can double for penalties. If he has a five card suit he may bid it at the three level, jumping if necessary. If he has no five card suit he can bid notrump with a stopper in the overcaller's suit (the minimum number of notrump with 12 to 15, or jump in notrump with 16 or more). If responder has no five card suit and no stopper in the opponent's suit, he may make a cue-bid, asking the opener to bid notrump if he has a stopper.

LITTLE ROMAN CLUB (Arno)

The Little Roman Club System, also called Arno, is similar to the Roman Club system, especially in its two-level opening bids. In the Little Roman System, all one-level openings, including one notrump, are forcing. The opening bid and responding style is canape.

One Club Opening

A forcing one club opening may be made on either of two types of hands. It may show a balanced hand with 12 to 16 points, or a one-suited or two-suited hand worth 17 to 20 points. If opener has a one-suiter, that suit is clubs; if he has a two-suiter, the shorter of the two is clubs.

A response of one diamond is negative, showing less than 10 points. If the opener rebids at the one level he shows a 12 to 16 point balanced hand.

Responses of one heart and one spade are positive, but not forcing to game. While natural, these responses may be made on as few as three cards, with a longer suit held in reserve. After the one heart or one spade response, if opener has a minimum hand he will raise with four-card support, or rebid one notrump if he lacks four-card support. For example, if opener's and responder's hands were

(Opener)
♠ K Q x   ♡ J x x   ◇ A x x   ♣ A x x x

(Responder)
♠ J x   ♡ A Q x   ◇ K Q x x x   ♣ x x x

226

the auction would go

Opener	Responder
1 ♣	1 ♡
1 Notrump	2 ♢
3 Notrump	

Having a maximum for his one notrump rebid and a fit for diamonds, opener may jump to three notrump over the two diamond bid. If he had had only 12 points, he would have rebid just two notrump.

If opener has 15 or 16 points, his automatic rebid is two clubs. The two club rebid does not promise length in clubs, but merely shows opener's point count. For example, if opener and responder had

(Opener)

♠ K Q x x   ♡ K x x x   ♢ A x x   ♣ A x

(Responder)

♠ J x   ♡ A Q x x   ♢ K Q x x x   ♣ x x

the bidding could go

Opener	Responder
1 ♣	1 ♡
2 ♣	2 ♢
2 ♡	4 ♡

Opener cannot raise responder's heart suit immediately, since that would show 12 to 14 points, and opener has 16. He therefore bids two clubs first, to show his maximum, then supports hearts. Since responder has four hearts, rather than the three he might have, and since he is not interested in slam even opposite a 16 point hand, he jumps to four hearts.

A response of two clubs or two diamonds over the one club opening is also positive, but again, not forcing to game. These responses also may be made on a three-card suit. If opener has 12 to 14 points he rebids a suit at the two level, even a three-card suit if necessary. If he has 15 or 16 points he rebids two notrump.

A one notrump response to one club shows 12 or more points and a balanced hand. This response is forcing to game. If opener has 12 or 13 points, he rebids a suit at the two level. If he has 14 to 16 points he raises to two notrump.

Jumps to two hearts, two spades, three clubs or three diamonds over one club show a long suit, and are forcing to game. These jumps ask opener to describe his strength and his support for opener's suit using one of the following four steps:

First   step = minimum hand, poor support

Second step = minimum hand, good support

Third   step = maximum hand, poor support

Fourth step = maximum hand, good support

If opener has a one-suited or two-suited hand with 17 to 20 points, he must rebid his longest suit one level higher than he would to show a 12 to 16 point hand. For example

Opener	*Responder*
1 ♣	1 ♡
3 ♣	

With a long club suit opener rebids three clubs; a two club bid would not have given any information with respect to opener's club suit, but would instead have promised 15 to 16 points in a balanced hand.

Openings of One Diamond, One Heart and One Spade

Openings of one diamond, one heart and one spade show 12 to 20 points, and are natural and forcing. The style is strongly canape, and the opening bid may be made in a three-card suit if the hand is worth 15 or more points.

A response in the next higher denomination over a one diamond, one heart or one spade opening is negative, showing 0 to 9 points. Thus a one heart response to a one diamond opening is negative, as is a one notrump response to a one spade opening.

All other suit responses are natural, and may be made on three card suits. A one notrump response to one diamond or one heart shows a balanced hand with 12 or more points. This response is forcing to game.

If opener has a 12 to 16 point hand, he makes a minimum rebid in his long suit. A rebid of one notrump after the negative response of one spade shows that opener has a five card spade suit.

If the one diamond opening is followed by a one notrump rebid by opener, it shows a balanced hand worth 17 to 20 high card points. After the notrump rebid, if responder has made the one heart negative response, a two club bid by responder is a relay, requiring the opener to bid two diamonds and to pass any rebid responder makes thereafter. For example:

Opener	*Responder*
1 ◇	1 ♡
1 Notrump	2 ♣
2 ◇	2 ♡
Pass	

Knowing that responder has one ace and at least four card spade support, opener bids the slam in spades.

Forcing One Notrump Opening

A one notrump opening shows either a balanced hand worth 21 to 24 points, or an unbalanced game-going hand. The one notrump opening is forcing. Any rebid by the opener other than in notrump shows the unbalanced hand and is forcing to game.

In response to the one notrump opening, the responder shows how many aces he has, Blackwood style:

$$2 \clubsuit = 0 \text{ aces}$$
$$2 \diamondsuit = 1 \text{ ace}$$
$$2 \heartsuit = 2 \text{ aces}$$
$$2 \spadesuit = 3 \text{ aces}$$

If opener has a balanced hand with 21 to 24 points he will rebid two notrump. Over two notrump, responder may bid three clubs as Stayman. Opener will rebid a four card major suit if he has one, or bid three diamonds if he has no four card major, or will bid three notrump if he has four cards in each major.

If responder rebids three diamonds over the opener's two notrump rebid, he asks opener about his point count. Opener rebids three hearts with 21 to 22 points, or three spades with 23 to 24. For example, opener's and responder's hands might be

(Opener)
♠ K Q x x   ♡ A K x   ◇ A K x   ♣ Q J x

(Responder)
♠ A x x   ♡ x x x   ◇ Q x x   ♣ A x x x

230

The bidding could go

Opener	Responder
1 Notrump	2 ♡
2 Notrump	3 ◇
3 ♡	3 Notrump

The two heart response showed two aces, but when opener rebid notrump, responder took control of the hand. His three diamond bid asked opener if he had a maximum or a minimum; opener's three heart bid showed 21 to 22 points. Responder therefore settled for three notrump.

After responder has shown his aces in response to the one notrump opening, if opener has an unbalanced hand he will rebid a suit. His bids will follow canape principle of bidding short suits before long suits. For example:

(Opener)

♠ K Q x x   ♡ A K   ◇ A K Q J x x   ♣ x

(Responder)

♠ J x x x x   ♡ Q x x   ◇ x x   ♣ A x x

With the partnership holding these hands the bidding could proceed

Opener	Responder
1 Notrump	2 ◇
2 ♠	3 ♣
3 ◇	3 ♠
6 ♠	

PRO SYSTEM
(Pattern Relay Organized System)

The Pattern Relay Organized, or PRO, system is a relatively natural bidding method that is designed principally to allow the stronger hand on any given deal is to take control of the auction and learn about his partner's strength and distribution. The PRO system uses only a few artificial conventions, although it uses several non-standard treatments.

Among the conventions used by the PRO system are a forcing one club opening bid, a virtually game-forcing one notrump response to a major suit opening, splinter bids, and the CLARAC slam try. The PRO system is devoted to auctions that do not involve game-forcing openings.

The Relay Principle

Using standard methods, unless opener has started with a strong two-bid type of opening with specialized responses, both opener and responder attempt to describe their strength and distribution as they search for the best contract. The PRO system allows the stronger hand to take control by making non-descriptive, information gathering "relay" bids. The relay is used only by the stronger hand, and only as a rebid; the opening bid or initial response is never a relay.

When used by the responder, the relay is the cheapest new suit rebid that the responder can make when his initial response has not limited his hand. For example, in the auction

(A) *Opener*   *Responder*
    1 ♣   1 ♠
    2 ♣   2 ◇

responder's one spade response is unlimited; therefore his two diamond bid over two clubs is a relay, asking opener to describe his hand further.

Similarly, in auctions in which responder's initial bid may have limited his hand, opener can sometimes use a non-descriptive type of bid that is designed to get more information from responder.

The major advantage of these relay bids is that they create a forcing situation at a low level of the auction, so that slam prospects may be assessed without getting the partnership out of its depth. In auction (A), for example, the partnership can start its slam investigations at the two level.

A second advantage is that when a forcing relay is available and some other non-jump bid is used instead, the latter bid is logically limited and non-forcing. For example, in the auction

Opener	Responder
1 ◇	1 ♡
2 ◇	3 ♣

responder's one heart response has not limited his hand; he could therefore have bid two hearts over two diamonds as a relay to create a forcing auction. Since he chose instead to bid three clubs, his bid was not forcing. If opener and responder hold, for example

(Opener)
♠ A 10 x   ♡ Q   ◇ A Q x x x x   ♣ J x x

(Responder)
♠ Q J x   ♡ A x x x x   ◇ —   ♣ K x x x

opener will pass three clubs, which may be the partnership's last makeable contract.

One Club Opening

The one club opening is forcing, and may be made with two types of hands. One club may be opened with an average hand with a club suit. If opener has this type of hand he will rebid clubs, or raise a suit bid by the responder.

One club may also be opened with a balanced hand worth 17 to 20 high card points. This hand may not include a five card suit other than clubs. If opener has this type of hand he will rebid notrump or a new major suit.

The negative response to the one club opening is one diamond. The one diamond response shows 0 to 6 points. Over the one diamond response opener may bid a four-card major suit if he has one, attempting to find a safe home at the one level.

Responses of one heart and one spade to the one club opening are constructive. If opener rebids one notrump, showing 17 to 20 points, the partnership is forced to game. Over the one notrump rebid, responder may bid two clubs as Stayman.

Opening Bids Other Than One Club

Opening bids are divided into three classes, according to strength. Minimum hands are those worth 13 points or less; intermediate hands are worth 14 to 16 points; strong hands are worth 17 to 20 points.

With minimum hands, the PRO system recommends opening in the highest ranking four-card suit, even if the hand contains a longer lower ranking suit. Thus, opener might hold

[A] ♠ A Q J x   ♡ x x   ◇ J x x x   ♣ K J x

or

[B] ♠ K Q x x   ♡ x   ◇ A Q x x x   ♣ J x x

Both Hand A and Hand B should be opened one spade. Opener shows a minimum hand by rebidding one notrump (unless he has opened one club), or rebidding a lower ranking suit, other than clubs, or making an immediate raise of responder's suit.

Balanced hands of intermediate strength—i.e., 14 to 16 points—are opened one notrump. Unbalanced hands are opened in the long suit. To show the intermediate strength of a hand opened in a suit, opener either rebids his suit, or rebids two clubs if his opening bid was not one club. The two club change of suit by opener is forcing, and does not promise a genuine club suit.

In addition, if responder's response was a two-level limited bid such as in the auction 1 ♠ - 2 ♠ or 1 ♠ - 2 ♡, a two notrump rebid by opener is forcing for one round. The two notrump rebid shows a generally balanced hand.

Reverses by opener are based on distributional playing strength rather than high card power. A reverse promises a concentration of at least ten cards in the two suits. The suit reversed into is usually at least five cards long. For example, with a hand such as

♠ A Q   ♡ A x x x x   ◇ A Q J x x   ♣ x

opener would open with one diamond, and then rebid his heart suit.

Limited Responses to Opening One Bids

One PRO treatment that differs from standard methods is that the two level response in a new suit over an opening bid is not forcing. Thus, the PRO partnership's auction may go

(A) *Opener*   *Responder*
  1 ♠   2 ♡
  Pass

(B) *Opener*   *Responder*
  1 ♠   2 ♢
  Pass

For his two heart bid in auction (A), responder might have

♠ x ♡ K Q x x x x ♢ x x ♣ J x x x

This treatment allows the responder to describe a weak hand completely naturally. For example, if responder has a hand such as

♠ A x ♡ x ♢ Q J x x x ♣ J 10 x x x

opposite a one spade opening, the bidding might go

Opener   *Responder*
1 ♠   2 ♢
2 Notrump   3 ♣
Pass

In addition, a jump shift by the responder is not forcing. Except when used by a passed hand, the jump shift shows 10 or 11 points and a solid suit. Opener need not rebid if he has a poor hand, or if the hand is a misfit.

The response of one notrump to a minor suit opening is a limited bid, showing a balanced hand worth 7 to 11 points. Opener is expected to pass with a minimum hand. If he has an intermediate or stronger hand, he may rebid two clubs, which initiates a Stayman type search for a major suit fit.

The response of one spade to a one heart opening bid is also limited to a maximum of 11 points. Since the one notrump response to one heart is used as a very strong forcing response, the one spade response is treated as limited.

Unlimited Responses to Opening One Bids

There are two responses in the PRO system that are used as completely unlimited bids. One is the one notrump response to a major suit opening bid; the other is a major suit response to a minor suit opening bid.

The one notrump response to a one heart or one spade opening immediately announces that responder probably has a game-going hand opposite the opening bid. Having created a forcing situation, this response allows a good deal of low level exploration. If the responder follows his notrump response with a relay bid, the partnership is committed to game. For example, if opener's and responder's hands were

(Opener)
♠ K J x   ♡ K J x x x   ◇ x   ♣ K 10 x x

(Responder)
♠ Q x x x   ♡ Q x   ◇ A x x   ♣ A Q x x

the bidding could go

Opener	Responder
1 ♡	1 Notrump
2 ♣	2 ◇
2 ♠	5 ♣

Responder's two diamond rebid, following his one notrump response, was a relay that was forcing to game. When opener rebid spades as well as clubs, he was marked with at most one diamond. Therefore, responder avoided notrump and bid game in clubs. His leap to the five level denied an interest in probing for slam.

Since a response of one notrump over a minor suit opening shows a hand limited to 11 points, the PRO system uses a major suit response to a minor suit opening to show either a hand worth 12 or more points, or a hand with a five-card or longer suit. Since responder usually has a five-card suit, opener may raise freely with three-card support. Thus, if responder has a hand such as

♠ K 10 x x x   ♡ A x x   ◇ x x   ♣ J x x

and has responded one spade only to hear his partner rebid one notrump, he need not worry about whether to pass or to rebid two spades, since opener has denied three-card support.

CLARAC SLAM TRY

The PRO system incorporates a convention called the CLARAC slam try, which uses a four club bid (or occasionally a three club bid by a responder who has shown a very good hand), to ask about aces, and to initiate further asking bids. The name CLARAC stands for CLub Asking, Respond Aces and Controls.

When the partner of the four club CLARAC bidder has shown a limited hand, the responses to four clubs are as follows: A four diamond bid shows no aces, and denies strong values such as kings or king and queen combinations. A four notrump bid also shows no aces, but promises reasonable king and king-queen values. Responses of four hearts, four spades and five clubs show one ace, plus first or second round control in the suit named. The control shown should be the lowest control held. Thus, a response of four spades would show one ace plus a spade control, and would deny a heart control in addition to the ace promised. The four spade response would not deny a club control.

Responses of five diamonds, five hearts, five spades and six clubs show two aces, plus a second round control in the suit named. For example a hand such as

$$\spadesuit \text{ A x x x} \qquad \heartsuit \text{ x} \qquad \diamondsuit \text{ Q J x x x} \qquad \clubsuit \text{ A J x}$$

if previously limited, would respond five hearts to the four club bid. A response of five notrump shows three aces and no other control.

If the partner of the CLARAC four club bidder has shown a good hand rather than a limited hand earlier in the auction, he must hold one ace more than the limited hand to make each of the responses described above, with the possible exception of the four diamond response. Thus, by a good hand, a response of four hearts, four spades or five clubs would show two aces plus control of the suit named; responses of five diamonds, five hearts, five spades or six clubs would show three aces and second round control of the suit named. Responses of six diamonds, six hearts or six spades would show four aces and second round control of the suit named.

If the CLARAC responder has made any bid other than four diamonds, the next suit bid by the four club bidder is an asking bid in that suit. For example, in the auction

(A) *Opener*   *Responder*
    1 ♢   2 Notrump
    4 ♣   4 ♡
    4 ♠

opener's four spade bid asks responder about his spade controls. With no control of the asked suit, responder bids the cheapest suit possible; with the king or a singleton, responder makes a minimum bid in notrump. A bid of a new suit by responder, other than the cheapest suit, shows the ace of the asked suit, plus second round control of the suit bid. If responder raises the asked suit, he shows two of the top three honors in that suit, with no other significant controls to show.

For example, in auction (A) shown above, if responder bid five diamonds over opener's four spade asking bid, he would be showing the ace of spades, and second round control of diamonds.

Following the CLARAC responder's answer to the asking bid, the CLARAC bidder may make a further asking bid. This process continues until slam is reached or until a negative response to an asking bid is given.

LEA SYSTEM

The Lea System uses a forcing one club opening to show an opening bid of 12 or more high card points. The responses use a series of six steps to show point count.

The one club opening may be made on all but two types of hands. It may not be made with a weak notrump type of hand. In addition, it may not be made with a hand worth 15 or 16 points, counting high cards plus distribution, with a six card suit; these hands are opened with one of a suit.

In response to a one club opening bid, responder shows his point count as follows:

$$1 \diamondsuit = 0 \text{ to } 5$$

$$1 \heartsuit = 6 \text{ to } 8$$

$$1 \spadesuit = 9 \text{ to } 11$$

$$1 \text{ NT} = 12 \text{ to } 14$$

$$2 \clubsuit = 15 \text{ to } 17$$

$$2 \diamondsuit = 18 \text{ to} \cdot 20$$

After a response of one notrump or higher, the partnership is forced to game.

After point count has been shown, rebids show natural suits. For example, suppose opener's and responder's hands were as follows:

(Opener)
♠ K Q x x x   ♡ Q 10 x   ◇ A Q   ♣ A x x

(Responder)

♠ x x   ♡ A K x x x   ♢ x x x x   ♣ x x

Using the Lea system, the auction would go

Opener	Responder
1 ♣	1 ♡
1 ♠	2 ♡
4 ♡	Pass

Responder's one heart response showed nothing about his heart suit, but simply promised 6 to 8 points. Opener's one spade rebid was natural, as was responder's two heart rebid.

SCHENKEN TWO DIAMONDS

The Schenken Two Diamond convention is a forcing opening bid that may be used with two types of hands. It may show a balanced, no-trump-type hand worth 23 points or more. In this event the opener's rebid will be in notrump, and is not forcing if the responder has responded two hearts.

The Schenken two diamond opening may also show a long, strong suit, and a hand with which a slam may be made if the responder has the right honor cards. In this event the opener will rebid a suit, and his rebid is forcing to game.

Showing Aces

The two diamond opening asks responder to show what aces, if any, he holds. The responder bids two hearts to show no aces. With one ace he makes a minimum response other than two hearts. If he has the ace of spades, or clubs or diamonds, he responds by bidding two spades, three clubs or three diamonds, respectively. If he has the ace of hearts, he responds two notrump.

If the responder has two aces he makes a jump response as follows: With touching aces, he jumps in the suit of the higher ranking ace. For these purposes, clubs and spades are considered touching suits, of which clubs is the higher ranking. If responder has non-touching aces, he jumps to three notrump. Thus, over a two diamond opening the responder would show his two aces as follows:

3 ♡ = aces of hearts and diamonds

3 ♠ = aces of spades and hearts

3 Notrump = aces of spades and diamonds, or the aces of hearts and clubs

4 ♣ = aces of clubs and spades

4 ◇ = aces of diamonds and clubs

If the responder should be so fortunate as to have three aces in response to the two diamond opening, his proper course is to make a double jump in the suit of his highest ranking ace.

Suppose the opener has a hand such as

♠ A K Q x x x x x   ♡ K Q x   ◇ —   ♣ A x

With this hand opener is assured of game, and if the responder has one or two key cards, the partnership will have a slam. After the hand is opened two diamonds, if responder jumps to three hearts, showing the aces of hearts and diamonds, opener can bid seven spades.

Showing Kings and Queens

After responder has shown his aces, the opener can ask about kings by rebidding the cheapest suit over responder's ace-showing bid. Thus, in the auction

Opener	Responder
2 ◇	2 Notrump
3 ♣	

responder has shown the ace of hearts and no other ace. Opener's three club bid asks about responder's kings.

Responder shows his kings in the same manner in which he

showed aces. The cheapest bid shows no kings; all other minimum bids show one king, in the suit bid. With two kings, the responder makes a jump response.

If the opener has the hand shown above,

♠ A K Q x x x x x   ♡ K Q x   ◇ −   ♣ A x

and the two diamond bid has elicited the information that the responder has the ace of hearts and no other ace, the opener can ask about kings. Thus, if the auction goes

Opener	*Responder*
2 ◇	2 Notrump
3 ♣	4 ♣

responder shows the king of clubs, and opener can now bid seven spades.

STAYMAN TWO CLUB AND TWO DIAMOND OPENINGS

The Stayman Two Club and Two Diamond openings are artificial forcing opening bids designed to enable the opener to show a full range of strong and intermediate hands. The two club opening is used for intermediate hands; the two diamond opening is used for stronger hands.

Two Club Opening

The two club opening is artificial and shows one of three types of hands. It may show a balanced 21 to 22 point hand. If opener has this hand his rebid will be two notrump.

The two club opening may also show a hand with a six-card or longer major suit, and eight to ten playing tricks. If opener has an 8-trick hand, he rebids two of his suit; if he has a 9-trick hand, he rebids three of his suit; if he has a 10-trick hand, he rebids four of his suit.

In addition, the two club opening may show a hand with at least five cards in each major suit, and eight to ten playing tricks. If opener has both major suits, his rebid will be in a minor suit. With an 8-trick hand, opener will rebid three clubs; with a 9-trick hand, he will rebid three diamonds. If opener has a 10-trick hand with 6-6 in the majors, he will rebid four of the minor suit in which he is void.

Suppose opener holds one of the following hands:

[A] ♠ A K Q 10 x x x   ♡ x x   ◇ A J x   ♣ x

[B] ♠ K Q   ♡ A K Q J x x   ◇ x   ♣ K Q J 10

[C] ♠ A K x   ♡ A Q x x x x x   ◇ A K x   ♣ —

[D] ♠ K Q J 10 x   ♡ A K x x x x   ◇ x   ♣ x

With Hand A, opener opens two clubs and rebids two spades, showing an 8-trick hand in spades. With Hand B, he would open two clubs and rebid four hearts, having a 10-trick hand in hearts. With Hand C, however, the opening bid should not be two clubs; it has the playing strength and defensive strength of a strong two-bid, and should be opened two diamonds.

With Hand D, opener should bid two clubs, and rebid three diamonds, showing a 9-trick major two-suiter.

Responses to Two Clubs

In responding to the two club opening, two diamonds is the usual bid; it is a waiting bid to see how the opener describes his hand. Other responses show very specific point count and suit length. Responder bids two of a major suit with a very weak hand—3 to 4 points—and a six-card suit. This response is not forcing.

If responder has a weak hand with a seven-card or longer minor suit, he may bid three of the minor. However, since the two club opening is so heavily major suit oriented, responder may not make the three club or three diamond response if he has as many as three cards in either major. Responder's bid of three clubs or three diamonds is not forcing.

If responder has a weak minor two-suiter, at least six-five, he may respond two notrump. This bid is not forcing. If opener has five cards in each of the major suits he will probably pass. He may rebid three of a minor with three card support. If opener has a good six-card suit, he will bid three of his major.

If responder has a stronger hand with both long minor suits, he may bid three notrump. Opener may pass or bid a three card minor suit.

If responder has a hand with a solid major suit at least five cards long, one that will run opposite a singleton without losing a trick, he may jump to three of his suit. If responder's running suit is a minor, he must jump to four.

Normally, however, responder will have none of these hands, and will bid two diamonds. Over the two diamond response opener has complete flexibility to show whether he has a notrump type hand, a single-suited or two-suited hand, and to show how many tricks he has.

If opener shows a major two-suiter with 8 or 9 playing tricks, responder can sign off in three of a major by taking a simple preference, or he can take his preference at the game level. Alternatively, responder can bid four diamonds, asking opener to bid game in his better suit. If responder bids four clubs over opener's three club or three diamond bid, his bid is Gerber, asking opener how many aces he has.

Two Diamond Opening

The two diamond opening is strong, artificial, and, except in two situations, forcing to game.

It may be made with a strong balanced notrump type hand, or with any other hand that is strong in high cards and defensive strength, and worth a forcing two-bid.

If opener has 23 or more high card points, he will open two diamonds and rebid in notrump. If the response is two hearts, and opener rebids two notrump, he shows 23 to 24 high card points; this rebid is not forcing.

Responses to Two Diamonds

In response to the two diamond opening, responder is expected to show whether or not he has high cards, i.e., aces and kings. The negative response is two hearts. This response has nothing to do with responder's heart suit or his point count; rather it says that he has fewer than two high cards. If responder has as little as two bare kings, he must make some other bid, bidding as naturally as possible.

For example, suppose responder holds one of the following hands in response to a two diamond opening:

[A]   ♠ K Q J x x   ♡ Q J x   ◇ Q J x   ♣ Q x

[B]   ♠ x x x   ♡ K x x   ◇ K x x x   ♣ x x x

With Hand A, although it has 14 high card points, responder must make the negative response of two hearts to show that he does not have two high cards. With Hand B, which has only 6 high card points, but has two kings, responder must make a positive response. Here, two notrump is best.

If responder bids anything other than two hearts in response to two diamonds the partnership is forced to game. If he responds two hearts, there are two situations in which the partnership may stop below game. One is when the opener rebids two notrump, showing 23 to 24 high card points. The other is when the opener bids a suit over two hearts, and rebids it after responder has made a second negative response. Thus, the following auctions are possible:

(A)   *Opener*   *Responder*
    2 ◇   2 ♡
    2 Notrump   Pass

(B) *Opener*   *Responder*
    2 ◇   2 ♡
    2 ♠   2 Notrump (or 3 ♣ if
    3 ♠   partnership is using a
                                   second negative
                                   convention)
                                   Pass

In auction (B), opener might have a hand such as

♠ A K x x x x   ♡ A Q x   ◇ K Q   ♣ A x

With this hand opposite two negative responses, opener has no assurance of making a game. If, however, responder has made a positive response over the two diamond opening, opener would have explored for slam.

MEXICAN TWO DIAMONDS

A part of the Romex System, the Mexican Two Diamond opening shows a relatively balanced hand with 19 to 21 points, and 4 to 6 losers. The two diamond opening normally promises distribution of 4-3-3-3, or 4-4-3-2, or 5-3-3-2; occasionally the opening may be used with 6-3-2-2 or 5-4-2-2 distribution. Typical hands for the two diamond opening would be

[A] ♠ K J x x   ♡ A J x   ◇ K Q x   ♣ A Q x

[B] ♠ A x x   ♡ K J x   ◇ A K J 10 x   ♣ K 10

[C] ♠ A Q   ♡ A Q   ◇ K x x   ♣ K J 10 x x x

The responses to the two diamond opening include transfers and asking bids.

Negative and Invitational Responses

With a hand worth 0 to 4 points, the responder makes a negative response. If he has a long diamond suit he may pass. The other negative responses are two hearts and two spades.

The two heart and two spade responses are transfer bids; they show nothing about the heart or spade suits in responder's hand. If responder has a long suit other than diamonds, his proper response is two hearts. The two heart response forces opener to rebid two spades. If spades is responder's long suit, he may pass. If he has instead a long club suit or a long heart suit, he rebids three clubs or three hearts over the opener's two spade rebid. For example, if responder has a hand such as

251

♠ x x   ♡ Q x x x x x   ◇ x x   ♣ x x x

the bidding will go

Opener	Responder
2 ◇	2 ♡
2 ♠	3 ♡
Pass	

If responder has 0 to 4 points with no long suit, he responds two spades. This response is also a transfer, and forces the opener to rebid two notrump which responder can pass. This transfer allows the strong hand to be the declarer at notrump.

If responder has 5 or 6 points he is allowed to make a semi-positive response. The semi-positive consists of the initially negative two heart response, followed by some bid other than the three club and three heart sign offs. For example, with a hand such as

♠ J x   ♡ x x x   ◇ Q J 10 x x   ♣ J x x

responder would bid two hearts over the two diamond opening, and over the opener's two spade rebid, responder would rebid two notrump. This sequence invites opener to bid game with a maximum.

If responder has invited game with the sequence

Opener	Responder
2 ◇	2 ♡
2 ♠	2 Notrump

opener may now use three clubs as a Stayman bid to find out whether or not responder has a four-card major suit. In response to three clubs, responder bids a four-card major if he has one, bids thee diamonds if he has neither, or bids three no-trump if he has both four-card majors.

If responder has 5 or 6 points with a long major suit, he invites game by responding two hearts to two diamonds, and then rebidding a suit. To invite game in spades, responder bids three spades over opener's two spade bid; to invite game in hearts, responder bids three diamonds over opener's two spade bid. Note that responder cannot make his game try by bidding three hearts over two spades, since that rebid shows 0 to 4 points. The game invitational sequences, therefore, are

(A) *Opener*   *Responder*
    2 ♦   2 ♡
    2 ♠   2 Notrump

(B) *Opener*   *Responder*
    2 ♦   2 ♡
    2 ♠   3 ♠

(C) *Opener*   *Responder*
    2 ♦   2 ♡
    2 ♠   3 ♦ (showing
                                        hearts)

Positive Responses

With a hand worth 7 or more points the responder should make a positive response. Positive responses are forcing to game. There are two types: those that are limited to game-going hands, and those showing slam interest.

With a hand of 7 to 9 points, the responder is interested in game, but not in slam. If he has any balanced hand (4-3-3-3, 4-4-3-2, or 5-3-3-2), or any mildly unbalanced hand (e.g., 5-4-2-2, 4-4-4-1, 5-4-3-1, 5-5-2-1), in the 7 to 9 point range, he makes the initially negative response of two spades. The two spade bid forces the opener to rebid two notrump; when responder makes any rebid over two notrump, the partnership is forced to game.

A rebid of three clubs by responder over opener's forced two notrump rebid is Stayman. Opener bids a four-card major suit if he has one, or bids three diamonds if he has no four card major, or bids three notrump if he has both majors. Thus, the auction could go

Opener	Responder
2 ♢	2 ♠
2 Notrump	3 ♣
3 Notrump	4 ♡
Pass	

Over the two notrump rebid, bids by the responder at the three level other than three clubs are natural, and show five-card suits. Thus if responder bids three clubs Stayman and then bids a major suit over the three diamond rebid, he promises five cards in the major suit he bids, and four cards in the other major.

If the responder has a six-card major suit with 7 to 9 points, he jumps to four diamonds or four hearts directly over the two diamond opening. These are Texas Transfer bids. The four diamond bid requires the opener to bid four hearts; responder's jump to four hearts forces opener to bid four spades.

If responder has 10 points or more and a broken six-card suit, he may bid it at the three level directly over the two diamond opening. If the opener has no slam interest, he should raise responder's suit with a fit, or rebid three notrump without a fit.

If opener is interested in a slam after responder's direct three-level response, he may cue-bid an ace. As an alternative, the partnership may agree that the opener will show key cards. Counting each ace, plus the king and queen of the responder's suit as key cards, opener would show how many key cards he had, using the following series of steps:

First suit step = 0 or 3 key cards

Second suit step = 1 or 4 key cards

Third suit step = 2 or 5 key cards

In counting steps, notrump is excluded, since that bid is used to deny fit and slam interest. In the auction

Opener	Responder
2 ◇	3 ◇
4 ♣	

opener's four club bid is the third step, promising two or five key cards. Opener's and responder's hands might be

(Opener)
♠ K J x x   ♡ K Q x   ◇ A x x   ♣ A Q J

(Responder)
♠ A x   ♡ J x   ◇ K 10 x x x x   ♣ K x x

After opener has shown his key cards, a bid of four notrump by the responder guarantees that the partnership possesses all six keys, and asks opener about his outside kings. If one key card is missing, responder may start cue-bidding in an effort to identify the missing key. With the above hands and auction, responder would know that the partnership is missing two keys, and would simply rebid his diamond suit.

If responder has a 10 point or better hand, either with relatively balanced distribution, or with a solid or semi-solid six-card suit, he may respond two notrump to the two diamond opening. Following the two notrump response a highly specialized sequence may occur.

Bidding After the Two Notrump Response

The two notrump response to the Mexican two diamond opening does not show that responder has any desire to play in notrump. It is a bid that asks opener to specify his point count. Opener answers in three steps:

$$3 \clubsuit = 19 \text{ high card points}$$

$$3 \diamondsuit = 20 \text{ high card points}$$

$$3 \heartsuit = 21 \text{ high card points}$$

If responder now bids the cheapest suit, he asks opener how many aces he has. Opener shows his aces in three steps, Roman style:

First step = 0 or 3 aces

Second step = 1 or 4 aces

Third step = 2 aces

If, after either of these inquiries has been answered, the responder rebids three notrump, that sets the final contract. If, instead of bidding three notrump, responder bids a suit, that is his lowest ranking four-card suit, and the partnership should bid four-card suits up the line in search of a fit. For example, if opener and responder hold

(Opener)
♠ A x   ♡ K J x x   ◇ K Q x x   ♣ A K x

(Responder)
♠ K Q x x   ♡ A Q x x   ◇ J x   ♣ x x x

the bidding could go

Opener	Responder
2 ◇	2 Notrump
3 ◇	3 ♡
4 ♣	4 ♡
5 ♡	6 ♡
Pass	

Responder's two notrump bid asked about opener's point count; opener's three diamond bid showed exactly 20 high card points. Responder's three heart bid asked how many aces opener held; the four club bid showed two aces. Then responder's four heart bid showed a suit; opener raised with his four hearts, and the partnership reached its slam.

If responder has 10 or more points and a solid or semi-solid six-card suit, he first responds two notrump over two diamonds, to learn opener's point count; then responder bids four clubs, which is treated as Modified Roman Gerber. The four club bid does not suggest that responder's suit is clubs; his suit is still undisclosed to opener. The four club bid asks opener how many aces he holds. Opener responds according to the following schedule:

4 ♦ = 0 or 3 aces

4 ♡ = 1 or 4 aces

4 ♠ = 2 aces of the same color

4 NT = 2 aces of the same rank

5 ♣ = 2 non-matching aces

Thus, with a hand such as

♠ K Q x x x x   ♡ –   ♦ K Q x x x   ♣ A x

responder can learn whether opener has three aces, and if he does not, whether or not opener has the right two aces for a grand slam.

If responder bids five clubs after opener's ace-showing bid, he asks about kings. If opener's bid was five clubs, five diamonds becomes responder's king-asking bid.

TAM II TWO CLUBS AND TWO DIAMOND OPENINGS

The TAM II Two Club and Two Diamond openings are artificial opening bids showing hands strong enough, or nearly so, to force to game. The two diamond opening is used only with balanced hands worth 22 to 25 high card points. The two club opening may be used with stronger balanced hands, or with unbalanced game-going hands.

Two Club Opening

The TAM II two club opening is forcing to game. It shows either a balanced hand with 26 to 29 high card points, or the equivalent of a strong two-bid in a suit. If opener has the balanced hand he will rebid notrump—the minimum number of notrump with 26 to 27 points, or a single jump in notrump with 28 to 29 points. If opener has instead the strong suit two-bid, he will rebid his suit.

Most of the responder's bids are designed to show opener whether or not responder's high cards fit opener's hand. If responder has less than one quick trick (an ace, or two kings, or a king and queen in the same suit), his proper response is two notrump. If he has one or more quick tricks, he bids the lowest suit in which he holds an ace or a king. For example, with

♠ A J 10 x x x   ♡ x   ♢ K x   ♣ x x x x

responder would bid two diamonds over the two club opening.

If responder has a six-card or longer suit headed by two of the top three honors, he may jump in that suit. For example, to bid three diamonds over two clubs, responder might have

♠ x x   ♡ x x   ◇ K Q x x x x   ♣ x x x

If opener rebids a suit, responder describes his hand further. If responder has fewer than three cards in opener's suit, he either bids a five card suit of his own, or he bids the minimum number of notrump if he has no five card suit. If responder has support for opener's suit he may show it in one of several ways, depending in part on the nature of his first response.

If responder has made an initial negative response of two notrump, he may show support for opener's suit by raising the suit if he has no king. If responder has a king, he may show support for opener's suit by jump shifting into the suit of his king. For example, in the auction

Opener	Responder
2 ♣	2 Notrump
3 ◇	4 ♠

responder's two notrump bid showed less than one quick trick; his four spade bid promised diamond support plus the king of spades. Neither of responder's bids has purported to describe his distribution.

If responder has made a positive response to the two club opening, and opener has rebid a suit, responder may show support for opener's suit in one of four ways. If he has no aces or kings in any suit other than the one he bid initially, he may give a simple raise of opener's suit. If responder has the ace or king of opener's suit in addition to the ace or king shown initially, but no ace or king in any unbid suit, he jump raises opener's suit. If responder has support for opener's suit and has an ace or a king in a suit he has not yet shown, he jump shifts into the latter suit. If responder has support for opener's suit and has 1½ to 2 quick tricks in the suit of his initial response, he jumps in his suit.

Suppose the auction has started

Opener	Responder
2 ♣	2 ◇
2 ♡	

and responder has one of the following hands:

[A] ♠ x x x   ♡ x x x   ◇ K Q x x   ♣ x x x

[B] ♠ x x x   ♡ K x x   ◇ K x x x   ♣ x x x

[C] ♠ x x x   ♡ x x x   ◇ K x x x   ♣ K x x

[D] ♠ x x x   ♡ x x x   ◇ A Q x   ♣ x x x x

With Hand A, responder raises hearts to the three level, having no more in aces and kings than he has already shown. With Hand B, responder shows his trump honor by jumping to four hearts. With Hand C, responder shows his king of clubs and his trump support by bidding three clubs. With Hand D, responder has trump support and one and a half quick tricks in the suit of his initial response. Therefore he jumps to four diamonds.

Two Diamond Opening

The TAM II Two Diamond convention uses an opening bid of two diamonds to show a balanced hand worth 22 to 25 high card points. The two diamond opening is forcing for one round, but not necessarily to game. Most of the responses are artificial; they include relays, Stayman, and transfers.

A response of two spades shows a hand with less than 3 high card points. It says nothing about responder's spade suit, but merely describes his point count. Opener may rebid three notrump if he is still optimistic about his prospects in game; otherwise he should rebid two notrump. Any rebid by responder in a suit over opener's two notrump rebid shows a long suit, but is not forward going; opener may nevertheless elect to bid game with a fit for a responder's suit. For example if opener's and responder's hands were

(Opener)
♠ A K x   ♡ A K x x   ◇ A x x x   ♣ A K

(Responder)
♠ x x x   ♡ 10 x x x x   ◇ x x x   ♣ J x

the bidding might go

Opener	Responder
2 ◇	2 ♠
2 Notrump	3 ♡
3 Notrump	

If, instead of the hand shown above, opener had held

♠ A K x   ♡ A K x   ◇ A K Q x x   ♣ Q x

he would have bid four hearts over three hearts in the above auction.

Responses of three clubs and three diamonds over the two diamond opening are Stayman-type bids. The three club bid shows less than 8 points in high cards, and asks opener to bid a four card major suit if he has one. With no four card major opener will rebid three diamonds, over which responder may bid a five card major suit if he has one.

If opener rebids the suit in which responder has four card support and responder has a hand worth a slam try, he may jump to five of the major suit. Opener is requested to bid slam with a maximum. For example, suppose opener's and responder's hands were

(Opener)
♠ A Q x x ♡ A J ◇ K Q J x ♣ A K x

(Responder)
♠ K x x x ♡ x x x ◇ A x ♣ x x x x

The bidding could go

Opener	Responder
2 ◇	3 ♣
3 ♠	5 ♠
6 ♠	Pass

The three diamond response to the two diamond opening shows 8 or more points, and also asks the opener to show a four card major suit if he has one. If opener has no four card major suit, he rebids three notrump with 22 to 23 points; if he has 24 to 25 points, he must either bid a five card minor suit if he has one, or bid four notrump with no five card minor.

If, over the three diamond response, opener rebids a suit in which responder has four card support, responder may raise to game with 8 or 9 points, or invite slam by jumping to five of the major with 10 points, or drive the hand to slam with a good 11 or more points. For example, in the auction

Opener	Responder
2 ◇	3 ◇
3 ♡	5 ♡

responder's five heart bid asks opener to bid a slam if he has an excellent minimum point count, or better. Responder might have either

[A] ♠ x x x   ♡ A J x x   ◇ J x x   ♣ K J x

or

[B] ♠ x x   ♡ A J x x   ◇ x x   ♣ K x x x x

Opener might hold a hand such as

[C] ♠ A x   ♡ K Q x x   ◇ A K Q x   ♣ A x x

or

[D] ♠ K J x   ♡ K Q x x   ◇ A K Q x   ♣ A x

With Hand C opener would continue to slam, having an ideal minimum. This hand should produce a slam opposite either Hand A or Hand B. With Hand D, opener would pass five hearts, having a less attractive minimum.

Note that in the auction

Opener	Responder
2 ◇	3 ◇
3 ♡	4 ♡

responder's four heart bid is not by any means a signoff bid since he has shown 8 or more points (by responding three diamonds), opposite a 22 to 25 point opening. If opener has a maximum, he should move toward slam.

If responder has a five card major suit and 8 or more high card points, he may jump to three of his major suit over the two diamond opening. With a minimum opening, opener rebids three notrump if he has a doubleton in responder's suit; or he raises to game in responder's suit if he has three- or four-card support. If opener has a maximum hand with a doubleton in responder's suit, he rebids four notrump. If opener has a maximum with trump support, he cue-bids his cheapest ace. For example, in the auction

Opener	Responder
2 ♢	3 ♡
4 ♣	

opener shows at least three hearts, and 24 to 25 high card points, including the ace of clubs, but excluding the ace of spades, since he bypassed three spades to bid four clubs.

If in response to the two diamond opening responder jumps to four diamonds or four hearts, his bid is a transfer. The jump to four diamonds requires opener to bid four hearts. Responder's jump to four hearts requires opener to rebid four spades.

If responder has a hand that is not suitable for either a Stayman bid or a transfer, or a natural jump to three of a major suit, he may use a response of two hearts as a non-descriptive relay. The two heart response to two diamonds shows nothing about responder's strength or his distribution, but simply asks opener to clarify his point count. Opener rebids two notrump with 22 to 23 high card points, or three notrump with 24 to 25 points. The two heart response is forcing to game.

To use the two heart relay, responder might have a minor suit oriented hand, or he might have a balanced notrump type hand. Responder's use of the relay with a notrump type hand serves to make the stronger hand the declarer in any notrump contract, and to allow minute specification of opener's point count. For example, if responder has a balanced hand he may raise notrump after opener's notrump rebid:

Opener	*Responder*
2 ◇	2 ♡
2 Notrump	4 Notrump

Opener's two notrump rebid showed 22 to 23 high card points. Responder's four notrump rebid showed about 10 points and asked opener to bid slam with 23 points.

Suit rebids by the responder, after opener has clarified his point count over the relay, are natural. Opener should either raise responder's suit or bid a suit of his own. Responder might have a hand such as

[E]   ♠ K x x x   ♡ x   ◇ A Q x x   ♣ J x x x

or

[F]   ♠ x x   ♡ x   ◇ A x x x x   ♣ Q x x x x

BIG DIAMOND SYSTEM

The Big Diamond System uses a combination of forcing one club and one diamond openings, together with specialized two- and three-level openings, to show general strength and distribution.

A one club opening shows one of two types of hands. It may show a hand with 12 to 16 points including high cards and distribution, with a club suit or a diamond suit, or with an unbiddable heart or spade suit. (Openings of one of a major suit promise five card suits and 12 to 16 points.)

One club may also be opened with a strong balanced hand with 17 to 19, or 22 or more high card points. The Bid Diamond notrump structure is therefore as follows:

14 to 16: open one notrump

17 to 19: open one club, rebid one notrump

20 to 21: open two notrump

22 to 23: open one club, rebid two notrump

24 to 26: open one club, rebid three notrump

27 to 29: open one club, rebid four notrump

Responses to One Club

In response to a one club opening, one diamond is the negative response, usually showing less than 7 points; however, the one diamond negative may be made with up to 10 scattered points. All other minimum suit bids are natural, showing at least four card suits, and are forcing for one round. A response of one heart or one spade shows 7 or more points; a response of two clubs or two diamonds shows 11 or more points with a good suit, usually five cards long.

Responses in notrump show balanced hands. A one notrump response shows 11 to 12 high card points with the major suits stopped, and the minor suits at least partially stopped. The one notrump response is not forcing. Higher notrump bids show stoppers in all suits. A response of two notrump shows 13 to 14 points and is forcing to game; a response of three notrump shows 15 to 16 points; a response of four notrump shows 17 to 18 points.

Responses of two hearts or two spades show 14 or more points with a good suit. Opener either rebids notrump if he has a balanced hand with 17 or more points, or shows his support for opener's suit if he has a 12 to 16 point hand. His support showing bids are as follows:

3 ♣ = singleton or small doubleton

3 ♢ = three small cards, or three cards headed by the jack

3 ♡ = two or three cards headed by the ace, king or queen

3 ♠ = two honors, no worse than the king and jack

In addition, opener may jump to four of responder's suit if he has four trumps headed by an honor, and a side suit singleton.

If opener and responder held the following hands

(Opener)
♠ K x   ♡ A Q J x   ♢ Q 10 x x x   ♣ K x

(Responder)
♠ A Q x x x   ♡ K x x   ♢ K x   ♣ Q J x

the auction would go

Opener	Responder
1 ♣	2 ♠
3 ♡	3 Notrump

Opener's three heart bid, showed two or three spades to an honor. Responder rebid three notrump, expecting opener to correct to four spades if he had three-card support.

Responses to one club at the three level show long semi-solid suits with little outside strength. A jump to three clubs or three diamonds may be made on a six- or seven-card suit; a jump to three hearts or three spades promises a seven-card suit. Responses to one club at the four level show solid seven-card suits with little outside strength.

Openings Above the One Level

Opening bids of two clubs and two diamonds show two-suited hands. See TWO CLUB OPENING FOR MINORS and TWO DIAMOND OPENING FOR MAJORS.

Opening bids of two hearts or two spades show intermediate strength, and are made with one-suited hands. These openings show long, solid or semi-solid suits, with approximately eight playing tricks. A typical hand might be

♠ A K Q 10 x x   ♡ x x   ◇ x x   ♣ A K x

The two heart and two spade openings are not forcing. A two notrump response shows slam interest. All other responses are natural.

An opening bid of three clubs or three diamonds shows 12 to

16 points with a six- or seven-card semi-solid suit. These openings deny possession of a four-card major suit. All responses are natural. A response of three hearts or three spades is forcing and opener should raise with as little as three small cards, or a doubleton honor. For a three diamond opening, for example, opener might have

♠ A x x   ♡ Q x   ◇ A K J x x x x   ♣ x

Over a response of three hearts or three spades, opener should raise to four.

One Diamond Opening

An opening bid of one diamond in the Big Diamond system shows an unbalanced hand worth 17 or more points including distribution. The only negative response is one heart, which usually shows 0 to 7 points; however, the negative response may be made with up to a scattered 9 count.

Responses of one spade, two clubs and two diamonds are natural, showing four card or longer suits, and 8 or more good points. A response of one notrump shows at least a four card heart suit with 8 good points. These responses are forcing to game.

Responses of two hearts and two spades show six-card suits headed by two of the top three honors, with little outside. Responses at the three level show solid six- or seven-card suits with nothing outside.

Rebids by the One Diamond Opener

If responder has bid one heart, showing a weak hand,

opener may rebid one spade with a good five-card suit and 17 to 21 points. A rebid of one notrump shows a good heart suit with 17 to 21 points. Rebids of two clubs and two diamonds promise good five card suits, and up to 9 playing tricks. None of these rebids is forcing.

Rebids of two hearts, two spades, three clubs or three diamonds show good suits with 22 points or more. These rebids are forcing for one round, and responder uses a series of steps to show his general strength and his support for opener's suit, as follows:

First   step = small doubleton or worse, weak hand

Second step = small doubleton or worse, some high card strength

Third   step = three small cards, weak hand

Fourth step = three small cards, some high card strength

Fifth   step = good trumps, weak hand

In addition, responder is allowed to jump to game in opener's suit if he has a weak hand with good trumps, and a singleton or void in a side suit.

If opener and responder held the following hands,

(Opener)
♠ A K x   ♡ A K x x x   ◇ Q x   ♣ A K x

(Responder)
♠ J x x   ♡ x x x   ◇ J x x   ♣ J x x x

271

the bidding could go

Opener	Responder
1 ◇	1 ♡
2 ♡	3 ♣
3 ♡	Pass

If opener jumps to three hearts, three spades, four clubs or four diamonds, he shows a game going hand, and asks responder to show his support for opener's suit in a series of steps as follows:

First step = void or singleton

Second step = doubleton

Third step = three small cards

Fourth step = four small cards

Fifth step = queen

Opener's and responder's hands might be

(Opener)
♠ A x   ♡ A K J x x x x   ◇ A K Q   ♣ x

(Responder)
♠ K x x x x   ♡ x x x   ◇ x x   ♣ A x x

The auction would start

Opener	Responder
1 ◇	1 ♡
3 ♡	4 ♣

Responder's four club bid, the third step, showed three-card heart support.

After responder has shown his holding in opener's suit, opener may ask whether or not responder has control in a side suit. Over the bid of a new suit by opener, responder is required to show his controls by steps as follows:

First   step = queen or worse

Second step = king

Third   step = king and queen

Fourth step = ace

Fifth   step = ace and queen

Sixth   step = ace and king

In the above auction, after opener learned that responder had three-card heart support, he could continue with asking bids in spades and clubs, as follows:

Opener	Responder
1 ◇	1 ♡
3 ♡	4 ♣
4 ♠	5 ♣
6 ♣	6 Notrump
7 ♡	

Opener's four spade asking bid elicits the information that responder has the king of spades. If responder had answered with the first step, denying the king of spades, opener would have persevered in hopes of finding responder with the ace of clubs for the small slam; on the other hand, if responder had answered with the third step, showing the king and queen of spades, opener would have immediately settled for the small slam, since for his initial negative response, responder would not have an ace, a king and a queen. Opener's six club asking bid, looking for the ace of clubs for the grand slam was safe, since if responder answered with the first or second step, the hand could be played in six hearts; and if he answered with the third step, six spades, the hand could be played in six notrump.

After the negative response of one heart to the one diamond opening, if opener rebids two notrump, he shows 22 to 24 points, with one suit, not clubs, unstopped. Responder has a variety of alternatives over two notrump. He may bid three clubs as Stayman; he may bid three diamonds to ask opener to bid his better major suit; or, with a game-going hand, responder may bid a five card or longer major suit.

If responder has bid one spade, one notrump, two clubs or two diamonds in response to the one diamond opening, opener must make a single raise of responder's suit if he has four card support, unless he has a self-supporting suit of his own. Opener's raise of responder's suit would set that as the trump suit, and subsequent bidding could proceed naturally. If opener has his own self-sufficient suit, he jump shifts in it, setting it as the trump suit.

If responder has shown a long solid or semi-solid suit (i.e., by jumping to two of a major or three of any suit), opener's bid of a new suit asks about responder's control of the new suit. Since responder's original response has denied strength outside his own suit, such control as he has will usually be shortness. His responses are as follows:

First   step = void or singleton

Second step = doubleton

Third   step = three small cards

Fourth step = four small cards

Fifth   step = queen

If opener's and responder's hands were

(Opener)
♠ K x   ♡ A K x x x x   ♢ K Q x   ♣ A x

(Responder)
♠ A Q x x x x   ♡ x x x x   ♢ J x   ♣ x

the bidding might go

Opener	*Responder*
1 ♢	2 ♠
3 ♡	4 ♢
6 ♡	

Opener's three heart bid asked about responder's heart control; if responder had shown three small hearts or worse, opener would have settled for game. But with responder having four hearts, slam became a good prospect, and much better in hearts than in spades.

DYNAMIC ONE NOTRUMP

The Dynamic One Notrump opening, an integral part of the Romex system, is a strong opening bid showing a relatively unbalanced hand. The Dynamic Notrump opening can be made on any distribution except 4-3-3-3, 4-4-3-2, or 5-3-3-2. It promises 18 to 21 points, including at least five controls, and has only four or five losers. This one notrump bid is forcing.

The opener may have a one-suited hand such as

♠ A K Q x x x   ♡ A K x   ◇ K x   ♣ x x

or a two suited hand such as

♠ K Q J x x   ♡ A K x x   ◇ A x   ♣ A x

or a three suited hand such as

♠ K Q x x   ♡ A K x x   ◇ A Q x x   ♣ x

Responses to One Notrump

In response to the one notrump opening the responder immediately shows how many controls he has. Counting each ace as two and each king as one, he bids in steps, as follows:

2 ♣ = 0 to 1 control, with 0 to 6 points

2 ◇ = 0 to 1 control with 7 to 15 points

2 ♡ = 2 controls, i.e., one ace or two kings; however, with one ace and less than 6 points, the proper response is two clubs

2 ♠ = 3 controls, i.e., one ace and one king, or three kings

2 NT = 4 controls in two suits, i.e., two aces, or an ace king combination and an outside king

3 ♣ = 4 controls in more than two suits, i.e., an ace and two kings all in different suits, or four kings

3 ♢ = 5 controls, i.e., one ace and three kings, or two aces and one king

3 ♡ = 6 controls, i.e., three aces, or two aces and two kings, or one ace and four kings

3 ♠ = 7 controls, i.e., three aces and one king, or two aces and three kings

If responder has fewer than two controls, and has a seven- or eight-card semi-solid major suit, with no void, he may make a natural jump to four of his suit.

Opener's Rebids over Two Club Response

After the responder has shown a very weak hand by bidding two clubs, the opener's first concern, with a minimum hand with poor game prospects, is to find a low level contract to play. If the opener rebids two of a major suit he shows a good five-card or longer suit. If he rebids three of a minor suit, he shows a good six-card or longer suit. If opener rebids four of a major suit he shows that he has game in his own hand.

Opener has available a number of rebids to show major two-suited hands and minor two-suited hands. With both minor suits and a hand with four losers, including at most two quick losers, or a hand with a total of three losers, the opener may rebid two notrump:

Opener	Responder
1 Notrump	2 ♣
2 Notrump	

Opener's distribution could be 5-5 or 5-4 in the minor suits, with the major suits being divided 2-1, 3-1 or 2-2. He might have a hand such as

♠ K J   ♡ K x   ◇ A K 10 x   ♣ A Q 10 x x

With a stronger minor two-suiter, opener may rebid three notrump:

Opener	Responder
1 Notrump	2 ♣
3 Notrump	

The three notrump bid promises at least ten cards in the minor suits, at most three losers, and no more than two quick losers. Opener might have a hand such as

♠ A   ♡ x   ◇ A K x x x x   ♣ A K x x x

If opener has five or more cards in each major suit, he has three descriptive bids available. If he has a four-loser hand, he may jump to three hearts over the two club response, allowing responder to choose a major suit at the three level. If opener has a three-loser hand, he jumps to three spades, requiring responder to state his preference at the four level. Or, if opener has a three loser hand with five cards in each major suit and three cards in a minor suit, he jumps to four of that minor suit.

Opener might have any of the following hands:

[A] ♠ K Q J x x   ♡ A J 10 x x   ◇ K x   ♣ A

[B] ♠ A Q J x x   ♡ A K Q 10 x x   ◇ x   ♣ Q

[C] ♠ A K J 10 x   ♡ K Q J 10 x   ◇ A x x   ♣ —

With Hand A, opener has four losers, and therefore jumps to three hearts. Responder may pass, or take a preference to spades; or if he has a few values, he may bid four of his better major suit. With Hand B, opener has a three-loser hand and no three card minor; he therefore bids three spades. With Hand C, opener rebids four diamonds, showing five cards in each major suit, three diamonds, and a void in clubs.

With a hand that does not fit any of these special rebids, opener rebids two diamonds. The two diamond bid does not mean that opener has diamonds; rather, it is a waiting bid. Opener might have two four-card major suits, or two five-card major suits with a five-loser hand; or he might have a six-card major suit and a four-card major suit, or he might have a long major suit and a long minor suit. His two diamond bid merely suggests that he does not know what to bid, and asks responder to help out.

Over opener's two diamond rebid, responder should bid a major suit if he has one. If responder has a four-card major suit or a weak five-card major suit, he bids two of that suit; if he has a good five-card major suit or a fair six-card major suit, he jumps to three of the major. If responder has no four-card major, he shows a five-card minor suit. If he has neither a five-card minor nor a four-card major, responder bids two no-trump.

If opener's and responder's hands were, for example

(Opener)
♠ A x   ♡ A x x x   ◇ A Q   ♣ K J x x x

(Responder)
♠ K J 10 x x x   ♡ J x   ◇ x x x   ♣ x x

the bidding would start

Opener	Responder
1 Notrump	2 ♣
2 ◇	3 ♠

Opener's Rebids over Two Diamond Response

If responder has bid two diamonds, or higher, in response to the one notrump opening, the partnership is forced to game. The opener's rebids are quite similar to his rebids over a two club response. The rebids that are different are two of a major suit and three of a major suit.

Over a two diamond response, of course, opener cannot use the two diamond waiting bid. Opener will rebid a four- or five-card heart suit whenever he has one, with two exceptions. If he also has a five-card spade suit he will show his spade suit first; if he has a six-card minor suit in addition to his heart suit, he will bid the minor suit first. With a hand such as

♠ A x   ♡ A x x x   ◇ A Q   ♣ K J x x

opener would rebid two hearts over the two diamond response:

Opener	*Responder*
1 Notrump	2 ◇
2 ♡	

But with one more club and one less spade, opener would rebid his clubs first over the two diamond response.

Similarly, if opener has a four- or five-card spade suit, he will bid it immediately unless he also has a heart suit that is longer than his spade suit, or has a six-card minor suit.

After the two-club response, the jump to three of a major suit showed at least five cards in each major, with three or four losers. However, after a two diamond response, the partnership is forced to game, so the opener can describe his hand in a more leisurely fashion. Thus with five spades and five hearts, he can bid his suits individually, without jumping. After the two diamond response, the jump by opener to three hearts or three spades is reserved to show specifically six cards in the major suit bid, and four cards in the other major.

All other rebids are the same as over the two club response. The two notrump rebid shows a moderately strong minor two-suiter. If the responder has at least one of the top three honors in either diamonds or clubs, he can bid three clubs over the two notrump rebid to ask the opener to describe his major suit distribution. Opener's answers to the three club inquiry are as follows:

3 ◇ = 2-2 in the major suits

3 ♡ = 3-card heart suit

3 ♠ = 3-card spade suit

3 NT = a singleton and doubleton in the majors

Thus, if opener's and responder's hands were

(Opener)
♠ A J 10   ♡ x   ◇ A K Q x x   ♣ A x x x

(Responder)
♠ x   ♡ x x x   ◇ J x x x   ♣ K Q J x x

the auction could go

Opener	Responder
1 Notrump	2 ◇
2 Notrump	3 ♣
3 ♠	4 ♣
4 ♠	6 ♣

Responder's three club bid asked opener to clarify his distribution; opener's three spade bid showed that he had three spades, leaving him with at most one heart. Responder's four club bid set the trump suit. Opener's four spade bid denied the ability to cue-bid four hearts, which he would have done with a heart void. Responder therefore inferred that the partnership had a heart loser, and settled for six clubs.

IV

Making Inquiries

There are few things more frustrating in bridge than having a hand that needs just one or two specific cards from partner to make a slam, and not knowing how to find out whether or not he has them. Sometimes the frustration occurs from the very outset of the hand, and some of the strong forcing opening bid conventions described in Chapter III are designed to elicit the information from the responder at his first turn to bid.

More often, however, the need to locate specific cards occurs after some exchange of information. Almost all of the conventions described below have their application some time after the opening bid, although some can be used as the opening bid itself.

The conventions described below fall into three general categories. The first group consists of conventions that ask partner how many aces, or how many aces and kings, he has. *See* BLACK-WOOD, ROMAN BLACKWOOD, KEY CARD BLACKWOOD, BABY BLACK-WOOD, GERBER, ROMAN GERBER, KEY CARD GERBER, SUPER GERBER, EX-TENDED GERBER, ACE IDENTIFICATION, BLACK AND RED GERBER, FANE FOUR CLUB CONVENTION, ACOL FOUR NOTRUMP OPENING, CULBERT-SON FOUR-FIVE NOTRUMP, SAN FRANCISCO, CULWOOD, CLARAC. A second group of conventions asks partner what sort of control he has of specific suits. *See* ASKING BIDS, ROMAN ASKING BIDS, CUL-

BERTSON ASKING BIDS, LEBOVIC ASKING BID, FOUR CLUB ASKING BID, FULWILER ASKING BIDS. *See also* D.I. A third category of conventions asks partner how good his trumps are. *See* GRAND SLAM FORCE, MALOWAN, BARON SLAM TRY, CULBERTSON TRUMP ASKING BIDS, ROMEX TRUMP ASKING BIDS, R/H FOUR NOTRUMP, WANG TRUMP ASKING BIDS.

BLACKWOOD

The Blackwood convention is one of the most widely used in the world. Its widespread acceptance is a tribute to its simplicity. In its basic form, it is a bid of four notrump to ask partner how many aces he has. The responses are as follows:

$$5 \clubsuit = 0 \text{ or } 4 \text{ aces}$$
$$5 \diamondsuit = 1 \text{ ace}$$
$$5 \heartsuit = 2 \text{ aces}$$
$$5 \spadesuit = 3 \text{ aces}$$

Although the five club bid is slightly ambiguous, the Blackwood bidder will normally be able to tell from his hand and from the previous bidding whether his partner has all of the aces or none. *See also* RESPONDING TO BLACKWOOD OVER OPPONENT'S INTERFERENCE, DOPI AND PODI, DEPO.

If, over the response to four notrump, the Blackwood bidder bids five notrump, he normally guarantees that the partnership is in possession of all of the aces, and is asking the responder to tell him how many kings he has. At duplicate bridge, the partnership might choose to agree that the five notrump bid does not guarantee possession of all the aces, since the Blackwood bidder might wish to try for a top score by bidding slam in notrump if the responder had the appropriate number of kings. However, on balance, the partnership is probably better off to agree that five notrump does guarantee all the aces.

Over five notrump, the responder shows his kings as follows:

$$6 \clubsuit = \text{no kings}$$
$$6 \diamondsuit = 1 \text{ king}$$
$$6 \heartsuit = 2 \text{ kings}$$
$$6 \spadesuit = 3 \text{ kings}$$
$$6 \text{ NT} = 4 \text{ kings}$$

The authorities are sharply divided as to the proper bid to show four kings. Several state that the six club bid shows either 0 or 4 kings, apparently on the theory that what is good enough for aces is good enough for kings. The majority, however, state that with four kings, the responder should bid six notrump. The rationale is that there is no need, as there is over four notrump, to conserve space. Since the Blackwood bidder is interested in a grand slam and the partnership has all of the kings, nothing is lost by making the fact quite clear with a bid of six notrump.

Over the five notrump rebid by the Blackwood bidder, the responder has the option, with a suitable hand, of jumping to a grand slam rather than just meekly showing his kings. For example, if he has a hand such as

$\spadesuit$ A x $\heartsuit$ 10 x $\diamondsuit$ Q x $\clubsuit$ A K Q J x x x

and the bidding has gone

Opener	Responder
1 $\spadesuit$	3 $\clubsuit$
3 $\spadesuit$	4 $\spadesuit$
4 Notrump	5 $\heartsuit$
5 Notrump	

responder should bid seven clubs. Once opener has certified that the partnership has all of the aces, responder can almost count thirteen tricks with his running club suit. He should, however, bid seven clubs rather than seven notrump since it is conceivable that he might need to ruff a spade to establish his thirteenth trick. Opener might have a hand such as

♠ K Q 10 9 x x   ♡ A x x   ◇ A x   ♣ x x

On occasion, such as with the hand above, the Blackwood bidder will rebid five notrump not so much to find out about kings, as to reassure the responder that all of the aces are held, just in case he can bid a grand slam upon learning that fact.

Playing in Five Notrump

Sometimes the Blackwood bidder, after hearing the ace-showing response, decides that the hand should not be played in slam, but should be played in five notrump. However, he cannot bid five notrump to play there, because that bid asks responder about his kings.

Assuming that there is a neutral suit higher than the suit of responder's ace-showing response, i.e., one that the responder could not take as a sign-off bid, the Blackwood bidder bids five of that suit. This bid requests the Blackwood responder to bid five notrump, which the Blackwood bidder can pass.

For example, at duplicate bridge, the partnership might try for slam in a minor suit, but need to retreat to notrump if that slam seemed out of reach:

Opener	*Responder*
1 ◇	3 ◇
4 Notrump	5 ◇
5 ♡	5 Notrump
Pass	

When Blackwood Should Not Be Used

The Blackwood convention is designed principally to help the partnership to stay out of a slam against which the opponents hold too many aces, rather than to help the partnership to reach a slam. The partnership's first tasks are to determine whether or not it has enough tricks and a solid enough trump suit to consider a slam. The use of Blackwood should follow, not precede, the making of these determinations.

Before bidding four notrump, the player should have thought through what he will do over any possible ace-showing response. Once he has embarked on Blackwood, he should bid a slam if the partnership is missing no more than one ace. If he learns that only one ace is missing and stops short of slam, he has misused the Blackwood convention.

A player should not bid Blackwood when the responses will not tell him what he needs to know. For example, if one hand has a small doubleton in a side suit, he needs to know whether his partner has control of that suit for slam purposes. If the owner of the small doubleton uses Blackwood and discovers that the partnership is missing one ace, he will not be able to bid slam with certainty, because the opponents may be able to cash the ace and king of his weak suit.

Blackwood should not be used when the partnership needs to learn specifically which aces it holds rather than just how many aces it holds. Thus, a hand containing a void should rarely bid Blackwood, for unless the partnership has all four aces, he will not know whether or not the essential aces are held. *But see* ROMAN BLACKWOOD.

As between the two partners, the Blackwood bid should be made by the one who has the greater playing strength, or the greater quantity of secondary values. For example, it does little good for a hand such as

288

♠ A x x x   ♡ K Q x   ◇ K x   ♣ A K x x

to bid Blackwood. Even if the partnership is shown to have all of the aces and kings, what guarantee could this hand have that the partnership had twelve tricks? It is much better for the four notrump bid to come from a hand such as

♠ K Q J x x x   ♡ x   ◇ K Q x x x   ♣ x

When a minor suit has been agreed upon as trumps, the four notrump bidder must be careful that the response to Blackwood cannot embarrass him. For example, if the hand is to be played in clubs, and the Blackwood bidder has only one ace, a response of five diamonds, showing one ace, would have the partnership too high. Similarly, if diamonds are to be the trump suit, and the Blackwood bidder has no aces, a response of five hearts, showing two aces would get the partnership too high.

On occasion, the bidding by the partner of the Blackwood bidder will have been so strong that the embarrassing responses are unlikely to be forthcoming, and Blackwood is really being used in search of a grand slam. In general, however, it is wise not to embark upon Blackwood without at least one ace when diamonds are to be trumps, and two aces if clubs are to be trumps.

When is Four Notrump Not Blackwood?

As simple as the responses to four notrump Blackwood may be, it is sometimes quite difficult to know whether or not a four notrump bid is indeed Blackwood or not. At one end of the scale, it is clear that four notrump is not Blackwood when the four notrump bid is made directly over an opening bid in notrump:

Opener	Responder
2 Notrump	4 Notrump

This four notrump bid is strictly quantitative, asking the opener to bid six notrump with a maximum hand.

At the other end of the scale, it is clear that a jump to four notrump when notrump has never been bid before is Blackwood:

Opener	Responder
1 ♠	3 ♠
4 Notrump	

Here, opener's four notrump bid is clearly Blackwood. But between these two extremes are many difficult cases. For example:

(A)
Opener	Responder
1 ♠	3 ♣
3 Notrump	4 Notrump

(B)
Opener	Responder
1 ♣	1 ♡
2 Notrump	4 Notrump

(C)
Opener	Responder
1 Notrump	2 ♣
2 ♡	4 Notrump

(D)
Opener	Responder
1 Notrump	3 ♡
3 Notrump	4 Notrump

Which of the four notrump bids in the above auctions are Blackwood?

There are several key questions that the partner of the four notrump bidder should ask himself in determining whether or not he is being asked to show his aces. The first is whether or not a trump suit has been agreed upon. If a trump suit has definitely been established, four notrump is usually Blackwood. For example, in the auction

Opener	Responder
1 ♡	3 ♡
3 Notrump	4 Notrump

hearts have been established as trumps. Therefore responder's four notrump bid is Blackwood. Similarly, in the auction

Opener	Responder
1 Notrump	3 ♠
4 ♢	4 Notrump

Opener has, by inference, agreed upon spades as trumps; therefore responder's four notrump bid is Blackwood. However, in the auction

Opener	Responder
1 Notrump	3 ♠
3 Notrump	4 Notrump

opener has not agreed on spades as trumps; therefore responder's four notrump bid could be taken as quantitative. However, since responder has no way, absent other conventions, to both establish his suit as trumps and ask about aces, the meaning of his four notrump bid in this auction is still the subject of debate.

When neither partner has supported the other's suit, four

notrump is more often a natural bid than Blackwood. For example:

Opener	Responder
1 ♠	2 ♣
2 ♡	4 ♣
4 Notrump	

Opener's four notrump bid is not Blackwood because no trump suit has been agreed upon. His four notrump bid was a natural bid. However, in the auction

Opener	Responder
1 ♡	3 ♢
3 ♡	4 Notrump

responder's jump to four notrump is Blackwood even though responder has never actually supported hearts. There being no natural meaning to the jump to four notrump when notrump has never before been bid, the bid must be Blackwood.

Another question the partner of the four notrump bidder must ask himself is whether the four notrump bidder has seemed content to play the hand in game. If he has, his four notrump bid is likely to be natural rather than Blackwood. For example:

Opener	Responder
1 Notrump	3 ♣
3 Notrump	4 ♢
4 Notrump	

Since opener was willing to play the hand in three notrump, his partner should not construe his four notrump bid as sudden interest in a slam. Similarly, if four notrump has been bid competitively, there is no reason to interpret it as Blackwood:

North	East	South	West
1 ♡	1 ♠	3 ♡	3 ♠
4 ♡	4 ♠	Pass	Pass
4 Notrump			

Since North was content to play the hand in four hearts, his four notrump bid cannot be Blackwood.

Another revealing question is whether the four notrump bidder has shown a weak hand earlier in the auction. If he has, his four notrump bid is not likely to be Blackwood. For example

Opener	Responder
2 ♠	2 Notrump
3 Notrump	4 Notrump

Responder has made a negative response to the strong two-bid. He is hardly likely to have a hand with which he can profitably ask about aces. More likely responder has a maximum point-count for his negative response, and perhaps one that is worth more than the normal minimum, but is lacking in quick tricks.

However, if responder has made a positive response to the strong two bid, there is no reason he cannot want to use Blackwood:

Opener	Responder
2 ♠	3 ♢
3 Notrump	4 Notrump

Here responder's four notrump bid should be taken as Blackwood.

Yet another question to be asked in assessing whether or not four notrump is Blackwood is whether four notrump was bid at the first genuine opportunity to use Blackwood, and if not, whether the four notrump bidder made a cue-bid apparently attempting to elicit information before bidding four notrump. If the answer to either of those questions is in the affirmative, the four notrump bid is more likely Blackwood than natural. For example

Opener	Responder
1 ♡	3 ♡
3 ♠	4 ♣
4 Notrump	

Opener's four notrump bid is Blackwood even though he did not use the convention at his very first opportunity, over three hearts. He cue-bid first and having received a return cue-bid, bid four notrump. His bid is clearly Blackwood.

Four notrump is also Blackwood if the four notrump bidder has opened with a strong two-bid, or if he has jump-shifted. For example

Opener	Responder
1 ♠	3 ♣
3 Notrump	4 Notrump

Responder's four notrump bid should be considered Blackwood since he made a jump shift response to the opening bid. Having made that response responder has no room to jump to four notrump, and he could well have the type of hand with which it is appropriate to ask for aces.

Four notrump is not Blackwood over an opponent's opening bid of four hearts or four spades. Over these preempts the four notrump bid is needed as a takeout bid. Over an opponent's preempt of four clubs or four diamonds, however, it is a close question as to whether four notrump should be considered to be natural or to be Blackwood.

The key to asking about aces in many of the above auctions in which the partner of the four notrump bidder had already bid notrump, is the use of the GERBER convention. Its use can clarify many otherwise troublesome auctions. *See also* COMBINING JACOBY WITH TEXAS.

Responding to Blackwood with a Void

The question of what the partner of the Blackwood bidder should do about a void divides into two questions: (1) whether or not he should show it, and (2) if so, how.

The void can never be simply counted as an ace and included in the ace-showing response. If the void is to be shown, it will have to be shown in some way out of the mainstream of responses.

The void should not be shown unless the responder has reason to think that it would be valuable for the Blackwood bidder to know about it. For example, a void in the Blackwood bidder's suit is usually not a helpful void. A void in the opponent's suit, however, is normally quite useful.

Another part of the question as to whether the void should be disclosed is whether it can be done without getting the partnership too high. Some partnerships agree, for instance, that a void cannot be shown by one who has opened the bidding or made a jump shift response unless he has two aces. If the Blackwood responder has not opened the bidding or made a jump shift, according to this agreement, he is allowed to show his void even if he has only one ace.

There are several ways in which the partnership could agree to show voids. First, the void could be shown by a jump to the six level, in the suit which the responder would have bid at the five level but for the void. For example, if the responder has one ace his response would have been five diamonds. With one ace and a void, his response would be six diamonds. A jump to six clubs would show no aces and a void, and a jump to six hearts would show two aces and a void.

While this method is precise with respect to the number of Aces held by the responder, it does not always reveal the location of his void. Another convention is designed to help identify which is the suit of the Blackwood responder's void. Using this second convention, the Blackwood responder would jump to six of his void suit unless it ranked higher than the partnership's agreed trump suit. In the latter event the responder would jump to six of the agreed trump suit. For example, if the bidding has gone

Opener	Responder
1 ♡	3 ♡
4 Notrump	6 ♣

using this method responder shows a void in clubs. If he had jumped to six hearts instead of six clubs, he would have been showing a void in spades.

When the trump suit is clubs or diamonds, a jump to six of the trump suit will be ambiguous as to which is the suit of the Blackwood responder's void. Moreover, regardless of what the trump suit is, this method does not allow the Blackwood responder to specify how many aces he has. Thus, in the above auction, responder has pinpointed a club void, but how many aces does he have?

A third method of showing voids requires the Blackwood responder to bid five notrump with two aces and a void, and to jump to the six level with one ace and a void. Using this method the responder will jump to six of his void suit if it ranks below the agreed trump suit, or to six of the trump suit if his void is higher ranking. These methods prevent the Blackwood bidder from asking about kings, but it is probably more valuable for him to know that his partner has two aces and a void, or one ace and a specific void, than to be able to inquire as to kings. Using this way of distinguishing between hands with two aces and hands with one also allows identification of the void suit more often in the situation in which locating the void is more likely to be crucial to a grand slam. When the responder has only one ace the location of the void is more likely to be a cardinal piece of information than it is when he has two aces and a void.

A somewhat similar method of showing voids involves the use of a three-step schedule of Blackwood responses. For example, in the Romex system, aces are shown as follows:

$$5 \clubsuit = 0 \text{ or } 3 \text{ aces}$$
$$5 \diamondsuit = 1 \text{ or } 4 \text{ aces}$$
$$5 \heartsuit = 2 \text{ aces}$$

If the responder has a void and at least one ace his responses will be higher than the five heart response. He will bid five spades if his void is in spades and he has one ace; he will bid five notrump if he has two aces and any void; he will jump to six of his void suit if it ranks below the agreed upon trump suit; or he will jump to six of the trump suit if his void ranks higher. Since responder can pinpoint a spade void when he holds one ace the only ambiguity as to where the void lies is if the trump suit is clubs and responder has a void in diamonds or hearts.

Yet another method of showing voids involves a temporizing bid by the Blackwood responder if he has two or more aces. With at least two aces and a void, the Blackwood responder should understate the number of aces he holds by two (assuming that his response will not land him in the agreed trump suit—if it would, he should respond normally). Thus, with three aces and a void, the response will be five diamonds; with two aces and a void, the response will be five clubs. When the Blackwood bidder returns to five of the trump suit, the responder now bids the suit of his void. The message to the Blackwood bidder is that his partner has two more aces than originally shown, and a void in the suit he has just bid. For example:

Opener	Responder
1 ♦	1 ♡
1 ♠	3 ♦
4 Notrump	5 ♣
5 ♦	6 ♣

Responder's six club bid reveals that he has two aces instead of none, and that he is void in clubs.

Using this method, if the responder has one ace and a void, and wants to be in slam, he can show his void in the following way: if his void suit ranks below the trump suit he jumps to six of the void; if his void suit ranks just above the trump suit he responds five notrump; and if his void suit ranks two suits above the trump suit he jumps to six of the trump suit. For example:

Opener	Responder
1 ♦	1 ♡
1 ♠	3 ♦
4 Notrump	6 ♦

Responder's six diamond bid shows that he has one ace and a

void in the suit ranking two higher than the trump suit, i.e., spades.

Using this method, if the Blackwood responder wants to bid a slam holding no aces and a void, his proper course of action is to respond as if he had three aces. If his desire to be in slam with no aces in his own hand is warranted, his partner will be able to tell that he has overstated the number of aces he holds. The Blackwood bidder in that auction is forced to rebid five notrump so that the responder can show the suit of his void as best he can. If his void ranks lower than the trump suit, he bids six of his void; if it ranks higher he bids six of the trump suit. Thus, the auction might go

Opener	Responder
2 ♣	2 ♠
3 ♡	4 ♡
4 Notrump	5 ♠
5 Notrump	6 ◇
7 ♡	

The opener's and responder's hands might be:

(Opener)
♠ A x   ♡ A K Q x x x   ◇ K x   ♣ A Q x

(Responder)
♠ K Q J 10 x   ♡ J x x x   ◇ —   ♣ K x x x

Suppressing Aces

When the responder to Blackwood has already shown one of his aces, a question arises as to whether he should show it again in responding to four notrump. For example, the Blackwood responder may have opened the bidding with a GAMBLING THREE NOTRUMP, showing a solid suit. Or he may have cue-bid the opponent's suit.

In general, unless the partnership has discussed it, the responder should show all of his aces. However, the more effective partnership agreement is to decline to include the ace of the opponents' suit in the Blackwood response when one member of the partnership has made a point of cue-bidding that suit to show a void.

For example, suppose North holds

♠ —   ♡ K J 10 x x x x   ◇ A Q J x   ♣ K x

and the bidding goes

North	East	South	West
1 ♡	1 ♠	3 ♡	Pass

North should cue-bid three spades, planning to follow with a Blackwood bid. Having taken the time to cue-bid first, the Blackwood bid would ask South to exclude the ace and king of spades from his responses. South might have either

[A] ♠ A x x   ♡ Q x x x   ◇ K x x   ♣ A x x

or

[B] ♠ Q x x   ♡ A x x x   ◇ K x   ♣ A x x x

Similarly, if the partner of the Blackwood bidder has made a cue bid that definitely shows first round control of the opponent's suit, he should exclude this ace from his considerations. If his cue-bid could have been made with less than first round control, however, he should show all of his aces and kings in response to Blackwood.

After a cue-bid by either partner has been followed by Blackwood and the appropriate response given, a rebid of five notrump by the Blackwood bidder asking about kings does not guarantee that the partnership has all four of the aces, but only all of the aces that matter for their suit contract.

ROMAN BLACKWOOD

One modification of the Blackwood convention which compresses the ace-showing responses in order to make room for the exchange of other information is called Roman Blackwood. Using this version, if the partner of the Blackwood bidder has two aces he has a choice of responses. If he feels that he has values he has not yet shown, he can respond five spades; otherwise he responds five hearts. The complete list of responses is as follows:

$$5 \clubsuit = 0 \text{ or } 3 \text{ aces}$$
$$5 \diamondsuit = 1 \text{ or } 4 \text{ aces}$$
$$5 \heartsuit = 2 \text{ aces without extra values}$$
$$5 \spadesuit = 2 \text{ aces with extra values}$$

For example, suppose the auction has proceeded

Opener	Responder
1 ♣	1 ♦
1 ♠	4 ♡*
4 Notrump	
*singleton heart	

and responder has the following hand:

♠ A Q x x   ♡ x   ◇ A x x x x   ♣ Q x x

Responder has the queen of trumps which in itself qualifies as an extra value; in addition he has the queen of opener's first bid suit. His hand is surely worth a five spade response.

Original Roman Responses

As originally devised, the five heart and five spade responses to Roman Blackwood were slightly different. A five heart response showed two "matching" aces, meaning aces of the same color or rank. There are four pairs of matching aces: clubs and diamonds, clubs and spades, diamonds and hearts, and hearts and spades. A five spade response showed two aces which did not match either in color or in rank. There are two pairs of these: hearts and clubs, and diamonds and spades.

This system of responses was valuable when the Blackwood bidder had one ace and his partner's response was five spades, showing non-matching aces—because the Blackwood bidder could always deduce which ace the partnership was missing. For example, if the Blackwood bidder had the ace of hearts and his partner held non-matching aces, they could only be the aces of diamonds and spades.

However, the five heart response occurred twice as often as the five spade response, and the Blackwood bidder who held one ace had to guess which two aces his partner held. He could always know one, but since there were two ways for that one ace to match another ace, the response was ambiguous.

Blue Team Roman Responses

An alternative method of showing aces is designed, in part, to cure the defect that plagued the original Roman Blackwood responses, and in part to provide the partnership with more room to explore after aces have been announced.

The Blue Team responses to Roman Blackwood are as follows:

5 ♣ = 1 or 4 aces

5 ♢ = 0 or 3 aces

5 ♡ = 2 aces of the same rank

5 ♠ = 2 aces of different ranks and different colors

5 NT = 2 aces of the same color.

Thus, the meanings of the five club and five diamond responses are the reverse of their standard Roman meanings. The rationale for reversing their meanings is that using the cheaper bid to show one ace conserves space when it is more likely to be needed. Further slam exploration is usually unnecessary when the Blackwood response has shown no aces; but it may be warranted if one ace has been shown.

The ambiguity of the original Roman five heart response has been cured by adding a five notrump response to show two specific pairs of aces. In this way the Blackwood bidder who has only one ace will know precisely which two aces his partner has.

This use of the five notrump bid may prevent the Blackwood bidder from inquiring about his partner's kings. This may be a disadvantage, since the number of kings held may be crucial to the determination of whether or not grand slam is a sound proposition. However, the advantage of using the five notrump response in this way is that Blackwood may now be bid by a player who has one ace and a void. If the response shows two aces, he will know whether or not one of the aces is in his void suit.

There does not appear to be any particular magic in maintaining the Rank-Mixed-Color order of responses set out above. The partnership could as easily agree to any ordering of the three groupings.

KEY CARD BLACKWOOD

When slam is to be played in a suit, the king of the trump suit is almost as important a card as any ace. If the partnership is lacking both an ace and the trump king, the slam is likely to be a poor proposition.

One convention intended to help the partnership to determine whether it has the trump king and sufficient aces to be in a slam is called Key Card Blackwood. This convention treats the king of the trump suit as a fifth ace. The responses to the four notrump bid are as follows:

$$5 \clubsuit = 0 \text{ or } 4 \text{ aces}$$
$$5 \diamondsuit = 1 \text{ or } 5 \text{ aces}$$
$$5 \heartsuit = 2 \text{ aces}$$
$$5 \spadesuit = 3 \text{ aces}$$

Use of Key Card Blackwood can help the partnership to bid grand slams that might otherwise be missed, or be bid without certainty that they had a solid trump suit, and to stay out of slams that might otherwise be bid. For example, suppose North held

♠ A Q x x x   ♡ x   ◇ A K Q x x   ♣ x

and the auction had started as follows:

North	South
1 ♠	3 ♠
4 Notrump	

The king of spades is crucial to the success of the grand slam, and use of Key Card Blackwood responses will reveal whether or not South has that king.

Again, suppose the North and South hands were as follows:

North:
♠ A J x x x x   ♡ A x x   ◇ x   ♣ K Q x

South (opener):
♠ Q x x x   ♡ K Q   ◇ A K Q x x   ♣ A x

Using Key Card Blackwood, the bidding would proceed

(A) *South*   *North*
    1 ◇   1 ♠
    4 ♠   4 Notrump
    5 ♡   6 ♠

Thus the partnership would easily avoid the grand slam.

Five Notrump Rebid

After the response to the four notrump Key Card Blackwood bid has been made, a bid of five notrump confirms that the partnership holds all five "keys". There are a number of ways to use the five notrump bid. The simplest is to ask the responder how many of the remaining kings are held. However, in bidding five notrump, the Blackwood bidder is exploring the prospects of grand slam, and with respect to grand slams, the question is usually not how many kings are held, so much as whether the right kings are held.

For example, North holds:

♠ A Q x x x x   ♡ x   ◇ x   ♣ A Q x x x

and the bidding has started

(B) *North*   *South*
     1 ♠   3 ♠
     4 Notrump   5 ♠
     5 Notrump

South's five spade bid shows three key cards, in this case two aces and the king of spades. North bids five notrump hoping to find out whether the partnership can make a grand slam. He needs to find out only about the king of clubs, however, and has no interest in how many other kings South might have.

The more useful treatment of the five notrump bid, therefore, is to guarantee that the partnership holds all of the aces plus the king of trumps, and to ask the responder to bid a grand slam if he thinks he has a suitable hand. If the responder does not think his hand is good enough to jump to the grand slam, but thinks he has extra values considering his previous bidding, he should make a cue-bid. This will usually show a king. With a hand that is not suitable to bid a grand slam, and that has no values in reserve, the responder would sign off in six of the trump suit.

For example, suppose South held one of the following hands, and the auction had proceeded as in B:

[C] ♠ K x x x   ♡ A K x x   ◇ A x x   ♣ J x

[D] ♠ K J x x   ♡ A J x   ◇ A x x   ♣ x x x

With Hand C South would cue bid six hearts over five notrump, having excellent controls, but not a hand that can guarantee enough tricks for a grand slam. With Hand D, South would simply bid six spades, having nothing in reserve.

However, if South has a hand such as

[E] ♠ K x x x   ♡ A x   ◇ A K Q J x   ♣ x x

and the bidding has started

North	South
1 ♠	3 ◇
4 ♣	4 ♠
4 Notrump	5 ♠
5 Notrump	

South would bid seven spades over five notrump, having a source of tricks in his own hand.

Which Suit is Trump?

The major disadvantage of Key Card Blackwood is that when it is not completely clear which suit has been agreed upon as trumps, there will be doubt as to which king is the key king. For example, in the auction

(F)	South	North
	1 ♡	2 ♣
	3 ♣	3 ♡
	4 Notrump	

neither partner will be sure, without specific discussion and agreement, which suit is to be the trump suit. If the responder fails to show the right king, the partnership may miss a lay-down slam. On the other hand, if the responder shows the wrong king, the partnership may go down in a slam for lack of enough aces.

The simplest solution to this problem is to adopt the general principle that the last suit bid is considered to be the trump suit for the purposes of responding to Key Card Blackwood. This principle should not apply, however, if the four notrump bidder has responded to the opening bid with a strong jump shift, for example:

(G) *South*   *North*
1 ♠   3 ♣
3 ♠   4 Notrump

North's bid of four notrump in sequence G should fix clubs as the trump suit for the purposes of South's responses. The partnership may yet play the contract in spades, but the key card is the king of clubs. North might hold, for example, either of these hands:

[H] ♠ x   ♡ A Q   ◇ A K x   ♣ A Q J x x x x

[I] ♠ K J x x x   ♡ x   ◇ K x   ♣ A Q x x x

With Hand I, if he can find the opener with three aces and the king of clubs, the responder will bid seven spades.

Instead of adopting the principle that the last suit bid fixes the key card, it is possible to a somewhat more complex set of guidelines, as follows:

(1) If only one suit has been supported, count the king of that suit.

(2) If two suits have been supported, count the king of the suit that was supported by the person who bid four notrump. For example, in Auction F, North should count the king of clubs, not the king of hearts.

(3) If the opening bid was a strong forcing bid such as two clubs, or a Schenken one club opening, count the king of the opener's bid suit. For example:

North	South
2 ♣	2 ♠
3 ♡	3 ♠
4 Notrump	

South should count the king of hearts, not the king of spades.

(4) If the responder made a strong jump shift response to the opening bid, count the king of his suit (as in Auction G).

(5) If none of the four rules stated above applies, count the king of the last bid suit. For example:

North	South
1 ♠	2 ♣
2 ♠	4 Notrump

North should count the king of spades, not the king of clubs.

It is also possible to use Roman type responses to Key Card Blackwood as follows:

$$5 \clubsuit = 0 \text{ or } 3 \text{ aces}$$

$$5 \diamondsuit = 1 \text{ or } 4 \text{ aces}$$

$$5 \heartsuit = 2 \text{ or } 5 \text{ aces}$$

For other conventions focusing on the trump king or on trump suit quality in general, *see* GRAND SLAM FORCE, MALOWAN, BARON SLAM TRY, CULBERTSON TRUMP ASKING BIDS, ROMEX TRUMP ASKING BIDS, RH FOUR NOTRUMP, WANG TRUMP ASKING BIDS.

BABY BLACKWOOD

Occasionally the use of Blackwood will get the partnership to an uncomfortably high contract. Some partnerships have adopted a low level Blackwood bid called Baby Blackwood. As it is normally used the Baby Blackwood convention is a bid of three notrump by the opening bidder after the responder has made a strong forcing raise of the opener's suit. For example,

Opener	Responder
1 ♠	3 ♠
3 Notrump	

Using Baby Blackwood, opener's three notrump bid asks for aces. This three notrump rebid by the opener is rarely put to any other use. But see WANG TRUMP ASKING BIDS.

The Baby Blackwood convention may be extended to have the responder's jump to three notrump over the opening bid of one heart or one spade ask for aces:

Opener	Responder
1 ♡	3 Notrump

This use of the three notrump bid would mean that three notrump could not be used in its natural sense, or as a strong forcing raise of the opener's suit as it is by many partnerships which use limit jump raises.

In addition, it is possible for the responder to use the Baby Blackwood convention by a jump to two notrump over his partner's one heart or one spade opening. When the partnership has agreed to use this version of Baby Blackwood, a series of notrump rebids by the responder can ask opener successively about his kings, queens and jacks:

Opener	Responder
1 ♠	2 Notrump ("how many aces?")
3 ♡	3 Notrump ("how many kings?")
4 ◇	4 Notrump ("how many queens?")
5 ◇	5 Notrump ("how many jacks?")

The use of the jump to two notrump as Baby Blackwood precludes use of that response as a natural bid showing a balanced 13 to 15 point hand, or as BARON TWO NOTRUMP or JACOBY TWO NOTRUMP, q.v.

RESPONDING TO BLACKWOOD OVER OPPONENT'S INTERFERENCE

When an opponent makes a bid directly over partner's four notrump Blackwood bid, he either usurps one of the bids available to the responder to show his aces, or bids a higher ranking suit than the suit in which the responder would properly have responded. For example:

South	West	North	East
1 ♢	3 ♡	4 Notrump	5 ♡

If South has no aces, or one or two aces, he can no longer make the bid he would have made without interference to show how many aces he has. If he has three aces and bids five spades, his partner cannot be sure, without some conventional understanding, what this bid means.

The standard way of dealing with interference over a Blackwood bid is to double the overcall whenever the size of the prospective penalty seems great enough to warrant abandoning the slam search. When the size of the probable penalty does not seem so attractive, the responder would pass to show that he has no aces, bid the next higher ranking suit over the overcall to show one ace, or bid the second suit above the overcall to show two aces, and so forth. In the above auction, for example, if South thought slam was still worth a try, he would pass to show no aces, bid five spades to show one ace, bid five notrump to show two aces, bid six clubs to show three aces, and bid six diamonds to show all four aces.

For other methods of dealing with opponents who interfere with the responses to Blackwood, *see* DOPI AND PODI, DEPO.

DOPI AND PODI

There are several conventions for bidding over Blackwood interference that do not use the double for penalties, but instead use it as part of a schedule of ace-showing bids. The simplest such convention is called DOPI (pronounced "dopey"). The DOPI convention uses a double to show no aces, a pass to show one ace, the bid of the cheapest suit over the overcall to show two aces, the bid of the second cheapest suit to show three aces, and so forth. The name DOPI might be called an alphanumeric acronym, since the D stands for Double and the P stands for Pass, and the O and I are numerals representing the number of aces held.

It is also possible to use Roman responses to DOPI. Using Roman DOPI, the partner of the Blackwood bidder acts as follows over the interference:

Double = 0 or 3 aces

Pass = 1 or 4 aces

Next suit = 2 aces

A similar convention is called PODI (or DIPO), in which the meanings of the double and the pass are reversed, the pass showing no aces and the double showing one ace. There seems to be little technical reason to prefer DOPI over PODI, or vice versa. However, DOPI is much more widely used, probably for psychological reasons. It seems more natural to double the opponents when there are no aces, making a slam seem more remote.

DEPO

Another Blackwood interference convention, one with a strictly alphabetical acronym, is called DEPO. Using DEPO the responder will double to show no aces, two aces or four aces, and will pass to show one ace or three. Since zero is considered to be an even number, the initials of DEPO stand for Double Even, Pass Odd.

The DEPO convention saves the partnership more room than DOPI or PODI, but has the disadvantage of being ambiguous. Usually the Blackwood bidder should be able to judge from his own hand and from the previous bidding how many aces the responder is showing, but he will not always be able to do so.

In order to retain accuracy as much as possible while saving space when it is most needed, some partnerships use DOPI at the five level, and use DEPO at the six level, where space is usually at a premium.

GERBER

Another ace-asking convention in widespread use is the Gerber convention. The Gerber convention uses a four club bid to ask about aces. One of the great advantages of Gerber is that it may allow the partnership to learn below the game level how many aces it has.

The responses to the Gerber four club bid are as follows:

$$4 \diamondsuit = 0 \text{ or } 4 \text{ aces}$$

$$4 \heartsuit = 1 \text{ ace}$$

$$4 \spadesuit = 2 \text{ aces}$$

$$4 \text{ Notrump} = 3 \text{ aces}$$

Originally, a bid of five clubs was used to show all of the aces. Most partnerships, however, use the four diamond bid to show 0 or 4 aces, just as the five club bid in response to Blackwood shows 0 to 4 aces. The reason is that it saves room, and that the Gerber bidder is unlikely to be unable to determine whether his partner holds all of the aces or none.

Some partnerships use the four club bid as Gerber in all auctions in which a trump suit has been agreed or where no-trump has been bid. For example

(A) *Opener*   *Responder*
    1 ♠   3 ♠
    4 ♣

(B) *Opener*   *Responder*
    1 ♡   3 ♡
    3 ♠   4 ♣

For these partnerships opener's four club bid in Auction A, and responder's four club bid in Auction B would both be Gerber.

Most experts, however, are unwilling to give up the use of four clubs as a cue-bid. They use Gerber only after notrump has been opened or responded or rebid. These partnerships tend to use Gerber freely in notrump auctions, in any situation in which a four notrump bid could be used in its natural or quantitative sense. For example

	Opener	*Responder*
(C)	1 Notrump	4 ♣

	Opener	*Responder*
(D)	1 ◇	1 ♠
	2 Notrump	4 ♣

	Opener	*Responder*
(E)	1 Notrump	2 ♣
	2 ♡	4 ♣

	Opener	*Responder*
(F)	1 ◇	2 Notrump
	4 ♣	

In each of the above auctions, C through F, the four club bid is the Gerber convention.

Further, in notrump auctions, only the partner of the notrump bidder may use the Gerber convention. The rationale is that the player who has shown a balanced hand by bidding notrump is almost never the partner who should ask about aces. Thus in the auctions

(G)	Opener	Responder
	1 Notrump	3 ♡
	4 ♣

(H)	Opener	Responder
	1 Notrump	2 ◇ (slam try)
	2 ♠	3 ♠
	4 ♣

opener's four club bids are cue-bids, not Gerber.

Over three notrump rebids, the four club bid is frequently needed as a natural bid. Some partnerships agree, therefore, that a Gerber bid must be a jump—either to four clubs or to five clubs. For example

(I)	Opener	Responder
	1 ♠	2 ◇
	2 Notrump	4 ♣

(J)	Opener	Responder
	1 ♠	2 ◇
	3 Notrump	4 ♣

In Auction I, responder jumped to four clubs; therefore his bid was Gerber. In Auction J, however, responder's four club bid was not a jump; therefore it is a natural bid, rather than Gerber. If responder wanted to use Gerber over opener's three notrump rebid, he would have to jump to five clubs:

| Opener | Responder
--- | --- | ---
 | 1 ♠ | 2 ◇
 | 3 Notrump | 5 ♣

Gerber for Kings

As the convention was originally devised, the Gerber bidder asked for kings by bidding the cheapest possible suit, other than the trump suit, over the ace showing response. For example

Opener	Responder
1 ♡	3 ♡
4 ♣	4 ♡
4 ♠	

Opener's four spade bid asked for kings.

To avoid misunderstandings, however, most partnerships agree that in order to ask about kings the Gerber bidder must rebid five clubs over the ace-showing response.

In response to the five club bid, kings are shown as follows:

$$5 ♢ = 0 \text{ kings}$$

$$5 ♡ = 1 \text{ king}$$

$$5 ♠ = 2 \text{ kings}$$

$$5 \text{ Notrump} = 3 \text{ kings}$$

$$6 ♣ = 4 \text{ kings}$$

As is the case with the Blackwood convention, the authorities are not in agreement as to the proper response to show all four kings. Most indicate that a response of five diamonds shows 0 or 4 kings. However, there appears to be little reason why it is not safer to bid six clubs with all of the kings, to avoid any ambiguity.

There are a variety of offshoots of the Gerber convention. *See* ROMAN GERBER, KEY CARD GERBER, SUPER GERBER, ACE IDENTI-

FICATION, BLACK AND RED GERBER, EXTENDED GERBER, CLARAC SLAM TRY, FANE FOUR CLUB CONVENTION.

Interference with Gerber

There are several methods of showing aces after interference by an opponent. See RESPONDING TO BLACKWOOD OVER AN OPPONENT'S INTERFERENCE, DOPI AND PODI, DEPO.

GERBER AFTER TWO NOTRUMP AND THREE NOTRUMP OPENINGS

When the bidding has been opened with two notrump—either directly or by way of an artificial two club opening, i.e.,

Opener	Responder
2 ♣	2 ♢
2 Notrump	

—a question arises as to how a genuine club suit may be shown. For example, suppose the bidding is opened with two notrump and the responder has a hand such as

♠ K x x   ♡ x   ♢ Q x x   ♣ K J 10 x x x

A bid of three clubs does not show the club suit because three clubs is normally used as Stayman. Some partnerships use the immediate jump to four clubs as Gerber, and in addition treat a bid of three clubs followed by four clubs as Gerber. These partnerships have no way to bid clubs naturally.

Since it is obviously useful for the responder to be able to check for aces after looking for a major suit fit, a response of three clubs followed by four clubs should be Gerber. There is no reason, moreover, why the responder should not always use this sequence when he wants to bid Gerber. In this way, the immediate jump to four clubs may be reserved to show a club suit. It should not matter that the opener will not know, when responder bids three clubs and then four clubs, whether responder has a four card major suit, or whether his three club bid was just temporizing, paving the way to Gerber.

Over a three notrump opening the question is not so much whether a four club response is natural, as which artificial bid it should be considered to be. Some partnerships use the four club response to a three notrump opening as the Stayman convention; some use it as the Gerber convention. Whichever use four clubs is put to, a four diamond response can be used for the other convention. It seems somewhat preferable to use the four diamond bid as Stayman, and to use four clubs as Gerber, giving the opener maximum room to show the number of aces he holds.

Some partnerships solve this problem by using four clubs as Stayman, and using a jump to five clubs as Gerber.

ROMAN GERBER

A variety of modifications and extensions of the Gerber convention have been devised. Some are patterned after modifications of the Blackwood convention. For example, it is possible to use Roman style responses to Gerber, as follows:

$$4 \diamond = 0 \text{ or } 3 \text{ aces}$$

$$4 \heartsuit = 1 \text{ or } 4 \text{ aces}$$

$$4 \spadesuit = 2 \text{ aces}$$

The Romex system uses a modification of Roman Gerber in which the pairs of aces are identified with greater particularity. The Romex responses are:

$4 \diamond = 0$ or 3 aces

$4 \heartsuit = 1$ or 4 aces

$4 \spadesuit = 2$ aces of the same color

$4 \text{ NT} = 2$ aces of the same rank

$5 \clubsuit = 2$ aces of different colors and different ranks

If the Gerber response is five clubs, five diamonds becomes the king-asking bid.

KEY CARD GERBER

As with Blackwood, the partnership may agree to use Key Card Gerber in which the king of the trump suit is counted as an ace. Using this modification the responses would be

$$4 \diamondsuit = 0 \text{ or } 4 \text{ aces}$$

$$4 \heartsuit = 1 \text{ or } 5 \text{ aces}$$

$$4 \spadesuit = 2 \text{ aces}$$

$$4 \text{ NT} = 3 \text{ aces}$$

See KEYCARD BLACKWOOD.

SUPER GERBER

One drawback to the use of the Gerber convention is that the four club bid cannot be used as a natural bid or as a cue-bid. Super Gerber is a convention that is designed to minimize this drawback. Super Gerber can use any suit bid between four clubs and five clubs, inclusive, depending on the previous bidding, to ask for aces.

Super Gerber is applicable to two situations. It may be used after a three notrump bid, or it may be used after a minor suit is agreed upon as trumps. If one partner has bid three notrump, Super Gerber is the bid of four of the lowest unbid suit. If all four suits have been bid, Super Gerber is a jump to five clubs. For example, in the auction

Opener	Responder
1 ♢	1 ♠
3 Notrump	4 ♣

responder's four club bid is Super Gerber since clubs have never before been bid. However, in the auction

Opener	Responder
1 ♣	1 ♢
3 Notrump	4 ♡

a four club bid by responder over three notrump would be natural rather than Gerber. Therefore, Super Gerber requires that responder bid four hearts, the lowest ranking unbid suit, to ask for aces. In the auction

Opener	Responder
1 ♠	2 ♦
2 ♡	3 ♣
3 Notrump	5 ♣

all of the suits have been bid. Therefore, four clubs would be used as a natural bid. Super Gerber uses a jump to five clubs to ask for aces.

In its second application, Super Gerber is used when a minor suit fit has been established. In this circumstance Super Gerber is a jump to four of the lowest ranking unbid suit. For example

(A)
Opener	Responder
1 ♦	3 ♦
4 ♡	

(B)
Opener	Responder
1 ♦	2 ♦
4 ♣	

In Auction A, opener's four heart bid, the jump to four of the lowest unbid suit, is Super Gerber. In Auction B, the four club bid is Super Gerber.

(C)
Opener	Responder
1 ♣	3 ♣
4 ♦	

(D)
Opener	Responder
1 ♡	2 ♦
3 ♦	4 ♠

In Auction C, opener's four diamond bid is Super Gerber. In Auction D, responder's four spade bid is Super Gerber.

Using this facet of Super Gerber, a minor suit is deemed to be agreed upon not only if it is supported, but also if it is rebid by one player. Thus, in the auction

Opener	Responder
1 ◇	1 ♠
3 ◇	4 ♡

responder's four heart bid is Super Gerber. Similarly, in an auction such as

Opener	Responder
1 ♣	2 ◇
2 Notrump	3 ◇
4 ♡	

opener's four heart bid is Super Gerber.

One advantage of Super Gerber over Blackwood when a minor suit is to be trump is that it keeps the auction from by-passing the partnership's game contract when there are not enough aces for slam.

The responses to Super Gerber are the standard series of four steps:

First step = 0 or 4 aces

Second step = 1 ace

Third step = 2 aces

Fourth step = 3 aces

Super Gerber may be used for kings by rebidding the Super Gerber suit. Thus, in the auction

Opener	Responder
1 ♣	2 ◇
2 Notrump	3 ◇
4 ♡	5 ♣
5 ♡	

responder's five club bid, the third step, showed two aces, and opener's five heart bid, repeating the Super Gerber suit, asked about kings.

An ambiguity may arise when five clubs has been used as the Super Gerber bid. Five clubs is used as Super Gerber only when all of the suits have been bid; therefore, if the Super Gerber bidder subsequently rebids six clubs, it may not be clear whether he is bidding clubs naturally, or is asking about kings. For example:

Opener	Responder
1 ♠	2 ◇
2 ♡	3 ♣
3 Notrump	5 ♣
5 ♠	6 ♣

Responder's six club bid is ambiguous.

In a few situations the use of Super Gerber precludes the use of splinter or fragment bids after a minor suit has been agreed. This effect is limited, however, to situations in which the Super Gerber bidder has not bid notrump showing a balanced hand, and where the singleton is in the lowest ranking unbid suit. For example

(E) *Opener*   *Responder*
   1 ♣   3 ♣
   4 ♦

(F) *Opener*   *Responder*
   1 ♣   3 ♣
   4 ♥

In Auction E, opener's four diamond bid would be Super Gerber. But in Auction F, there is no reason why his four heart bid (or a four spade bid) could not be used to show a singleton.

ACE IDENTIFICATION

The Ace Identification convention is an extension of the Gerber convention, used after the responder has shown one or two aces, showing the Gerber bidder that the partnership is missing one ace. After the Gerber response, a bid of four notrump asks for further information, identifying the ace or aces held.

If the response to Gerber has shown one ace, the four notrump bid asks the responder to bid the suit in which he holds the ace. If the response to Gerber has shown two aces, the four notrump bid asks the responder to bid as follows:

$$5 \clubsuit = \text{two aces of the same color}$$

$$5 \diamondsuit = \text{two aces of the same rank}$$

$$5 \heartsuit = \text{two aces of different colors and different ranks}$$

The use of the Ace Identification extension may help the partnership to decide whether or not to bid a slam. If the Gerber bidder has a void, this convention may assist in reaching a grand slam. For example, if South holds

♠ A K Q x   ♡ x x   ◇ K Q x x x x x   ♣ —

and his partner opens the bidding with one notrump, the auction could go

North	South
1 Notrump	2 ♣
2 ♠	4 ♣
4 ♠	4 Notrump
5 ♣	7 ♠

South's four club bid was Gerber, and North showed two aces. South's four notrump bid asked which two aces North held, and North's five club bid showed that his aces were the same color. Knowing that opener had the aces of hearts and diamonds, South could count thirteen tricks and bid the grand slam. If North had shown any other two aces, South would have settled for six spades.

BLACK AND RED GERBER

Another modification of the Gerber convention is designed primarily to solve the problem of how to ask for aces when the agreed suit is clubs. Blackwood might get the partnership too high, while the Gerber convention would be ambiguous. The Black and Red Gerber convention uses a four club bid as Gerber only if a red suit has been agreed upon as trumps. If a black suit has been agreed, the Gerber bid is four diamonds. For example

Opener	Responder
1 ♠	2 ♣
4 ♣	4 ◇

Responder's four diamond bid would be Gerber.

The responses to either Gerber bid are the normal series of four steps:

First   step   =   0 or 4 aces

Second   step   =   1 ace

Third   step   =   2 aces

Fourth   step   =   3 aces

After aces have been shown, a variety of possibilities arise. The Gerber bidder may rebid the Gerber suit to ask for kings. Or he may rebid four notrump to ask his partner to clarify which aces he holds: see ACE IDENTIFICATION. Or he may cue-bid. For example, suppose opener holds the following hand:

♠ x   ♡ A K J x x x   ◇ A   ♣ A Q x x x

The bidding might go

Opener	Responder
1 ♡	3 ♡
4 ♣	4 ♡
4 ♠	5 ♣
7 ♡	

Responder's four heart bid showed one ace. Opener cue-bid four spades, hoping to find responder with a club control. When responder was able to cue-bid clubs, opener could bid the grand slam.

FANE FOUR CLUB CONVENTION

The Fane four club convention seeks to determine how many aces the responder holds, and which ones they are. The responder to the four club bid starts by bidding his lowest ranking ace. The responses are as follows:

$4 \diamondsuit$ = ace of diamonds

$4 \heartsuit$ = ace of hearts

$4 \spadesuit$ = ace of spades and no other ace

4 NT = ace of clubs

If the responder to four clubs has either no aces or four aces, he must bid five clubs.

After the response to four clubs, if the four club bidder rebids five clubs, he asks how many aces are held. The responses are

$5 \diamondsuit$ = 1 ace

$5 \heartsuit$ = 2 aces

$5 \spadesuit$ = 3 aces

After a four spade response to four clubs, showing only the ace of spades, a five club bid can be used as a cue-bid, asking the responder to show his lowest ranking king.

If the player who has bid four clubs and five clubs rebids five notrump, he asks how many kings are held. The responses are

$$6 \clubsuit = 0 \text{ kings}$$

$$6 \diamondsuit = 1 \text{ king}$$

$$6 \heartsuit = 2 \text{ kings}$$

$$6 \spadesuit = 3 \text{ kings}$$

$$6 \text{ NT} = 4 \text{ kings}$$

If the partner of the four club bidder has what he considers to be a useful void, he can show a void and the number of aces he holds by jumping to the five level in response to four clubs:

$$5 \diamondsuit = \text{a void and one ace}$$

$$5 \heartsuit = \text{a void and two aces}$$

$$5 \spadesuit = \text{a void and three aces}$$

In order to sign off, the four club bidder may either bid the agreed trump suit or bid four notrump; his partner is required to pass either of these bids. After a five level response, the four club bidder may sign off by bidding an unbid suit, which asks his partner to return to five notrump.

One of the drawbacks of this convention is that the four club bid cannot be used to initiate a normal cue-bidding sequence. Another, is that the partnership may be at the five level with unsuitable hands before it knows how many aces and what controls, are missing. For example, if opener's and responder's hands were

(Opener)
♠ A K Q J x x   ♡ J x x x   ◇ —   ♣ A K x

(Responder)
♠ 10 x x x   ♡ Q x x   ◇ A K Q x   ♣ Q J

the bidding would go

Opener	Responder
1 ♠	3 ♠
4 ♣	4 ◇ (diamond ace)
5 ♣	5 ◇ (only one ace)
5 ♠	Pass

With these hands five spades is in jeopardy of being set with a heart ruff.

ACOL FOUR NOTRUMP OPENING

The Acol four notrump convention uses an opening bid of four notrump to ask the responder if he has any aces. If he has one ace he is expected to identify it. The proper responses are

$$5 \; \clubsuit \;\; = \;\; 0 \text{ aces}$$
$$5 \; \diamondsuit \;\; = \;\; \text{ace of diamonds}$$
$$5 \; \heartsuit \;\; = \;\; \text{ace of hearts}$$
$$5 \; \spadesuit \;\; = \;\; \text{ace of spades}$$
$$6 \; \clubsuit \;\; = \;\; \text{ace of clubs}$$

If the responder should be endowed with two aces opposite this opening, his proper response is five notrump.

Probably the most useful type of hand with which to use this convention is one that contains a void, such as

$$\spadesuit \text{ A K Q J x x x} \qquad \heartsuit \text{ K Q J x} \qquad \diamondsuit - \qquad \clubsuit \text{ A K}$$

The Acol four notrump opening can be coordinated with standard Blackwood. An Acol four notrump opening could not, for example, be made with a hand such as

$$\spadesuit \text{ x} \qquad \heartsuit \text{ K Q J} \qquad \diamondsuit \text{ A K Q J x x x x} \qquad \clubsuit \text{ x}$$

because any one-ace-showing response would get the partnership out of its depth. However, with this hand, the opener could start things off with a forcing two-bid, planning to bid Blackwood later.

CULBERTSON FOUR-FIVE NOTRUMP

Normally when the Blackwood convention is used, the four notrump bidder becomes the "captain" of the partnership for the remainder of the auction, and the responder simply does as he is told. The Blackwood bidder may have any of a number of hands, and there is little way that the responder can have enough information to sensibly exercise any judgment.

The Culbertson Four-Five Notrump convention sets certain minimum standards for the bid of four notrump. Thus, the bid gives information to the responder, as well as extracting it from him, and allows both partners to use their judgment in assessing slam prospects.

Using the Culbertson convention, the bid of four notrump guarantees either three aces, or two aces plus the king of a suit genuinely bid by the partnership. A suit that has been cue-bid does not count as a genuinely bid suit.

Responding to Four Notrump

The responses to the four notrump bid are as follows. If the partner of the four notrump bidder has either two aces, or one ace and the kings of all of the suits bid by the partnership, his proper bid is five notrump. Whichever of these two hands the responder has, the partnership is guaranteed that it possesses all four aces.

If the responder either has the kings of all the partnership's suits but no ace, or has the ace of a suit bid by the partnership but does not have all of its kings, he has a choice of responses: he may either bid six of the agreed trump suit, or bid five of one of the partnership's suits, so long as it is not their cheapest suit. Which bid he selects will depend on how he evaluates his hand. For example, North might hold

[A] ♠ K x x x x   ♡ K x x   ◇ A x x   ♣ x x

or

[B] ♠ K x x x x   ♡ K x x   ◇ A x   ♣ K x x

with the auction having proceeded

South	*North*
1 ◇	1 ♠
3 ♠	4 ◇
4 Notrump	

North is allowed to bid either five spades or six spades in response to four notrump. He knows that the partnership may be missing either one ace, or the king of diamonds. With Hand A he would bid five spades, not being sure that he wants to be in slam. Opener's hand might be

♠ A Q x x   ♡ A x   ◇ Q J x x x   ♣ A x

With Hand B, responder should bid six spades, having extra values.

If the partner of the four notrump bidder has an ace or a void in a suit not genuinely bid by the partnership, but does not have all of the kings in the partnership's suits, his assigned response is five of the suit in which he holds the ace or void. For example, suppose North held:

[C] ♠ K x x x x   ♡ K x   ◇ J x   ♣ A Q x x

and the auction started

South	North
1 ◇	1 ♠
3 ♠	4 ♣
4 Notrump	

The four club bid by North was a cue-bid, and did not promise a suit. Therefore, North's proper response to four notrump is five clubs. If South, holding a hand such as

[D]   ♠ A Q x x   ♡ A x   ◇ K Q x x x   ♣ x x

now signs off in five spades, North can nevertheless carry on to six spades with the Hand C above, having values in reserve.

If the partner of the four notrump bidder has neither an ace nor the kings of all of the partnership's suits, he will normally bid five of the partnership's lowest suit.

None of the above Culbertson responses is absolutely forced upon the responder. Since responder knows that his partner's hand must meet certain minimum requirements to have allowed him to bid four notrump, the responder is free to evaluate his own hand in that light. With one exception, if the responder's overall values are poor, he may choose a response that shows less than he actually holds. The exception is that if he holds two aces, or one ace and the kings of all of the partnership's bid suits, he must act aggressively, bidding at least five notrump. Conversely, if his values probably fit exceptionally well with his partner's hand he may choose to overbid.

If the partner of the four notrump bidder has two aces and a king of a side suit, he is allowed to show this by bidding either five or six of the suit in which he has the king. In the event that he bids five of the suit and his partner has the ace, his partner may infer initially that responder has a void in that suit. However, his next response will clarify that he had instead an especially good hand with useful features in the suit he has bid. For example, if he possesses both the king and queen of this side suit he may bid five to show the king, and then rebid six of the suit to show the queen. For example:

Opener	Responder
1 ♢	1 ♡
4 ♡	4 Notrump
5 ♣	5 ♡
6 ♣	

Opener might have a hand such as

♠ A x x   ♡ K Q x x   ♢ A Q x x   ♣ K Q

If he had held the queen of spades instead of the queen of clubs, he would have jumped directly to six clubs instead of bidding first five and then six clubs.

Rebids by the Four Notrump Bidder

If the partner of the four notrump bidder has responded at the five level, a rebid of five notrump by the four notrump bidder guarantees that the partnership has all of the aces. If the response to four notrump has been five notrump, the four notrump bidder may show interest in a grand slam by making any bid other than six of the agreed trump suit. For example, if North holds

♠ A K Q x x x   ♡ A x   ◇ x   ♣ K Q x x

and the auction starts

South	North
1 ◇	2 ♠
3 ♠	4 Notrump
5 Notrump	

North knows from the five notrump response that South has the ace of diamonds and the ace of clubs. But he cannot yet count to thirteen tricks. North therefore cue-bids six clubs over five notrump, hoping that his partner will have a king to cue-bid.

South, for example, might have any of the following hands:

[A]   ♠ J x x   ♡ Q x x   ◇ A Q J x x   ♣ A x

[B]   ♠ x x x x   ♡ K x x   ◇ A Q x x   ♣ A x

[C]   ♠ x x x   ♡ x x x   ◇ A K Q x x   ♣ A x

With Hand A, South would content himself with bidding six spades, having no undisclosed controls to bid. With Hand B, South would cue-bid six hearts over six clubs. And with Hand C, South would cue-bid six diamonds, planning to bid again if necessary to get to the grand slam. North, opposite South's cue-bids with Hands B and C, would need no further information to bid seven spades.

Choice Between Four Notrump and a Cue-Bid

When one is interested in a slam and has the choice between bidding Culbertson four notrump and making a cue-bid, a principal consideration is the frugal use of bidding space. For example, if the bidding starts

Opener	Responder
1 ♣	2 ♡
3 ♡	

responder has room to cue-bid before making the Culbertson four notrump bid. By cue-bidding he may gain valuable information.

On the other hand, if the auction starts

Opener	Responder
1 ♣	1 ◇
1 ♡	4 ♡

there is insufficient room to cue-bid, have partner make a cue-bid in turn, and bid four notrump. In such a situation the Culbertson four notrump bid should be made in preference to the cue-bid, for otherwise partner will infer that the cue-bidder lacked the values required to bid four notrump.

SAN FRANCISCO

The San Francisco convention, like the Culbertson Four-Five Notrump convention, imposes minimum requirements on the four notrump bidder. The San Francisco convention, sometimes called the Warren convention, requires that the four notrump bidder hold at least two aces.

The responder simultaneously shows how many aces and kings he has. Counting each ace as three points and each king as one point, the normal responses are as follows:

5 ♣ = fewer than 3 points (no ace, at most 2 kings)

5 ◇ = 3 points (1 ace and no kings, or 3 kings)

5 ♡ = 4 points (1 ace and 1 king, or 4 kings)

5 ♠ = 5 points (1 ace and 2 kings)

5 NT = 6 points (1 ace and three kings, or 2 aces)

6 ♣ = 7 points (2 aces and 1 king, or 1 ace and 4 kings)

6 ◇ = 8 points (2 aces and 2 kings)

6 ♡ = 9 points (2 aces and 3 kings)

6 ♠ = 10 points (2 aces and 4 kings)

If the four notrump bidder has opened the bidding with a strong two-bid, the responses are altered to reflect the reduced potential of the responding hand. In this event, the five club response shows no points, five diamonds shows one point, five hearts shows two points, and so on.

One drawback to the San Francisco convention is that the responses are much more complicated than those for some other ace-asking conventions. Another defect is that several of the responses are ambiguous since they can be made with more than one combination of aces and kings. Usually the four no-trump bidder will be able to tell which holding responder has, but sometimes he will not.

CULWOOD

The Culwood convention, as its name might imply, is something of a combination of Blackwood and the Culbertson Four-Five Notrump convention. The Culwood convention places the same requirements on the four notrump bidder as does the Culbertson convention, but uses some of the Blackwood responses.

The Culwood four notrump bidder is required to have either three aces, or two aces and the king of a suit bid by himself or his partner. The responses are as follows:

5 ♣ = 0 aces

5 ♢ = 1 ace

5 ♡ = 2 aces

5 ♠ = the partnership has all the aces, and the kings of the bid suits

5 NT = the partnership has all of the aces, and the responder has two of the top three trumps in his own hand.

For example, suppose opener's and responder's hands were the following:

(Opener)
♠ K Q x x   ♡ A Q J x x   ♢ A x   ♣ x x

(Responder)
♠ A J x x x   ♡ K x x   ♢ x   ♣ A K x x

Using the Culwood convention the bidding would start

Opener	*Responder*
1 ♡	1 ♠
3 ♠	4 Notrump
5 Notrump	

Opener's five notrump bid promises that the partnership has all of the aces, and that opener has two of the top three trump honors.

EXTENDED GERBER

Extended Gerber is a variation of the Gerber convention in which the responses to the four club bid show how many controls, i.e., aces and kings are held. Thereafter, the four club bidder may ask how many kings and queens are held in any two specific suits.

Asking for Aces and Kings

The Extended Gerber convention starts with a four club bid after notrump has been bid, or after a trump suit has been agreed upon. The four club bid asks partner to announce his controls in accordance with the following schedule:

4 ◇ = 0 or 1 controls, or 5 or 6 controls, or 10 or 11 controls

4 ♡ = 2 or 7 controls

4 ♠ = 3 or 8 controls

4 NT = 4 or 9 controls

Thus, if the bidding has gone

Opener	*Responder*
1 ♡	3 ♡
4 ♣	4 ◇

responder's four diamond bid shows either 0 or 1 control, or 5 or 6 controls, or 10 or 11 controls. Opener asks for further clarification by bidding the next suit, four hearts. Responder will bid four spades if he has the lower of any pair of controls, i.e., 0, 5 or 10 controls. He will bid four notrump if he holds the upper of any pair of controls, i.e., 1, 6 or 11 controls. Opener should be able to tell from his own hand and from the previous bidding whether his partner has nearly all of the controls (there being a total of twelve in the deck), or virtually no controls, or something in between.

If the response to Extended Gerber has been four diamonds, any four level bid except four hearts is a sign off. If the response to Extended Gerber has been anything other than four diamonds, a bid by the four club bidder of four notrump or four of the trump suit is a sign off.

Signing Off at the Five Level

In order to sign off in five diamonds, five hearts or five spades after the ace and king showing response to Extended Gerber has been given, the four club bidder uses a relay. If the four club bidder bids five clubs, the responder is forced to bid five diamonds. This forced response enables the four club bidder to pass, allowing the partnership to play in five diamonds. Similarly, if the four club bidder rebids five diamonds, the responder is forced to bid five hearts; the forced five heart bid may be passed, or the Extended Gerber bidder may bid five spades as a sign off. For example:

Opener	Responder
1 ◇	1 ♡
1 ♠	3 ♠
4 ♣	4 Notrump
5 ◇	5 ♡
5 ♠	Pass

Responder's four notrump response showed either four or nine controls. If opener had a hand such as

♠ K Q x x   ♡ A x   ◇ K Q J x x x   ♣ x

he would know that responder must have four controls, rather than nine. Unless his controls were specifically the aces of spades and diamonds, slam would be a poor proposition. Therefore opener bid five diamonds, forcing responder to bid five hearts, and to pass opener's five spade sign off.

This somewhat convoluted method of signing off leaves other five level bids free to be used as other asking bids.

Asking for Kings and Queens

After the ace and king asking bids have been completed, the four club bidder may ask his partner how many kings and queens he holds in two specified suits. Counting each king as two points and each queen as one, the responder shows his kings and queens in the designated suits in a series of seven steps. The first step shows no points, the second step shows one point, the third step shows two points, and so forth through the seventh step, which shows all six points in the two suits.

There are six pairs of suits that may be asked about. Each pair is asked about by means of a different five-level bid or series of bids, as follows:

Suits of Inquiry	Asking Bids
spades and hearts	direct five notrump bid
spades and diamonds	direct five spade bid
hearts and diamonds	direct five heart bid

spades and clubs	five club bid, followed by a five spade bid
hearts and clubs	five club bid followed by a five heart bid
diamonds and clubs	five club bid followed by a five notrump bid

For example, in the auction

Opener	Responder
1 ♡	3 ♡
4 ♣	4 Notrump (4 or 9 controls)
5 ♣ (relay)	5 ◇ (forced)
5 ♡	6 ♡

opener's five heart bid after the five club relay shows that he did not want to sign off after all, but that he wants to know about responder's kings and queens in hearts and clubs. Responder's six heart bid, the fifth step, shows that he has four points in those suits—i.e., either both kings or one king and both queens. Opener might have a hand such as

♠ A x   ♡ A x x x x   ◇ x   ♣ A K x x

Responder's four notrump bid has told him that responder has four controls, which must be the ace of diamonds and two kings. Opener uses the five club-five heart asking combination of bids to learn whether his trump suit and side suit are solid.

D.I. ("Declarative Interrogative" or "Declarative Informatory")

The D.I. convention is a general slam exploration bid that lies somewhere between the conventions that ask about aces and kings in bunches, and the conventions that ask about specific controls in individual suits. D.I. is a four notrump bid that is not natural and does not ask how many aces are held, but rather asks partner to show a previously undisclosed feature.

There are several situations in which a four notrump bid cannot be D.I. A jump to four notrump is never D.I. Such a jump is either natural or Blackwood. A bid of four notrump over three notrump is also not D.I. In addition, if four notrump is bid by either the opener or the responder at his first or second turn to bid, it is not D.I. For example

Opener	Responder
4 ♡	4 Notrump

Responder's four notrump bid is Blackwood, not D.I. Similarly in the auction

Opener	Responder
1 ♠	4 ♠
4 Notrump	

opener's four notrump bid is not D.I. but Blackwood.

In its original form, a four notrump D.I. bid promised at least two aces if made by an unlimited hand; it promised at least one ace if bid by a limited hand. For example:

(A)	Opener	Responder
1 ♠	3 ♠
4 ♣	4 ◇
4 Notrump

(B)	Opener	Responder
1 ♠	2 ◇
2 ♡	4 ◇
4 ♠	4 Notrump

In Auctions A and B the four notrump bids promise at least two aces, since four notrump was bid by a hand that is not yet limited. In the following auction, however,

Opener	Responder
1 ♠	2 ♠
4 ♣	4 ◇
4 ♡	4 Notrump

the four notrump bid does not promise more than one ace since responder has already limited his hand.

In addition, some partnerships agree that in order to bid four notrump as D.I. one must have at least second round control of his own suits and any unbid suits. For example, in Auction A above, opener would promise two aces and no worse than K x or a singleton in clubs and hearts; but he might have three small diamonds.

Responses to D.I.

The D.I. responder may make any of three types of responses: negative, encouraging, or positive. To respond nega-

354

tively to D.I. the responder simply bids five of the agreed trump suit. For example, if opener has

♠ K J x x   ♡ A J x x   ◇ Q x   ♣ J x

and the auction goes

Opener	Responder
1 ♠	2 ♣
2 ♡	3 ♠
4 ♠	4 Notrump

opener has no reason to want to encourage responder in his slam interest. Therefore he should respond five spades to responder's four notrump D.I. bid.

To make an encouraging response, the D.I. responder bids a control or value at the five level, below the agreed trump suit. Although this is encouraging, it does not necessarily show extra values. For example, if opener had

♠ A Q x x x   ♡ K Q x x   ◇ x x   ♣ K x

in the above auction, he would bid five clubs in response to the D.I. bid.

Any bid by the D.I. responder higher than five of the trump suit is a positive response. A five notrump response is the strongest of all positive responses. It promises two aces, and maximum strength for the previous bidding. For example, if opener had

♠ A K x x x x   ♡ A K Q x   ◇ x x   ♣ x

he could bid five notrump, having two aces, a six-card suit, and solid hearts.

The weakest positive response is a jump to six of the agreed trump suit. This bid suggests that a grand slam would probably be a poor proposition.

Positive responses, above five of the agreed trump suit, other than a bid of six of the trump suit, show extra values, commit the partnership to a small slam, and encourage exploration of grand slam possibilities. For example, suppose opener had

♠ A K x x x ♡ K Q x x ◇ K x ♣ x x

in the auction

Opener	Responder
1 ♠	2 ♣
2 ♡	3 ♠
4 ♠	4 Notrump
6 ◇	

Opener definitely wants to be in slam, but he cannot bid five no-trump because he has only one ace. He therefore bids six diamonds in order to show a diamond control and extra values. His six diamond bid denies the ability to show a club feature. Responder might have a hand such as

[A] ♠ Q x x x ♡ A x ◇ A x x ♣ A x x x
or
[B] ♠ Q x x x ♡ A x ◇ A x x ♣ A K x x

With Hand A, responder should bid six spades, knowing that the partnership may well have a club loser. With Hand B, responder should bid seven spades. Since the opener has shown extra values including a diamond control, the grand slam rates to be a good proposition.

Rebids

If the four notrump D.I. bidder rebids five notrump, he promises one ace more than he originally guaranteed, and he is asking for further information with an eye on grand slam. Responder may bid a grand slam directly over five notrump if he has extra values such as a solid suit, or extra queens, or well placed doubleton kings. Alternatively, the D.I. responder may encourage by showing a low-ranking feature. If he has no reasons to encourage, he signs off at six of the trump suit.

Blue Team D.I.

As most often used today, the D.I. convention does not place as stringent requirements on the D.I. bidder in terms of the number of aces he holds, or the control of his own suits or the unbid suits. Rather, the convention is used principally as an aid to cue-bidding toward slam.

When used in this way, a four notrump bid in the midst of cue-bidding is a general slam try asking for further information. Some of the adherents of D.I. are fond of saying that D.I. stands for "Do-something Intelligent." Suppose, for example, that North holds

♠ Q   ♡ K J x x x x   ◇ A x x   ♣ A Q x

and opens the bidding with a Precision one club bid, showing at least 16 high card points. Thereafter the bidding proceeds:

North	South
1 ♣	1 ♠
2 ♡	3 ♡
4 ♣	4 ♠
4 Notrump	

North's two heart bid showed his suit; South's one spade bid was natural, as was his raise to three hearts. After opener had cue-bid four clubs and responder had cue-bid four spades, opener bid four notrump as D.I., to enable responder to show a minor suit king if he had one. Using standard methods a four notrump Blackwood bid would be unsatisfactory because there are too many things opener needs to find out. A cue-bid by opener of either minor suit over responder's four spade bid might prevent responder from showing his minor suit control. The D.I. bid therefore gave the partnership the greatest flexibility.

The D.I. bid can also be used to determine whether or not the partnership has two losers in a side suit. For example, if opener's and responder's hands were

(Opener)

♠ —   ♡ A x   ♢ A K 10 x x x   ♣ Q J 10 x x

(Responder)

♠ A K x x x   ♡ K x   ♢ J x x x   ♣ x x

the auction might be

Opener	Responder
1 ♢	1 ♠
3 ♣	4 ♢
4 ♡	4 ♠
4 Notrump	5 ♢
Pass	

Responder's five diamond bid in response to D.I. denied a club control. Therefore slam was out of the question.

The D.I. four notrump bid may also be made in a sequence

that makes it clear that control of a particular suit is crucial. For example

Opener	Responder
1 ◇	2 ♡
3 ♡	4 ♣
4 ◇	4 Notrump

Responder's four notrump bid showed an inability to cue-bid spades. Responder's hand might be

    ♠ x x   ♡ A K J x x x   ◇ x   ♣ A K Q x

If opener has a hand such as

    [A] ♠ x   ♡ Q x x x   ◇ A K Q x x x   ♣ x x

he will bid six hearts. However, if he has

    [B] ♠ Q J x   ♡ Q x x x   ◇ A K Q J x   ♣ x

which is stronger in high cards, but has no spade control, he must sign off in five hearts.

    The problem with this use of D.I. is that if opener has a hand such as

    [C] ♠ K x   ♡ Q x x x   ◇ A K Q x x   ♣ x x

the hand belongs in six notrump from opener's side of the table.

CONTROL ASKING BIDS

Asking bids in general are not widely used. The genuine need to use an asking bid tends to arise fairly infrequently. It is only with relatively freakish hands that one needs to find one particular control in partner's hand, and sometimes that information may be obtained in other ways such as cue-bidding. And because the need to use an asking bid arises infrequently, the agreement to use them places a perhaps unprofitable strain on the memory, as to which bids are asking bids, and what the responses are.

On the other hand there are certain situations in which the use of asking bids seem to make more sense than cue-bidding. Cue-bidding is a cooperative process that normally works well when there is not great disparity between the playing strengths of the two hands. In situations, however, where one hand is known to be much stronger than the other—a fact that is sometimes established at an elevated level of the auction—cue-bidding is less satisfactory. The situations in which asking bids seem *a priori* appropriate include cases in which the hand has been opened with a strong two-bid. After the opening and response, there may not be enough room for the opener to cue-bid all of his treasures in an effort to elicit the one piece of information he needs from his partner. Here the opener is likely to be able to pinpoint his interest with a single bid. And opposite a very strong hand, the needed value may be something that is not susceptible to cue-bidding, such as *third* round control of a suit.

Similarly, when one partner opens with a preemptive bid at the three level or the four level, and the other is interested in slam despite the preemptor's announced weakness, asking bids are more appropriate than cue-bids. The partner of the preemptor should be the captain of the hand, rather than one of the crew.

Asking Bids after Strong Two-Bids

For these reasons some partnerships use new suit bids by the opener as asking bids whenever the bidding has been opened with a strong two-bid; they use new suit bids or jumps by the responder as asking bids when the opening bid has been a high-level preempt. For example, suppose opener has

♠ A K x x x   ♡ A K x x   ◇ A K   ♣ x

and the bidding goes 2 ♠ - 4 ♠, with responder's four spade bid denying first or second round control of any suit. Opener would still like to know if responder has the queen of hearts or a doubleton. Thus some partnerships would treat opener's five heart bid in the auction

Opener	Responder
2 ♠	4 ♠
5 ♡	

as an asking bid in hearts, asking responder to bid six spades with third round control of hearts.

If, in response to the two spade opening bid above, responder had raised to three spades, which the partnership had agreed did not deny first or second round controls, opener would again be hard pressed to get the desired information by cue-bidding, because he needs to know not only about the ace of clubs, but again about third round heart control. Thus some partnerships would use the bid of a new suit at the six-level after Blackwood as an asking bid. For example, in the auction

Opener	Responder
2 ♠	3 ♠
4 Notrump	5 ◇
6 ♡	

361

opener's six heart bid would ask about third round heart control. *See also* ROMAN ASKING BIDS, CULBERTSON ASKING BIDS, LEBOVIC ASKING BID, FOUR CLUB ASKING BID, FULWILER ASKING BIDS.

One drawback to asking bids is that they may reserve a bid that could be put to better use in another way. See, e.g., BARON SLAM TRY. The major disadvantage of asking bids is that they pinpoint the weakness to the defenders as well as to the partnership. Even drowsy defenders will frequently lead the suit of the asking bid, and they will generally be right.

Asking Bids over Preempts

When a player wants to try for a slam opposite a preemptive opening by his partner, he normally has no more than one weak spot in his hand. Some partnerships therefore use asking bids over opening preempts.

In response to an opening preempt at the four level, the bid of any new suit would be an asking bid. The opener should show his control of that suit as follows:

First   step = no first or second round control

Second step = king or singleton

Third   step = ace

Fourth step = singleton ace, ace and king, or a void

For example, if the responder held

♠ A x x   ♡ A K x x x x   ◇ x x   ♣ A x

opposite a four spade opening bid, he would bid five diamonds. Over a five heart response, the first step, responder would sign off at five spades. Over a five spade response, the second step, responder would bid six spades. And over any higher step, responder could bid the grand slam.

When the bidding has been opened with a preempt at the three level, standard practice is to treat any new suit bid by the responder on the three level as forcing. A jump response, therefore, is an idle bid. Some partnerships use the jump response over a three-level preempt as an asking bid.

For example, if responder has

♠ Q J x x x   ♡ A Q x   ◇ A K Q x x   ♣ —

opposite a three heart opening, the bidding could start

Opener	Responder
3 ♡	4 ♠

Opener should show his spade control according to the above schedule.

In making one of these asking bids, of course, the asker should take care to have sufficient values that the partnership will not be unduly high if the opener lacks control of the asked suit.

ROMAN ASKING BIDS

In order to reduce the taxing of the memory as to what bids are asking bids, some partnerships use unusual jumps in previously unbid suits to ask about controls. These jumps, called Roman asking bids, may be one level higher than that of a jump shift, as in the auction

Opener	Responder
1 ◇	1 ♡
4 ♣	

Or they may be one level higher than that of a cue-bid, as in the auction

Opener	Responder
1 ♠	3 ♠
5 ♣	

The unusual jump asking bid may be used by the responder as well as the opener. For example

Opener	Responder
1 ◇	1 ♡
1 ♠	4 ♣

The unusual jump asking bid may be used in the suit of an opponent's overcall. For example,

North	East	South	West
1 ♡	2 ♣	4 ♣	

Or it may be used in response to an overcall. For example

North	East	South	West
1 ♠	2 ♣	Pass	3 ♠

Responses to Roman Asking Bids

There are essentially two sets of responses to choose from. The older version uses a series of four steps:

First   step = no first or second round control

Second step = king or singleton

Third   step = ace or void

Fourth step = ace and king

One modern variation would use the fourth step, rather than the third step, to show a void.

Suppose opener and responder had the following hands:

(Opener)
♠ A K Q 10 x x   ♡ A   ◇ A x x x   ♣ K Q

(Responder)
♠ J x x x   ♡ x x x x   ◇ x   ♣ x x x x

Using the above responses the auction would be

Opener	Responder
2 ♣	2 ◇ (negative)
2 ♠	3 ♠
5 ◇	5 ♠
6 ♠	

Responder's five spade bid, the second step, showed the king of diamonds or a singleton diamond.

The newer series of responses to Roman asking bids uses a six step schedule designed to clarify the nature of the control. The responses are:

First   step = no first or second round control

Second step = singleton

Third   step = king

Fourth step = ace

Fifth   step = void

Sixth   step = ace and king

If it is known that the responder cannot be short in the suit asked about, the second and fifth steps are eliminated.

Using these responses with the hands set out above, the auction would have been exactly the same. The responder would have bid five spades over the five diamond asking bid. The difference is that the opener would know that responder had a singleton rather than the king—perhaps a crucial question if the asker is looking for solidification of a suit rather than just control.

A player who makes an asking bid does not guarantee first round control of all of the other suits. Sometimes he makes the asking bid in order to determine whether or not it is safe to use Blackwood. For example, opener might have

♠ A K Q x   ♡ A   ◇ K Q x x x x   ♣ x x

in an auction that starts

Opener	*Responder*
1 ◇	1 ♠

Opener cannot afford to bid Blackwood, because he has a small doubleton club. Therefore, he jumps to four clubs, an unusual jump, to ask responder if he has a club control. If responder bids four diamonds, denying control, opener will settle for four spades. If responder bids anything but four diamonds, opener will bid four notrump Blackwood.

Any partnership using asking bids should be sure to discuss and agree, if Blackwood is to be used after an asking bid response shows an ace, whether that ace is to be included in the Blackwood ace-showing responses.

For alternative uses of unusual jumps, see SPLINTERS, FRAGMENTS.

CULBERTSON ASKING BIDS

A Culbertson asking bid, initially, is any bid of a suit other than trumps at or above the four level after a suit has been raised, or any unusual jump to the three level or higher. If no suit has been raised, an unusual jump by inference agrees on the previous suit as trumps. Examples of Culbertson asking bids are:

(A) *Opener*
    1 ♠
    4 ♦
                              Responder
                              3 ♠

(B) *Opener*
    1 ♣
    4 ♦
                              Responder
                              1 ♠

(C) *Opener*
    1 ♣
    3 ♠
                              Responder
                              1 ♠
                              4 ♦

(D) *Opener*
    1 ♣
                              Responder
                              3 ♠

Responses to Culbertson Asking Bids

The responses to Culbertson Asking Bids are intricate, showing both control of the suit asked about, and other controls in addition. First round controls include aces and voids, except when the prescribed response is a notrump bid, in which case only aces are counted. Second round controls are kings or singletons; third round controls are queens or doubletons.

If the responder does not have first or second round control of the asked suit, he signs off with a minimum bid in the agreed trump suit. Or, even if he has first or second round control of the asked suit, if he has no first round control in any other suit, he must sign off.

If the responder has first or second round control of the asked suit, and in addition has two aces, he bids the minimum number of notrump.*

If the responder has first or second round control of the asked suit, and in addition has three aces, he jumps in notrump.

If the responder has first or second round control in the asked suit, and in addition has either one ace or a void, he bids the suit in which he has the ace or void. If his ace is in the agreed trump suit, he must jump in it.

If the responder has a void in the asked suit, and has two aces, he jumps in one of the suits in which he has an ace; if one of his aces is in the trump suit, he must jump in the other suit to avoid confusing his response with that which shows lesser values.

In the auction

Opener	*Responder*
1 ♠	2 ◇
2 ♠	4 ♡

responder's four heart bid is an asking bid, agreeing on spades as trumps. Suppose opener had one of the following hands:

[A]   ♠ A Q 10 x x x   ♡ x x   ◇ x x   ♣ A x x

---

*An Australian modification to this response is that when the responder holds a singleton in the asked suit and two aces, he jumps in the suit of the lower ranking ace.

369

[B] ♠ A Q 10 x x x   ♡ x   ◇ x x x   ♣ A x x

[C] ♠ A J 10 x x x   ♡ x   ◇ A x x   ♣ A x x

[D] ♠ A J 10 x x x   ♡ —   ◇ K x x   ♣ K Q x x

[E] ♠ A J 10 x x x   ♡ —   ◇ x x x   ♣ A K x x

[F] ♠ K Q J x x x   ♡ —   ◇ x x x   ♣ K Q J x

With Hand A, in which opener lacks control of hearts, he returns to four spades, the agreed trump suit. With Hand B, opener has control of hearts and has two aces; his proper bid is four notrump. The additional ace in Hand C requires opener to jump to five notrump.

With Hand D, opener must show his heart control and one ace by bidding the suit of the ace. However, since the ace is in the trump suit, and a four spade bid would be negative, opener must jump to five spades. With Hand E, opener must jump to six clubs. With Hand F, opener has control of hearts, but he has no other first round controls; therefore he must sign off with a four spade bid.

Further Asking Bid in the Same Suit

The Culbertson asking bidder may make additional asking bids after the response to the first asking bid. He may ask about the same suit, whether the first response was positive or negative. Or he may ask about a new suit.

If the asking bidder rebids the asked suit after a negative response, he asks the responder to clarify his negative response. If the responder has second round control of the asked suit but has no outside ace, he bids the minimum number of no-trump. If the responder has only third round control of the asked suit but has one or more outside aces, he shows this by bidding an outside ace. If the responder has neither control of the asked suit nor an ace, he bids the minimum number of the trump suit.

Thus, in the auction

Opener	Responder
1 ♠	2 ◇
2 ♠	4 ♡
4 ♠	5 ♡

opener might hold

[A] ♠ A J 10 x x x   ♡ x x   ◇ x x   ♣ A x x

[B] ♠ K Q J x x x   ♡ x   ◇ x x   ♣ K Q J x

[C] ♠ K Q J x x x   ♡ x x   ◇ x x   ♣ K Q J

With Hand A opener would bid six clubs, showing third round control of hearts and the ace of clubs. With Hand B, opener would bid five notrump showing second round control, but no aces. With Hand C, opener would bid five spades, denying both control and aces.

If the asking bidder rebids the asked suit after a positive response, he asks whether his partner has third round control of the asked suit, as well as the first or second round control he has already shown. For example, a singleton, or K x, or K Q x constitutes second and third round control. A singleton ace, or A x, or A Q x constitutes first and third round control.

With no third round control, i.e., holding either A x x (x) or K x x (x), the partner of the asking bidder simply signs off in the agreed trump suit. If he has third round control, he should either bid an undisclosed void, or bid a second round control in another suit; or if he has neither of those features, he should bid the minimum number of notrump. Thus, in the auction

Opener	Responder
1 ♠	2 ♢
2 ♠	4 ♡
4 Notrump	5 ♡

opener has shown two aces, plus first or second round control of hearts. Suppose opener's hand is one of the following:

[D] ♠ A J 10 x x x   ♡ K x x   ♢ x x   ♣ A x

[E] ♠ A J 10 x x x   ♡ x   ♢ x x x   ♣ A K x

[F] ♠ A J 10 x x x   ♡ x   ♢ x x x   ♣ A Q x

With Hand D, opener lacks third round control of hearts; therefore he signs off in five spades. With Hand E, opener has third round control of hearts and second round control of clubs. He must bid six clubs. With Hand F, although he has third round control of hearts, he has neither a void nor a side second round control to cue-bid; he must bid five notrump.

Further Asking Bid in a New Suit

If the asking bidder bids a new suit after receiving a positive response to the original asking bid, it asks about second round control of the new suit. If the responder lacks second round control, he signs off in the agreed trump suit. If the responder has second round control, he cue-bids either an undisclosed void, or a second round control in another suit; or if he has neither of those features, he should bid the minimum number of notrump.

If the asking bidder bids a new suit after receiving a negative response to his first asking bid, it is an asking bid in the new suit, and the responses are the same as for the original asking bid. For example, suppose opener has

♠ A J 10 x x x   ♡ x x x   ◇ x   ♣ A x x

The auction would start

Opener	Responder
1 ♠	2 ◇
2 ♠	4 ♡
4 ♠	5 ◇
5 Notrump	

Opener's four spade bid over the four heart asking bid was a negative response. The five diamond bid was a new asking bid, this time in diamonds. Opener's five notrump bid showed first or second round control of diamonds and two aces in addition. If responder had a hand such as

♠ K x x x   ♡ A x   ◇ A 10 x x x x x   ♣ —

he could jump to seven spades over the five notrump bid.

Using Culbertson asking bids, the question as to which should be the suit of the first asking bid is often quite tricky. With the above hand, the responder had no way to make an immediate asking bid in diamonds since no suit had been agreed as trumps, and a jump in diamonds would not have been unusual. Therefore with the above hand, a temporizing asking bid was made in hearts, followed by an asking bid in the real suit of interest.

However, so great is the complexity of these asking bids that when this very hand and this very sequence arose in a 1937 team of four match in Vienna, Josephine Culbertson did not recognize the five diamond bid as an asking bid, and passed. Seven spades was in fact laydown, and was reached at the other table by the Viennese pair—using Culbertson asking bids.

LEBOVIC ASKING BID

The Lebovic Convention is an asking bid designed to deal with the problem of how to determine whether or not the partnership has control of a certain suit when the trump suit is a minor. When a minor suit has been agreed upon, and two other suits have been bid, the Lebovic convention uses a jump in the fourth suit to ask about control in that suit. For example

Opener	Responder
1 ♣	1 ♡
1 ♠	3 ♣
4 ◇	

opener's four diamond bid asks about control of that suit.

The minor suit may be agreed by inference when it has been rebid by one player. For example, in the auction

Opener	Responder
1 ◇	1 ♠
2 ◇	3 ♣
3 ◇	4 ♡

responder's four heart bid agrees on diamonds as trumps, and asks opener about his control of the heart suit. Responder might have a hand such as

♠ A K Q x x x   ♡ x x   ◇ Q x   ♣ A x x

The responses to the Lebovic asking bid are as follows: if the responder has neither first nor second round control of the asked suit, he makes the minimum bid in the trump suit. If the responder has a singleton in the asked suit, he bids six of the trump suit. If the responder has K x or longer in the asked suit, he bids four notrump. If the responder has the ace or a void in the asked suit, he bids five of that suit.

In exceptional cases the Lebovic convention may be extended to auctions in which two suits remain unbid. If one partner has made a strong jump bid, a subsequent jump by the other in a new suit may be used as a Lebovic asking bid, even if another suit also is unbid. For example

Opener	*Responder*
1 ♣	1 ♠
3 ♣	4 ♡

Responder's four heart bid agrees on clubs, and asks about hearts.

FOUR CLUB ASKING BID

The Four Club Asking Bid convention is a three-stage series of asking bids designed to elicit information about short suits, aces, and trump honors. The convention uses a four club bid as an asking bid in two situations: first, when it is a jump to four clubs, and second, when four clubs is bid immediately after a jump raise in a suit. For example

(A)	Opener	Responder
	1 ♡	3 ♡
	4 ♣

(B)	Opener	Responder
	1 ◇	1 ♡
	2 ♡	4 ♣

The four club bid asks whether partner has a singleton or void anywhere in the hand. If he does, he bids the short suit. Lacking a singleton or void, he bids four of the trump suit.

After the response to the shortness asking bid, if the four club bidder makes the lowest ranking non-trump bid (including notrump), he asks his partner to reveal how many aces he holds. The responses are

First   step = 0 or 4 aces

Second step = 1 ace

Third   step = 2 aces

Fourth step = 3 aces

After the ace showing response, if the four club bidder

bids the lowest ranking non-trump bid, he asks about the quality of partner's trumps. The responses are

First   step   =   0 or 3 of the top three honors

Second step   =   1 of the top three honors

Third   step   =   2 of the top three honors

If the auction proceeds as follows

Opener	*Responder*
1 ♠	4 ♣
4 ♡	4 Notrump
5 ◇	5 ♡
5 ♠	

opener's four heart bid showed a singleton heart. Responder's four notrump bid, being the cheapest non-trump bid, asked about aces. Five diamonds by opener showed one ace. Responder's five heart bid, again the cheapest bid, asked about the quality of the trump suit. Opener's five spade bid promised all or none of the top three honors.

FULWILER ASKING BIDS

The Fulwiler Asking Bid is a control asking bid that may be used even at a very low level of the auction. Used after the trump suit has been established, the Fulwiler asking bid is any minimum bid by either opener or responder in another suit. For example

(A) *Opener*   *Responder*
     1 ♠   2 ♠
     3 ♦

(B) *Opener*   *Responder*
     1 ♦   1 ♡
     2 ♡   2 ♠

Opener's three diamond bid in A is a Fulwiler asking bid, asking about diamond control. Responder's two spade bid in B asks about opener's spade control.

The responder to the asking bid shows his controls in a series of six steps:

First   step = no first or second round control

Second step = singleton

Third   step = void

Fourth step = king

Fifth   step = ace

Sixth   step = ace and king

The use of such low level bids as asking bids, of course, precludes the use of these bids as natural bids or short suit game tries. When the opener's bid is raised to two, he is more often concerned with whether or not he should bid a game, rather than whether the responder has a particular suit controlled for purposes of a slam.

GRAND SLAM FORCE

The single most important consideration in determining whether or not to bid a grand slam is the solidity of the trump suit. It is even more important than that also important question as to whether the partnership has first round control of all side suits, for sometimes aces are not cashed.

Of the trump quality asking bids, the grand slam force is the most widely used. The use of this convention commits the partnership to at least a small slam. For conventions that may be used in determining whether or not to bid even a small slam, *see* BARON SLAM TRY, CULBERTSON TRUMP ASKING BIDS, ROMEX TRUMP ASKING BIDS, R/H FOUR NOTRUMP, WANG TRUMP ASKING BIDS. *See also* PRECISION CLUB SYSTEM.

In its simple form, the grand slam force is a jump to five notrump after a suit has been agreed on as trump, in which the five notrump bidder asks his partner to bid a grand slam if he has two of the top three trump honors. For example, if responder has a hand such as

♠ A K   ♡ Q 10 x x x x   ◇ K Q 10 x x   ♣ —

and the auction has started

Opener	Responder
1 ♣	1 ♡
3 ♡	4 ♣
4 ◇	

After opener's cue-bid of four diamonds, the only thing of interest to the responder is whether or not his partner has the ace and king of hearts. This is an appropriate hand for the grand slam force.

Before using the grand slam force, however, one must be mindful of certain prerequisites. First, the hand must be able to produce thirteen tricks if the partner of the grand slam force bidder has two of the top three trump honors. Similarly, it is advisable to be sure that the partnership has no side suit losers. Discovery of trump suit solidity is a pyrrhic victory if the grand slam goes down because an opponent cashes an ace, or because the partnership has only twelve tricks.

In order to use the grand slam force, the grand slam force bidder himself must have one of the top three trump honors. Otherwise the partnership could reach a grand slam missing the ace of trumps. Further, since the grand slam force commits the partnership at least to a small slam, the grand slam force bidder should be sure that it will be safe to play at the six level even if his partner has none of the trump honors. For example, if the grand slam force bidder has only the queen of trumps, and his partner turns up with neither the ace nor the king, a small slam is rather iffy.

Which Suit is Trump?

To be effective, both the grand slam force bidder and his partner must be aware what suit has been agreed as trumps. When only one suit has been supported, that suit is trumps. If each partner has supported the other's suit, a five notrump bid will be ambiguous unless the partnership has discussed and agreed on which suit should be deemed trumps. In the absence of specific agreement, the trump suit should probably be deemed to be the suit that was supported second. For example in the auction

Opener	Responder
1 ♡	2 ♣
3 ♣	3 ♡
5 Notrump	

opener's five notrump bid should ask about heart honors. If opener had been interested in club honors he might have been able to jump to five notrump directly over the two club response. In the auction

Opener	Responder
1 ♡	2 ♣
3 ♣	3 ♡
3 ♠	5 Notrump

responder's five notrump bid should ask about hearts.

If no suit has been supported, but the grand slam force bidder has opened with a strong two-bid or its equivalent, or has made a strong jump shift response, his suit should be deemed trumps. If no other rule applies, the last bid suit should be deemed trumps, assuming that the grand slam bidder can be deemed to be supporting that suit. For example,

(A)

Opener	Responder
1 ♠	3 ♠
5 Notrump	

(B)

Opener	Responder
1 ♠	5 Notrump

(C)

Opener	Responder
1 ♠	3 ♡
3 ♠	5 Notrump

In Auctions A and B, it is clear that the five notrump bid asks about spades. In Auction C, neither suit has been supported; however, since the grand slam force bidder has made a jump shift response, he should be deemed to be using the grand slam force for his own suit. If he had wanted to use the grand slam force for spades, he could have done so directly over the one spade opening, as in Auction B.

In the Auctions D, E and F none of the five notrump bids is the grand slam force:

(D)	*Opener*	*Responder*
	1 ♣	1 ♡
	2 ♠	3 ♡
	3 Notrump	5 Notrump

(E)	*Opener*	*Responder*
	2 Notrump	3 ♡
	3 Notrump	5 Notrump

(F)	*Opener*	*Responder*
	1 ♢	1 ♠
	3 ♠	4 ♣
	4 ♠	5 ♠
	5 Notrump	

(G)	*Opener*	*Responder*
	1 ♠	3 ♠
	4 ♣	4 ♡
	5 ♣	5 ♢
	5 Notrump	

In Auction D, no suit has been agreed on, although both partners had opportunities to support each other's suits while forcing to game. Responder's five notrump bid therefore should be construed giving opener a choice among the possible small slam contracts.

In Auction E, the five notrump bid by the responder cannot be a grand slam force because it is virtually impossible that his hand is such that the solidity of the trump suit is his only concern. Responder's five notrump bid gives opener a choice between six hearts and six notrump. In Auction F, opener's five notrump bid cannot be the grand slam force since over four clubs he appeared to be willing to play in four spades. His five notrump bid is therefore a suggestion that the hand be played in six notrump with himself as declarer. He might have the K x of hearts to protect. In Auction G, opener's five notrump bid is ambiguous.

Responses to Five Notrump

If the partner of the grand slam force bidder has two of the top three honors in the trump suit, he should bid a grand slam. However, many partnerships agree that the proper bid with two of the top three honors is always seven *clubs*. If the grand slam force responder can be counted on to bid seven clubs rather than seven of what he has been led to believe is the trump suit, the grand slam force can be used to ask about a suit other than the one in which the grand slam force bidder actually wants to play.

For example, if the responder had a hand such as

♠ K x x   ♡ A K Q J 10 x x   ♢ A x x   ♣ —

and his partner opened one spade, responder would want to be in a grand slam if opener had as little as

♠ A Q x x x   ♡ x   ◇ K x x x x   ♣ x x

But responder does not want the hand played in seven spades, which could be defeated by a 4-1 spade break. The hand should be played in seven hearts, which is a good deal safer. Responder would thus like to establish the solidity of the spade suit and end up in hearts, by means of the following auction:

Opener	Responder
1 ♠	5 Notrump
7 ♣	7 ♡
Pass	

If the partner of the grand slam force bidder does not have two of the top three trump honors, he should attempt to use whatever space there is between five notrump and six of the trump suit to describe just what he does have. Further description could be advantageous because if the partners have between them ten trumps headed by the ace and king, they are unlikely to lose a trump trick; thus the grand slam could be bid even absent the trump queen.

The Culbertson recommended responses to the grand slam force vary according to the trump suit. If spades are trumps, the responses are

6 ♣ = five spades; no ace, no king

6 ◇ = four spades headed by the ace or king

6 ♡ = five spades headed by the ace or king

6 ♠ = four spades; no ace, no king

If hearts are trumps, the Culbertson responses are

6 ♣ = four hearts headed by the ace or king

6 ◇ = five hearts headed by the ace or king

6 ♡ = four or five hearts; no ace, no king

If diamonds are trumps, the responses are

6 ♣ = five diamonds headed by the ace or king

6 ◇ = any other holding

The principle adopted by most partnerships today as to how to respond holding fewer than two of the top three honors, is the better the suit, the higher the bid. Codifying this principle, the Blue Team responses to the grand slam force are as follows, with spades as trumps

6 ♣ = none of the top three honors

6 ◇ = queen

6 ♡ = no more than four spades by the ace or king

6 ♠ = five spades headed by the ace or king

With hearts as trumps the Blue Team responses are:

6 ♣ = queen or worse

6 ◇ = no more than four hearts headed by the ace or king

6 ♡ = five hearts headed by the ace or king

With diamonds as trumps, the responses are:

6 ♣ = queen or worse

6 ◇ = any number headed by the ace or king

Suppose opener and responder had the following hands:

(Opener)
♠ A Q x x   ♡ A 10 x x x x   ◇ A K   ♣ x

(Responder)
♠ K x   ♡ K x x x   ◇ Q x x   ♣ A J x x

Using the Blue Team responses, the bidding would go

Opener	Responder
1 ♡	3 ♡
3 ♠	4 ♣
4 ◇	4 ♠
5 Notrump	6 ◇
7 ♡	

Some partnerships reverse the meanings of the six-level bids after the five notrump grand slam force bid, so that the cheaper responses show the better trump holdings. This practice has the advantage of allowing the showing first of honor cards, and second of length, since a further asking bid can sometimes be made. For example, in the Romex system, the responses to the grand slam force are

6 ♣ = ace or king

6 ◇ = queen

6 ♡ = none of the top three honors

388

Using these responses the auction might go

Opener	Responder
1 ♠	3 ♠
4 ♣	4 ◇
4 ♡	5 Notrump
6 ♣	6 ◇

Responder's six diamond bid asks opener to bid the grand slam with extra length in his suit.

Triggers Other Than Five Notrump

In order to provide more room for description of fair-to-good trump holdings when a suit other than spades has been agreed on, some partnerships use bids other than five notrump as the grand slam force for other suits. For example, after hearts have been agreed, a jump to five spades can be used as the grand slam force; after diamonds have been agreed, a jump to five hearts can be used as the grand slam force; after clubs have been agreed, a jump to five diamonds can be used as the grand slam force.

Each of these grand slam force triggers allows four steps for description of various trump holdings. The possible four-step gradations would be those described previously for situations in which spades have been agreed on and five notrump is used as the grand slam force.

To use any of these bids as the grand slam force, the bid must be a jump, in order to avoid confusion and interference with ordinary cue-bidding. For example, in the auction

(A) | Opener | Responder |
|--------|-----------|
| 1 ♠ | 2 ♣ |
| 3 ♣ | 3 ♡ |
| 3 ♠ | 4 ♡ |
| 5 ◇ | |

North's five diamond bid is a simple cue-bid. However, in the auction

(B) | Opener | Responder |
|--------|-----------|
| 1 ♠ | 2 ♣ |
| 3 ♣ | 3 ♡ |
| 5 ◇ | |

North's jump to five diamonds can be used as the grand slam force in clubs. North and South might have hands such as

North:
♠ A K Q 10 x   ♡ x   ◇ A x x   ♣ K x x x

South:
♠ x x   ♡ A Q x x   ◇ x   ♣ A J x x x x

If five notrump were used as the grand slam force and South had the above hand, he would have to content himself with a six club response, even though seven is makeable. In auction (B), however, South has room to show that he has one of the top two trump honors plus extra length. Thus, the auction might go

Opener	Responder
1 ♠	2 ♣
3 ♣	3 ♡
5 ◇	6 ♣
7 ♣	

Use of these specific jumps as the grand slam force means, of course, that they cannot be used as splinter or fragment bids. Since splinter or fragment jumps are most frequently used below the game level, however, this seems a modest price to pay for having extra room to show potentially adequate non-maximum trump holdings.

MALOWAN
(Grand Slam Force after Blackwood)

Sometimes the partnership is not able to find out, without using Blackwood, whether or not it has all of the side suits controlled. If Blackwood is used, five notrump cannot be used as the grand slam force, since that bid asks about kings.* In this situation, the Blackwood bidder may usually use the Malowan convention as the grand slam force.

The Malowan convention is a bid of six clubs after the ace-showing response to Blackwood, to ask the Blackwood responser to bid a grand slam if he has two of the top three trump honors. If he does not have two of the top three trump honors, he should again try to use the space between six clubs and six of the trump suit to clarify his trump holding.

If the agreed trump suit is clubs, of course, the Malowan convention does not work. An alternative is for the Blackwood bidder to bid a new suit over the Blackwood response, forcing the Blackwood responder to bid five notrump. Over five notrump, the Blackwood bidder can bid six clubs as the grand slam force.

---

*In the Romex system, a new suit bid after the ace-showing response to Blackwood is used to ask for kings; the five notrump bid is therefore always the grand slam force, whether or not Blackwood has been bid.

BARON SLAM TRY

Sometimes the decision between game and slam, or between a small slam and a grand slam, does not depend on finding partner with two of the top three trump honors, but on finding him with some lesser holding such as one honor, or extra length. The Baron slam try is an invitation to bid slam if the trump suit is "good." The device by which the invitation is issued is a jump to five or six of the suit below the trump suit. For example, if spades is the trump suit, a jump to five hearts would invite a small slam in spades; a jump to six hearts would invite a grand slam in spades.

The partner of the Baron bidder must examine his trump holding in light of the previous auction. If his trumps are no better than he has already suggested, he should decline the invitation. For example, in the auction

Opener	Responder
2 ♣	2 ♢ (negative)
2 ♠	3 ♠
5 ♡	

Responder's trumps might be no better than three small cards. If he has the queen of spades or four small spades, he should accept the invitation. Opener's hand might be

♠ A K x x x x   ♡ x   ♢ A K Q x x   ♣ A

If responder's hand were as "good" as

♠ x x x x   ♡ x x x   ♢ x x x   ♣ x x x

slam would be a fine proposition.

The Baron grand slam try may be made as a non-jump bid after Blackwood has been used. Suppose opener held

♠ K Q x x x   ♡ A 10 x x   ◇ K x x   ♣ x

and the auction proceeded

Opener	Responder
1 ♠	3 ♡
4 ♡	4 Notrump
5 ◇	6 ◇

Responder's six diamond bid, being the suit below the agreed trump suit, invites opener to bid seven hearts with extra trump values. With the hand given, opener should bid the grand slam. He has the ten of trumps, and more importantly, he has four trumps, when he might have raised with only three. Responder is likely to have a six-card heart suit headed by the king. His Blackwood bid has elicited the fact that opener has the ace of trumps; all he needs now is extra length.

CULBERTSON TRUMP ASKING BIDS

Culbertson Trump Asking Bids are usually used in conjunction with CULBERTSON ASKING BIDS. After a four-level response to a Culbertson asking bid, such as

(A) *Opener*   *Responder*
     1 ♣   3 ♠
     4 ♣

(B) *Opener*   *Responder*
     1 ♦   3 ♦
     4 ♣   4 ♥

a bid of four notrump by the asking bidder (responder in Auction A, opener in Auction B) asks about the quality of the trump suit. The partner of the trump asking bidder shows how many of the top three trump honors he has:

5 ♣ = none of the top three honors

5 ♦ = 1 of the top three honors

5 ♥ = 2 of the top three honors

5 ♠ = all three top honors

If the four notrump bidder rebids five notrump, he asks his partner how many trumps he holds. With the minimum number, considering the previous bidding, the asking bid responder can bid six clubs, and bid one extra step for each additional card held.

If the response to the Culbertson control asking bid was at

the five level, a bid of five notrump by the asking bidder can be used as the trump asking bid. The five notrump bid, however, asks only about trump honors in accordance with the above schedule; there is no way to ask about trump length.

ROMEX TRUMP ASKING BIDS

In the Romex system, a two club opening bid is artificial and is forcing to game. Having established a game force, the opener need not jump in his suit without a special purpose. The Romex system uses a jump rebid after a two club opening as a bid that sets that suit as trumps (at least temporarily), and asks responder how many cards he has in the suit. For example

Opener	Responder
2 ♣	2 ◇
3 ♠	

Responder shows his trump length as follows:

First   step = void or singleton

Second step = doubleton

Third   step = three cards

Fourth step = four or more cards

Fifth   step = singleton ace, king or queen

After receiving a response of the second, third or fourth step, if the opener bids notrump, he asks responder to reveal the number of top trump honors he holds. The responses are

First   step (♣) = none of the top three honors

Second step (◇) = 1 of the top three honors

Third   step (♡) = 2 of the top three honors

Fourth step (♠) = all three top honors

For example, in the auction

Opener	Responder
2 ♣	2 ♦
3 ♠	4 ♦
4 Notrump	5 ♣

responder's four diamond bid showed three card support for spades; his five club bid showed that he has none of the top spade honors.

If the response to the first trump asking bid was the first or second step, the minimum bid of a new suit by the opener changes the trump suit, and is a trump asking bid in the new suit. The responder shows his length in the new suit in the same way he did to the first trump asking bid:

Opener	Responder
2 ♣	2 ♦
3 ♠	3 Notrump
4 ♣	4 Notrump

Opener's four club bid changes the trump suit to clubs, and asks responder about his length in clubs. Responder's four notrump bid showed four card support for clubs. However, if responder had bid the first or second step in response to the club asking bid, opener could have changed the trump suit again, and made a trump asking bid in a third suit.

THE R/H FOUR NOTRUMP CONVENTION

The R/H four notrump convention uses a non-jump bid of four notrump after a trump suit has been established, to ask about the three top trump honors. This convention is best used after the partnership has had an opportunity to cue-bid first round controls in the side suits.

To show his trump honors, the partner of the four notrump bidder either bids five of the trump suit with none of the top three trump honors, or bids five notrump with all three honors, or bids a non-trump suit with one or two honors, as follows:

Lowest side suit = king or queen

Middle side suit = ace

Highest side suit = any two of the top three honors

Opener's and responder's hands might be

(Opener)
♠ K J x x x   ♡ K x x   ◇ A K Q x x   ♣ —

(Responder)
♠ Q x x x x   ♡ Q J x x   ◇ x   ♣ A K J

The auction would be

Opener	Responder
1 ♠	3 ♠
4 ♣	4 ♠ (no red ace to cue-bid)
4 Notrump	5 ♣ (king or queen)
5 ♠	

WANG TRUMP ASKING BIDS

Wang trump asking bids use a variety of bids at relatively low levels of the auction to ask about trump honors. The responses are given in three steps as follows:

First   step = none of the top three honors

Second   step = one of the top three honors

Third   step = two of the top three honors

The bids that can be used as Wang trump asking bids are varied. A three notrump rebid after a strong raise to the three level may be used as a trump asking bid:

Opener	*Responder*
1 ♠	3 ♠
3 Notrump	

Suppose opener has a hand such as

♠ A x x x x   ♡ A K x x   ◇ x   ♣ K Q x

After the auction has started 1 ♠ — 3 ♠, opener wants to ask about aces and about trump honors. If he uses Blackwood first and responder shows two aces, opener can use the grand slam force (six clubs). But if responder shows only one ace, opener has no way to find out whether responder's trumps are good enough for a small slam. Therefore, with this hand the opener uses the trump asking bid first, and follows with four notrump Blackwood:

Opener	Responder
1 ♠	3 ♠
3 Notrump	4 ♡ (two of the
4 Notrump	top three
	honors)

Similarly, a three notrump rebid after a limit raise could be used as a trump asking bid. The asking bid could also be used by responder if his suit is raised to the three level:

Opener	Responder
1 ◇	1 ♡
3 ♡	3 Notrump

Wang trump asking bids can be used at even lower levels of the auction. For example, when game forcing Stayman is being used, the simple raise of a major suit can be a trump asking bid:

Opener	Responder
1 Notrump	2 ◇
2 ♡	3 ♡

After an inverted minor suit raise, the bid of the cheapest suit may be used as a trump asking bid. For example

Opener	Responder
1 ◇	2 ◇
2 ♡	

The immediate jump raise of a positive response to an artificial forcing one club opening may be used as a trump asking bid. For example

Opener	Responder
1 ♣	1 ♠
3 ♠	

(See PRECISION system, in which a simple raise of a positive suit response is a trump asking bid.)

V

Competitive Bidding

Bidding by the opponents is a double-edged sword. It can be very annoying; some of the best planned auctions become unusable because an opponent has bid—especially when he has preempted.

On the other hand, when the opponents have bid, additional possibilities may facilitate the exchange of information. The opponent's bid may make available a double or a cue bid, or the use of any of a number of conventions designed to allow description of a two-suited hand with one bid.

Conventions for coping with interference with the Blackwood convention have been described above. The conventions described below deal with opposition bidding at somewhat lower levels of the auction.

TAKEOUT DOUBLES

The takeout double is so widely used that most people no longer think of it as a convention, but instead unconsciously accept it as a natural part of bidding. It is nevertheless a convention, since, by agreement, it has a meaning other than the desire to penalize the bidder in the suit he has bid.

A takeout double is a double of a suit bid, usually at a low level of the auction, before the partner of the doubler has made a bid.* Absent agreement, a double of a notrump bid, exception in one situation, is always for penalties, never for takeout. The one exception occurs when a one notrump response to an opening bid is doubled. For example:

North	East	South	West
1 ♠	Pass	1 Notrump	Double

West's double in this auction is a takeout double.

A takeout double asks the partner of the doubler to bid one of the unbid suits. The doubler promises strength at least roughly equivalent to that of an opening bid. (*See also* TAKEOUT DOUBLES OF PREEMPTS.) He suggests that he is short in the suit doubled and has at least three-card support for any other suit that his partner might choose to bid. The doubler also suggests strongly that he has four cards in any unbid major suit. However, what the doubler lacks in distribution can be compensated for by extra high-card strength. For example, a takeout double of a one heart opening bid could be made with either of the following hands:

---

*See also NEGATIVE DOUBLES, RESPONSIVE DOUBLES, COMPETITIVE DOUBLES, DOUBLES FOR SACRIFICE, *below.*

♠ A Q x x   ♡ x   ◇ K J x x   ♣ J x x x

♠ A K x   ♡ x x   ◇ A K x x   ♣ Q x x x

Because of the modern tendency to use cue-bids as light two-suited takeout bids, the range of the takeout double for some partnerships has increased tremendously. In these partnerships, for any hand that is too strong for a simple overcall, a takeout double must be made. For example:

[A]   ♠ A Q x   ♡ A K Q x x x   ◇ x   ♣ A x x

[B]   ♠ A K x   ♡ K Q x   ◇ A J x x   ♣ K J x

With Hand A one would double an opening bid, planning to rebid hearts. With Hand B, one would double an opening bid planning to rebid notrump. Thus, in modern practice, there is virtually no upper limit to the strength of the takeout double.

Responses

Unless and until the doubler makes some more revealing rebid, his partner must assume that the takeout doubler has the garden variety, support-for-all-suits type hand, having about the strength of an opening bid. The doubler's partner's possible responses fall into three categories: dutiful, encouraging and enthusiastic.

With a hand worth less than about 9 points, the doubler's partner should make a simple bid in his best suit. (See also HERBERT.) For example, in the auction

North	East	South	West
1 ♡	Double	Pass	

West might have one of the following hands:

[A] ♠ K x x x   ♡ x x x   ♢ J x x x   ♣ K x

[B] ♠ x x x x x   ♡ x x x   ♢ x x   ♣ x x x

[C] ♠ x   ♡ J x x x x x   ♢ x x x   ♣ x x x

With Hands A and B, West should bid one spade. Spades is his best suit and he has less than 9 points.

With Hand C, West should bid two clubs. The partner of the doubler has a duty to bid, and he should not pass the double simply because he has a weak hand, or simply because he has length in the opener's suit. He should pass only if he has good reason to believe he will punish the opponents. When his partner has doubled at the one level, he will need a very good hand and strong trumps to pass the takeout double for penalties. A hand such as the following would suffice to pass a takeout double of one heart:

♠ K x   ♡ A J 10 9 x   ♢ K x x   ♣ x x x

With about 6 to 8 points, the partner of the takeout doubler should make his response even if an opponent bids over the double. For example, in the auction

North	East	South	West
1 ♢	Double	2 ♢	

West should bid two spades with a hand such as

♠ K J x x   ♡ Q x x   ♢ x x x   ♣ J x x

If he has a long suit and can make his bid at the one level, the partner of the double may do so even with less than 6 points. In the auction

North	East	South	West
1 ◇	Double	1 ♡	

West should bid one spade with

♠ Q J x x x   ♡ x x x   ◇ x x   ♣ J x x

If the partner of the doubler has the opponent's suit stopped and has an 8 point hand or better, he may bid notrump. All notrump bids by the partner of the doubler are encouraging; the bid of one notrump therefore may not be made on a poor hand. For example in the auction

North	East	South	West
1 ♠	Double	Pass	

suppose West held one of the following hands:

[D] ♠ A Q x x   ♡ x x x   ◇ x x x   ♣ x x x

[E] ♠ K J x x   ♡ J x   ◇ A x x x   ♣ x x x

[F] ♠ K J x x   ♡ K x   ◇ K Q x   ♣ x x x x

Hand D, although it has a good spade stopper, is not strong enough for the encouraging bid of one notrump. West must therefore bid a suit. Having the same length in all of the unbid suits, he must bid the cheapest. With Hand D, therefore, West should bid two clubs.

With Hand E, West should bid one notrump. This bid describes West's high card strength and his holding in the opponent's suit. Hand F is too strong for the one notrump response, and therefore West must jump to two notrump. The two notrump bid shows a hand of some 12 to 14 points. This bid is very encouraging, but is not forcing.

If the partner of the doubler has a hand worth about 9 to 12 points, without a secure stopper in the opponent's suit, he should jump in the suit he prefers. For example, over a takeout double of one diamond, he should jump to two hearts with

♠ K x x   ♡ A J x x x   ◇ Q x   ♣ x x x

Like the notrump responses, this response is encouraging, but not forcing.

With a hand worth about 11 or 12 points but with no clear preference as to suits, the partner of the doubler may make a cue-bid of the opponent's suit, asking the doubler to bid his best suit. For example

North	East	South	West
1 ◇	Double	Pass	2 ◇

West might have a hand such as

♠ K x x x   ♡ A J x x   ◇ J x   ♣ Q x x

This cue-bid is highly encouraging, and forces the doubler to bid. However, it is not forcing to game.

If the partner of the doubler has the equivalent of a sound opening bid, he is allowed to become downright enthusiastic. With such a hand he can cue-bid, and follow with forcing bids driving the hand to game.

Doubler's Rebids

If the doubler rebids over a non-forcing response, other than in a competitive auction, he shows a hand stronger than the 12 to 15 points he has already promised. Any bid of a new suit shows a hand that was too strong to make an overcall. Any bid of notrump shows a hand that was too strong for a 16 to 18 point notrump overcall.

If the doubler raises his partner's suit he promises at least four card support. If the response has been a simple suit bid, a single raise by the doubler shows a sound opening bid of about 16 to 19 points. A jump raise would show about 19 to 23 points, or a hand with which the doubler wants to be in game if his partner has as much as four or five points.

For example, in the auction

North	East	South	West
1 ◇	Double	Pass	1 ♡
Pass			

East might hold one of the following hands:

[A] ♠ A Q x x   ♡ K J x x   ◇ x   ♣ K x x x

[B] ♠ A K x   ♡ K x x x   ◇ x   ♣ A Q x x x

[C] ♠ K x x x   ♡ A K x x   ◇ x   ♣ Q x x x

With Hand A, East has a total of 16 points, counting three points for the singleton diamond. He has just enough for a raise to two hearts. Hand B is good enough for a raise to three hearts. With Hand C East should pass.

If the partner of the doubler makes any bid other than a

dutiful response, and thereby shows more than 8 points, the doubler should evaluate his hand to see whether or not the combined hands can reach the 25- or 26-point game level. If the doubler can tell that they do reach that level, he should bid game or force to game. If he still is uncertain whether or not the combined hands reach that level, he should invite game.

After an encouraging response, a change of suit by the doubler is forcing for one round.

STRONG CUE BIDS

For many years the cue-bid of an opponent's opening bid was used as the strongest possible competitive call. It showed the equivalent of a forcing two-bid, promised first or second round control of the suit cue-bid, and was forcing to game.

More modern treatment for the strong cue-bid is to use it with very strong hands with good game prospects, although not to treat it as forcing to game. Second round control of the opponent's suit is not mandatory if the rest of the hand is strong enough. Any of the following hands would be appropriate for a strong cue-bid:

[A] ♠ K x   ♡ A K Q x x x x   ◇ A K   ♣ x x

[B] ♠ K Q J x x x   ♡ —   ◇ A   ♣ A K J x x x

[C] ♠ A K x x   ♡ A K Q J x   ◇ x   ♣ A x x

[D] ♠ K Q 10 x   ♡ A K x   ◇ A Q x x   ♣ A J

The strong cue-bid is forcing on partner, and any change of suit by the cue-bidder is forcing. The partner of the cue-bidder should bid naturally. If the cue-bidder bids the same suit twice, or rebids notrump, or supports his partner's suit below game, he strongly invites game.

For example, with Hand A, West would cue-bid two clubs over South's one club opening bid, and the auction might proceed as follows:

South	West	North	East
1 ♣	2 ♣	Pass	2 ◇
Pass	2 ♡	Pass	2 ♠
Pass	3 ♣		

West has forced East to bid by cue-bidding two clubs. West then showed his heart suit, over which East was forced to bid again. If West had rebid three hearts over East's two spade bid, his bid would not have been forcing. Therefore, having visions of either a three notrump contract or a four heart contract, West cue-bid three clubs, wanting his partner to bid notrump with a club stopper, or to raise to four hearts without a stopper. East might have a hand such as:

♠ Q x x x   ♡ x   ◇ J x x x x   ♣ x x x

or

♠ J x x x   ♡ x   ◇ J x x x x   ♣ Q 10 x

With a hand such as

[B]   ♠ K Q J x x x   ♡ –   ◇ A   ♣ A K J x x x

West would cue-bid over a one diamond or one heart opening bid. The auction might proceed:

South	West	North	East
1 ♡	2 ♡	Pass	3 ◇
Pass	3 ♠	Pass	3 Notrump
Pass	4 ♣	Pass	5 ♣
Pass	6 ♣	Pass	Pass

East might have a hand such as

♠ x   ♡ Q J x x   ◇ Q x x x x   ♣ Q x x

With a hand such as

[C] ♠ A K x x   ♡ A K Q J x   ◇ x   ♣ A x x

West would cue-bid two diamonds over a one diamond open-ing, or two clubs over a one club opening, and the bidding might go

South	West	North	East
1 ◇	2 ◇	Pass	2 ♡
Pass	3 ♡	Pass	Pass

East might hold

♠ x x x   ♡ x x x   ◇ Q x x x x   ♣ x x

With a hand such as

[D] ♠ K Q 10 x   ♡ A K x   ◇ A Q x x   ♣ A J

West would cue-bid over any opening bid by South, and would rebid two notrump. This sequence shows a balanced hand worth about 22 to 24 points.

CUE-BID AS A LIGHT TAKEOUT

It is possible to use an immediate cue-bid of an opponent's opening bid as a weak takeout bid for the other three suits. The cue-bidder might, for example, bid two diamonds over a one diamond opening bid with the following hand:

♠ K x x x   ♡ K x x x   ◇ x   ♣ Q x x x

This use of the cue bid is designed to reserve the takeout double for stronger hands having greater defensive values. It is, more valuable, however, to use the cue-bid to show a two-suited hand.

TWO-SUITED TAKEOUTS—IN PROFILE

Two-suited hands are generally difficult to describe after an opponent has opened the bidding. All too frequently it occurs that either the opponents bid too much too soon for both of the suits to be shown, or everybody passes too soon for both suits to be shown.

Many conventions have been devised to convey in a single competitive bid the information that the bidder has two long suits. Most of these overcalls or cue-bids are intended principally for use as obstructive bids, either to preempt the space in which the opponents wish to exchange information, or to lead to a sacrifice against their contracts. See MICHAELS CUE-BID, UPPER SUITS CUE-BIDS, TOP AND BOTTOM CUE-BIDS, COLORFUL CUE-BIDS, UNUSUAL NOTRUMP OVERCALL, UNUSUAL ONE NOTRUMP OVERCALL, ASTRO CUE-BIDS, ROMAN JUMP OVERCALLS, COPENHAGEN, UNUSUAL NOTRUMP & MINORS, TRUSCOTT, SIMPLIFIED TAKEOUT OVER STRONG ARTIFICIAL OPENINGS.

Being designed to hinder the opponents, two-suited takeouts may be made on quite limited high-card values. Their strength should range from about 6 to 10 high card points, with less than two defensive tricks. A hand such as

[A] ♠ K J x x x   ♡ Q 10 x x x   ◇ x x   ♣ x

would be suitable for a non-vulnerable major suit takeout.

Ideally, the two-suited takeout would promise at least five cards in each of the suits shown. If the takeout is for both major suits, however, it is permissible to make the bid with five cards in one major suit and four cards in the other.

Since high level sacrifice is a definite possibility after a two-suited takeout, the texture of the two suits shown by the takeout should be good, for the sake of safety. And such high card strength as there is should be concentrated in the two suits. For example, a hand such as

♠ A   ♡ K x   ◇ J x x x x   ♣ Q x x x x

is inappropriate for a two-suited takeout bid.

In that two-suited takeouts are essentially preemptive in character, it is generally unwise to try to make them do double duty as constructive bids looking for a game or slam. For example, if a two-suited cue-bid or overcall is permissible on a hand such as Hand A above, using it also with a hand such as

[B]   ♠ A K J x x   ♡ K Q 10 x x   ◇ K x   ♣ x

makes its range so wide that partner has considerable difficulty in coping with it. He may neglect to try for game when game could be made opposite Hand B. Or he may fail to sacrifice when he should opposite Hand A. Or, opposite Hand B, he may sacrifice when the opponents cannot make their contract.

When to Use

Two-suited cue-bid and overcall conventions are normally used only over the opponent's one-level opening bids, and only in the direct position, as for example:

(A) *North*   *East*   or   (B) *North*   *East*
   1 ♡   2 ♡   1 ◇   2 ◇

Because most two-suited cue-bid and overcall conventions are fundamentally preemptive devices, they are not needed in the pass-out position:

(C)	*North*	*East*	*South*	*West*
	1 ♡	Pass	Pass	2 ♡

West is obviously not interested in either preempting or sacrificing. The cue-bid in this position usually means that the cue-bidder has a strong hand, perhaps two-suited, but primarily a hand with which he felt he could not afford to have his partner pass a takeout double. Thus in the Auction C above, the West hand might be

♠ A K Q x x   ♡ —   ◇ K x   ♣ A x x x x x

A special situation deserves attention. When the opponents have bid two suits, the cue-bid of a minor suit bid by either of them should not be used to show a weak two-suiter.

For example, in the auction

North	*East*	*South*	*West*
1 ◇	Pass	1 ♠	2 ◇

West's two diamond bid should simply show a hand worth an overcall, with a long diamond suit. There is no need to use the cue-bid in this situation to show two suits, for when the opponents have bid two suits, a takeout double will call for the other two suits.

If North had opened the bidding with a major suit, however, especially playing five card major suit openings, West's cue-bid would be for takeout, showing a very strong two-suiter:

North	East	South	West
1 ♡	Pass	1 ♠	2 ♡

Conventional two-suited cue-bids or overcalls also are not used when the bidding has been opened with a weak two bid. For example, in the auction

North	East	South	West
2 ♡	3 ♡		

East may have a two-suiter, but the cue-bid suggests primarily that East did not want to risk having West pass a takeout double for penalties. East might have a hand such as

♠ A K Q x x   ♡ —   ◇ K x   ♣ A x x x x x

Responding to the Two-Suited Takeout

The partner of the cue-bidder should, if at all possible, take a preference for one of the cue-bidder's suits. Having a weak hand and two long suits, the cue-bidder is rarely interested in hearing what his partner has to say about a third suit.

Moreover, since the cue-bid is principally an obstructive device, the partner of the cue-bidder should take his preference at an appropriate level. For example:

North	East	South	West
1 ♡	2 ♡	Double	

Suppose East's cue-bid shows a two-suiter in spades and clubs, and West has one of the following hands:

[A]   ♠ Q x x x   ♡ 10 x x x   ◇ x x   ♣ K x x

[B]   ♠ x x   ♡ Q J x x   ◇ K Q x x   ♣ A x x

With Hand A, West should jump to four spades. The opponents are likely to make four hearts, so a sacrifice is in order. With Hand B, West should simply take his preference by bidding three clubs. The opponents do not seem likely to make a game, so West has no thought of sacrificing.

A Double-Edged Sword

A final word of caution on two-suited bids is in order. These bids are quite useful if they help to take away most of the opponents' bidding room so that they cannot adequately exchange information, or if they lead to a profitable sacrifice.

However, if the side that has made the two-suited bid does not buy the contract, the bid will have become a liability, since it has drawn a blueprint for the declarer as to how the defenders' cards are distributed.

See also DEFENSE AGAINST OPPONENTS' TWO-SUITED CALLS.

MICHAELS CUE-BIDS

The Michaels Cue-bid is usually used as a two-suited takeout bid, although some partnerships use it as a weak three-suited takeout bid. *See* CUE-BID AS A LIGHT TAKEOUT. Over an opponent's minor suit opening bid, the Michaels cue-bid shows both major suits. It promises a total of at least nine cards in those two suits, and preferably ten, with five in each major. See TWO-SUITED TAKEOUTS—IN PROFILE.

For the auction

South	West	North	East
1 ♣	2 ♣		

West might have a hand such as

♠ Q J x x x   ♡ K J x x x   ◇ x   ♣ x x

Over an opponent's major suit opening bid, the Michaels cue-bid also shows a two suited hand. It promises at least five cards in the unbid major suit, and at least five cards in one of the minor suits. Since the partnership may be forced to the three level to find its fit, the Michaels cue-bid over a major suit opening may be made on a stronger hand.

For example, for the auction

North	East	South	West
Pass	Pass	1 ♡	2 ♡

West might have a hand such as

[A]   ♠ K Q x x x   ♡ x   ◇ x x   ♣ K Q x x x

or

[B] ♠ A Q x x x   ♡ x   ◇ x   ♣ Q J 10 x x x

The partner of the Michaels cue-bidder should support his partner's major suit if he can. Any three card support will suffice.
If he cannot support the major suit, he may bid two notrump
to ask the Michaels bidder to name his minor suit. For example,
in the auction

North	East	South	West
1 ♡	2 ♡	Pass	

West might hold either of the following hands:

[C] ♠ K Q x   ♡ K x x x   ◇ Q J x x   ♣ Q x

[D] ♠ x x   ♡ K x x x   ◇ J x   ♣ A x x x x

With Hand C, West would bid two spades. He has spade
support, but has no particular desire to play the hand at any
higher level, since neither his side nor the opponents seem likely
to make very much. With Hand D West cannot support spades,
so he bids two notrump to ask his partner which minor suit he
has. He expects East will bid three diamonds, in which case
West will pass. But if East should bid three clubs, West will be
able to bid five clubs to sacrifice against the opponents' probable four heart game.

The Michaels cue-bid is the most flexible of all the two-
suited cue-bids (*but see* ROMAN JUMP OVERCALLS). The only
two-suited hand it cannot possibly handle, given an appropriate
opening bid by the opponents, is the hand with both minor suits.
An agreement by the partnership to use Michaels cue-bids in
combination with the UNUSUAL NOTRUMP OVERCALL, calling for

the lowest unbid suits, would give the partnership the greatest flexibility to show two-suited hands. Using this combination of conventions, the partnership would be able to handle ten of the twelve possible combinations of unbid suits, as shown by the following chart:

| | Opponent's Opening Bid | | | |
Two Suits Held	♣	♦	♥	♠
♠ & ♥	Michaels Cue-bid	Michaels Cue-bid	—	—
♠ & ♦	(GAP)	—	Michaels Cue-bid*	—
♠ & ♣	—	(GAP)	Michaels Cue-bid*	—
♥ & ♦	Unusual Notrump	—	—	Michaels Cue-bid*
♥ & ♣	—	Unusual Notrump	—	Michaels Cue-bid*
♦ & ♣	—	—	Unusual Notrump	Unusual Notrump

---

*Initially ambiguous as to which minor suit held.

UPPER SUITS CUE-BIDS

Some partnerships, disliking the ambiguity of the Michaels cue-bid over a major suit opening bid, use the cue-bid always to show the two highest unbid suits. If the bidding is opened in a minor suit, of course, the suits shown by the cue-bid are the majors. This is the equivalent of the Michaels cue-bid.

If the bidding is opened in a major suit, however, the cue-bid shows specifically the other major suit and diamonds—the two highest unbid suits. The effect of this agreement is that the cue-bidder may never have clubs as his second suit.

The price of certainty, therefore, is a decrease in flexibility. Never being allowed to show a club suit as one of the two suits, there are only three suit combinations that can be shown using Upper Suit cue-bids. For its initial ambiguity, Michaels has the advantage of handling five different combinations, depending on the opponent's opening bid.

For strength and distribution requirements, responses, etc., *see* TWO-SUITED TAKEOUTS—IN PROFILE.

TOP AND BOTTOM CUE-BIDS

The Top and Bottom Cue-bid requires that the cue-bidder's two suits be the highest unbid suit and the lowest unbid suit. If used over all opening suit bids, these cue-bids would have the following meanings:

> 1 ♣ — 2 ♣ shows spades and diamonds
>
> 1 ♢ — 2 ♢ shows spades and clubs
>
> 1 ♡ — 2 ♡ shows spades and clubs
>
> 1 ♠ — 2 ♠ shows hearts and clubs

The chief drawback in using this convention over all openings is that the cue-bid may never be made holding both major suits.

In order to preserve the ability to show both major suits, the partnership should agree to use Michaels cue-bids over opponents' minor suit opening bids, and restrict Top and Bottom cue-bids to the opponents' major suit opening bids. The effect of such an agreement would be that the cue-bid could never show a two-suiter that included diamonds.

For strength and distribution requirements, responses, etc., *see* TWO-SUITED TAKEOUTS—IN PROFILE.

COLORFUL CUE-BIDS

Colorful Cue-bids are used over an opponent's opening bid in a major suit. The cue-bidder promises two long suits of the same color, the color opposite that of the opening bid. Thus a cue-bid of two hearts over one heart would show spades and clubs; a cue-bid of two spades over one spade would show hearts and diamonds.

For strength and distribution requirements, responses, etc., *see* TWO-SUITED TAKEOUTS—IN PROFILE.

UNUSUAL NOTRUMP OVERCALL

There are a variety of competitive bidding situations in which, as a matter of logic, a notrump bid cannot signify a desire to play the hand in notrump. As a convention, the Unusual Notrump Overcall is a bid that by agreement, rather than by inference, is a takeout for two suits.

By an unpassed hand, the Unusual Notrump Overcall is a jump to two notrump over an opening bid, to show a two-suited hand. (*See also* UNUSUAL ONE NOTRUMP OVERCALL.) If the opening bid was one heart or one spade, the two notrump bid shows length in both minor suits.

When the opening bid is one club or one diamond, there are two schools of thought as to which suits should be shown. Some partnerships, in recognition of the growing use of five card major suit openings and the consequent frequent openings in a three card minor suit, always use the two notrump overcall to show the minor suits. For these partnerships, the auction

North	East	South	West
1 ◇	2 Notrump		

would show that East has a long club suit and a long diamond suit.

The majority of the partnerships which use The Unusual Notrump convention, however, use it to show length in the two lowest unbid suits. Thus, over a one diamond opening bid a jump to two notrump will show hearts and clubs; over a one club opening bid, a jump to two notrump will show hearts and diamonds. For strength and distribution requirements, responses, etc., *see* TWO-SUITED TAKEOUTS—IN PROFILE.

The partner of the Unusual Notrump overcaller may in

turn make an unusual notrump bid. For example, if West has a hand such as

♠ x x   ♡ Q J x   ◇ K x x x   ♣ Q x x x

in an auction such as

North	East	South	West
1 ♠	2 Notrump	4 ♠	

West should bid four notrump. The four notrump bid tells East that West wants to play in five of a minor suit, but that he has no real preference; he asks East to bid his longer suit.

In the absence of special partnership agreement, the Unusual Notrump overcall is not used over the opponent's opening bids at the two level or higher, except over strong forcing two-bids. Thus, consider the following auction:

North	East	South	West
2 ♡	2 Notrump		

If North and South are using strong two-bids, East's two notrump bid is the Unusual Notrump showing at least five cards in each minor suit.

If North and South are using weak two bids, East's two notrump bid is not for takeout, and does not show a two-suited hand. Instead, East simply indicates a desire to play the hand in notrump. He shows a hand worth a one notrump opening bid or overcall.

By a passed hand, the Unusual Notrump overcall can be made at any level, including the one level. For example:

North	East	South	West
Pass	Pass	Pass	1 ♠
1 Notrump			

Since North did not have a strong enough hand to open the bidding, he cannot show the normal 16 to 18 points with his notrump overcall. His bid, by inference, is unusual. By agreement, the Unusual Notrump overcall at the one level is a two-suited takeout, normally for the two lower unbid suits.

UNUSUAL ONE NOTRUMP OVERCALL

By special agreement the partnership may use Unusual Notrump overcalls at the one level by an unpassed hand, as in the following auction:

North	East	South	West
Pass	1 ♡	1 Notrump	

As to which two suits are shown by South's one notrump bid, this too is a matter for special partnership agreement.

Some partnerships, for example, use the one-level Unusual Notrump to show the highest and lowest ranking unbid suits. If these partnerships are also using Upper Suit Cue-bids, and the jump to two notrump to show the two lowest ranking unbid suits, the addition of the one-level Unusual Notrump gives them complete coverage of all two-suited hands:

Two Suits Held	Opponent's Opening Bid			
	♣	◇	♡	♠
♠ & ♡	Cue-bid	Cue-bid	—	—
♠ & ◇	1 Notrump	—	Cue-bid	—
♠ & ♣	—	1 Notrump	1 Notrump	—
♡ & ◇	2 Notrump	—	—	Cue-bid
♡ & ♣	—	2 Notrump	—	1 Notrump
◇ & ♣	—	—	2 Notrump	2 Notrump

For strength and distribution requirements, responses, etc., *see* TWO-SUITED TAKEOUTS—IN PROFILE.

ASTRO CUE-BID

Astro Cue-bids are used to describe two-suited hands that include one major suit and one minor suit. The cue-bid shows the lower unbid major suit and the lower unbid minor suit. Specific cue-bids show the following two suits:

1 ♣ – 2 ♣ shows hearts and diamonds

1 ♦ – 2 ♦ shows hearts and clubs

1 ♡ – 2 ♡ shows spades and clubs

1 ♠ – 2 ♠ shows hearts and clubs

Unlike Michaels, Top and Bottom, Upper Suit, and Colorful Cue-bids, and unlike the Unusual Notrump overcall, Astro cue-bids do not suggest that the same length is held in both of the bidder's suits. Astro cue-bids are designed principally to facilitate the description of hands containing a four-card major suit and a five card minor suit; these hands are difficult to describe bidding naturally.

Thus, the Astro cue-bidder promises more cards in the minor suit than in the major suit. He may have, for example, a four-card major suit and a five-card minor suit, or a four-card major suit and a six-card minor suit, or a five-card major suit and a six-card minor suit. Occasionally he may have five or six cards in each suit, but the convention envisions a minor suit that is longer than the major suit. For example, a cue-bid of two diamonds over one diamond, or two spades over one spade, might show

♠ x   ♡ K Q x x   ◇ J x   ♣ A J 10 x x x

432

Because the Astro cue-bid is intended to make it easier to bid a hand in which one of the suits could not be bid as an over-call, the strength of the Astro cue-bid may vary more than it should for other cue-bids such as Michaels. Therefore while the Astro bid may be made on a hand that is worthy only of a pre-empt, it may also be made on hands that have excellent game and slam potential.

ROMAN JUMP OVERCALLS

Roman Jump Overcalls are two-suited bids, showing the suit in which the jump is made, and the next higher unbid suit. For these purposes, clubs are ranked over spades as well as under diamonds. Thus, over a one diamond opening, for example, a jump overcall of two hearts would show hearts and spades, a jump to two spades would show spades and clubs.

This system has the advantage that, with a single convention, there is no combination of suits that cannot be shown, regardless of the suit in which the opening bid was made. Its disadvantage, however, is that it precludes use of single-suited jump overcalls. Weak jump overcalls can be very useful, both defensively in preempting the opponents, and offensively in limiting the weakness with which one-level overcalls will be made. Hands with which weak jump overcalls can be made occur considerably more frequently than hands warranting a two-suited jump overcall.

As with most of the cue-bids discussed in this section, the Roman jump overcall is essentially an obstructive bid. For strength and distribution requirements, responses, etc., *see* TWO-SUITED TAKEOUTS—IN PROFILE.

Strong Two-Suiters

With a strong two suited hand, the Roman system uses a jump to two notrump. The jump to two notrump forces the hand opposite to bid the lowest unbid suit. If the two notrump bidder now bids three notrump, he shows that his two suits still are unbid; the three notrump bid forces his partner to take a preference at the four level. For example:

North	East	South	West
1 ♣	2 Notrump	Pass	3 ◇
Pass	3 Notrump		

East's two notrump bid shows a strong hand with two long suits. West's three diamond bid is forced; West may or may not have length or strength in diamonds. East's three notrump bid shows that he did not have diamonds, and that he therefore has both major suits. West is forced to bid four of his better major. East might have a hand such as

♠ K Q J x x   ♡ A Q J x x x   ◇ x   ♣ x

In the above auction, if East had bid a suit instead of rebidding three notrump, his bid would have shown the suit that he bid and the suit his partner had been forced to bid:

North	East	South	West
1 ♣	2 Notrump	Pass	3 ◇
Pass	3 ♡ or		
	4 ♡		

East's heart bid means that he has both hearts and diamonds. His three heart bid would be highly invitational, but not forcing.

COPENHAGEN

The Copenhagen convention is a system of jump overcalls designed to show two-suited hands. It uses a jump to two notrump over the opening bid to show the two lowest unbid suits, a jump to three clubs to show the lowest unbid suit and the highest unbid suit, and a jump to three diamonds to show the two highest unbid suits.

This system has the advantage that it can show any two suited hand after an opening bid in any suit. One of its disadvantages is that it necessarily propels the bidding immediately to the three level regardless of which two suits are held. Other conventions sometimes give the partnership a chance to play at the two level. A second disadvantage is that the three-club and three-diamond overcalls cannot be used in their natural senses.

For strength and distribution requirements, responses, etc., *see* TWO-SUITED TAKEOUTS—IN PROFILE.

UNUSUAL NOTRUMP AND MINORS

The unusual Notrump & Minors convention is a part of the Lea System. Using this convention all non-jump notrump and non-jump minor suit overcalls are unusual, showing two-suited hands.

Using this convention, the non-jump notrump overcall shows the lowest ranking unbid suits. A non-jump overcall in clubs shows the lowest ranking unbid suit and the highest ranking unbid suit. A non-jump overcall in diamonds shows the two highest ranking unbid suits. The Unusual Notrump & Minors conventions uses these overcalls over any opening bids, whether in suits or in notrump, and at any level.

When the convention is used over an opponent's notrump opening bid, it arbitrarily assumes that the opponents' suit is clubs, and the other three suits are deemed to be the unbid suits. Some examples:

(A) *North*   *East*
     1 ♡   2 ♣

(B) *North*   *East*
     1 ◇   1 Notrump

(C) *North*   *East*
     1 Notrump 2 ◇

(D) *North*   *East*
     1 ♣   2 ♣

In Auction A, East's two club overcall shows the lowest and the highest unbid suits, clubs and spades. In Auction D, the two club overcall shows diamonds and spades. In Auction B,

437

the one notrump overcall shows the two lower unbid suits, clubs and hearts. In Auction C, the two diamond overcall shows the major suits.

For strength and distribution requirements, responses, etc., *see* TWO-SUITED TAKEOUTS—IN PROFILE.

TRUSCOTT OVER STRONG
ARTIFICIAL OPENINGS

The Truscott convention is a system of two-suited overcalls used principally over strong artificial club and diamond opening bids. Using the Truscott convention, any non-jump overcall shows the suit overcalled plus the next higher ranking suit. Thus, over an artificial one club opening, West would show the following suits:

South	West
1 ♣	1 ◇ shows diamonds and hearts
1 ♣	1 ♡ shows hearts and spades
1 ♣	1 ♠ shows spades and clubs
1 ♣	2 ♣ shows clubs and diamonds

A double of the artificial opening bid shows the suit doubled and the non-touching suit. Over a Schenken one club opening, for example, a double would show clubs and hearts. A notrump overcall would show the combination of non-touching suits that is not shown by the double of the suit opened. Thus a notrump overcall over one club would show diamonds and spades.

Over a Schenken two diamond opening bid, or over a negative one diamond response to one club, the double would show diamonds and spades, and a notrump overcall would show clubs and hearts.

For strength and distribution recommendations, responses, etc., *see* TWO-SUITED TAKEOUTS—IN PROFILE.

SIMPLIFIED TAKEOUT OVER STRONG
ARTIFICIAL OPENINGS

As a defense to an opponent's strong artificial opening bid of one club, many partnerships play a simple combination of two-suited takeout bids. These partnerships use a double to show both major suits, and a one notrump overcall to show both minor suits. This system may also be used against opponents' strong artificial openings of one diamond, two clubs, and two diamonds.

For strength and distribution recommendations, responses, etc., *see* TWO-SUITED TAKEOUTS—IN PROFILE.

EXCLUSION OVERCALLS

If the bidding is opened naturally in a suit and the next player is short in that suit, frequently a takeout double may be made. When an artificial opening bid is made, however, it leaves all four suits unbid, and thus precludes a three-suit takeout double.

To compensate for being deprived of the takeout double over an opponent's artificial opening bid, some partnerships use "exclusion" bids. An exclusion bid is the bid of a short suit promising length in all of the other suits.

For example, suppose North and South are using the Precision Club system, and East and West are using exclusion bids. In the auction

North	*East*	*South*	*West*
1 ♣	1 ♠		

East's one spade bid shows a hand that is short in spades. Had the bidding been opened with a natural one spade bid, East would probably have made a takeout double.

The partner of the exclusion overcaller may respond as he would have to a takeout double of the short suit.

BALANCING TWO CLUB BID (for takeout)

Using standard methods of balancing over an opening bid of one in a suit, all bids in an unbid suit are natural. For example:

North	East	South	West
1 ♠	Pass	Pass	2 ♣

West's two club bid promises length in clubs. A balancing double usually shows close to an opening bid, with support for the unbid suits.

The Roth Stone system uses a balancing bid of two clubs as a forcing takeout. If the bidding has been opened one diamond, one heart, or one spade, the balancing bid of two clubs shows 6 to 9 high card points, with support for the other unbid suits. For example, in the auction

North	East	South	West
1 ♡	Pass	Pass	2 ♣

West might have

[A] ♠ Q x x x   ♡ x x   ◇ A x x x   ♣ x x x

The two club bid is technically forcing for one round; however, the partner of the two club bidder may pass if he has a long club suit, without length in either unbid suit.

The purpose of this use of the two club bid is to provide a takeout bid with weak hands, while reserving the takeout double for hands with at least 10 high card points. The availability of both calls for takeout gives the partner of the balancer a better idea of the partnership's potential. For example, if West

were allowed to make a balancing takeout double with both
Hand A above, and a hand such as

    [B] ♠ K x x x   ♡ x x   ◇ A Q 10 x   ♣ A 10 x

East would be hard pressed to know whether he should act aggressively or cautiously with a hand such as

    ♠ J x x   ♡ A Q x x   ◇ K x   ♣ K J x x

LANDY

It is especially dangerous to overcall over notrump opening bids. The overcaller is bidding largely in the dark, and may find his partner with a weak hand and a singleton in his suit. In contrast, the responder knows the strength of his partner's hand, and knows he has at least two cards in the overcaller's suit. The responder to a notrump opening bid thus has much less difficulty in deciding whether or not to double the overcall in these circumstances than he has over an overcall of a suit opening bid.

Having a two-suited hand greatly increases the safety of overcalling over the notrump bid, because it allows the overcaller's partner to take his choice of suits, thereby decreasing the likelihood of suffering a severe penalty double. The Landy convention is one of several conventions designed to describe two-suited hands over the opponent's one notrump opening. *See also* RIPSTRA, ASTRO, MODIFIED ASTRO, ROTH STONE ASTRO, PINPOINT ASTRO, BROZEL, TWO CLUBS FOR MINORS & TWO DIAMONDS FOR MAJORS, UNUSUAL NOTRUMP & MINORS.

The Landy convention is a two club bid over the opponent's one notrump opening bid to show both major suits. The two club bidder should have at least four cards in each major suit.

The strength needed to overcall varies with the vulnerability. Normally the Landy bidder should have a hand counting to at least 13 total points, counting high cards plus distribution. He might have a hand such as

[A]   ♠ A K 10 x   ♡ Q J x x   ◇ A x x   ♣ x x

or

[B]   ♠ A Q x x x   ♡ K x x x x   ◇ x x   ♣ x

With a hand that is weak in high cards and not especially freakish in distribution, he should pass:

[C] ♠ Q 10 x x x   ♡ A J x x   ◇ x x   ♣ x x

Using Landy, the two club bid does not show anything about the overcaller's club suit; it merely asks his partner to choose his better major suit.

Responses to Landy

Holding four of either major suit, the partner of the Landy bidder should bid that suit. Lacking a four card major, he should bid a three card major. If the partner of the Landy bidder has a very long club suit and no more than two cards in either major suit, he is allowed to pass the two club bid. Similarly, lacking as much as three-card support for a major suit, the partner of the Landy bidder is allowed to bid two diamonds if he has a long diamond suit, for example:

♠ x   ♡ x x   ◇ K J x x x x x   ♣ x x x

In responding to the two club bid with a major suit, a bid at the two level is a simple preference; a bid at the three level invites the Landy bidder to go on to game. In evaluating their hands for game, both the Landy bidder and his partner should be optimistic with very uneven distribution and a concentration of their high cards in the major suits.

For example, in response to the two club bid, West might have one of the following hands:

[A]   ♠ x   ♡ A Q x x x   ◇ x x x   ♣ x x x x

[B]   ♠ x x   ♡ Q x x x x   ◇ K J x   ♣ K Q x

With Hand A West should jump to three hearts. His hand is not robust, but he has excellent trump honors and a singleton in his partner's second suit. A crossruff might well bring in ten tricks.

With Hand B, West should bid just two hearts. Although he has almost twice the high card count he had in Hand A, they are all, except for the queen of hearts, in the wrong places. Kings and queens and jacks do not carry their full weight opposite partner's singletons.

446

If his partner has taken a simple preference, and the Landy bidder has a very distributional hand with good high cards in his suits, he may try for game by raising the suit his partner has chosen. For example, the Landy bidder should raise two spades to three with

♠ K J x x x   ♡ A Q x x x x   ◇ x   ♣ x

but should pass with a balanced hand such as

♠ K Q x x x   ♡ A Q x x   ◇ K x   ♣ x x

Over Weak Notrumps

The mechanism for the use of the Landy convention is the same over weak notrump openings as it is over strong notrumps, and the strength requirements for the two club overcall are the same. However, over weak notrumps it pays to be more aggressive in trying for game. Thus the Landy convention should be used over weak notrumps even on some balanced hands that would be strong enough to double a strong notrump opening.

If the partner of the Landy bidder has a good fit for one of the major suits and about 9 to 11 points concentrated in the major suits, he should invite game by jumping to three of his major suit. If he has the equivalent of an opening bid and a four card major suit, he should jump to four of the major. With the equivalent of an opening bid but no four-card major suit, for example,

♠ A x x   ♡ K x x   ◇ x x x   ♣ A Q x x

the partner of the Landy bidder should bid two notrump:

North	East	South	West
1 Notrump	2 ♣	Pass	2 Notrump

West's two notrump response is forcing on East for one round. If East can bid a five card major suit, West will raise to game. If East bids three diamonds, West will bid three notrump. If East bids three clubs, clubs may well be the partnership's best suit.

With a long solid or semi-solid minor suit and a good hand, the partner of the Landy bidder should bid three of his suit. The Landy bidder will bid again unless he has a very distributional hand with a misfit for his partner's suit.

Positional Considerations

While some partnerships use Landy only in the position directly over the notrump bidder, the convention can be used in both positions. In addition, some partnerships use the two club bid as Landy only if the two club bidder is an unpassed hand. Their reasoning is that a passed hand can double for the major suits without fear that he is showing a hand worth 16 or more points. This frees up the two club bid for use as a natural overcall showing clubs, and allows the partner of the doubler to pass with a moderately good hand that was not strong enough for a penalty double on its own. For example, suppose East had passed, holding

♠ K Q x x   ♡ K J 10 x   ◊ Q x x   ♣ x x

and the bidding proceeded

North	East	South	West
Pass	Pass	1 Notrump	Pass
Pass	Double		

East should be able to double for the major suits rather than bidding two clubs. If West held, for example,

♠ x x   ♡ Q x x   ◇ A x x x   ♣ K Q x x

he could pass for penalties.

RIPSTRA

The Ripstra convention is very similar to the Landy convention, in that it shows at least eight cards in the major suits over the opponent's notrump opening. The difference is that the Ripstra convention uses the two club bid as the takeout bid only when the overcaller's clubs are as strong as, or stronger than, his diamonds; it uses a two diamond bid as the takeout bid when his diamonds are stronger. For example, the Ripstra bidder would overcall two clubs with a hand such as

♠ K J x x   ♡ A Q x x   ◇ x   ♣ K x x x

but he would overcall two diamonds with a hand such as

♠ K Q x x   ♡ A Q x x x   ◇ J x x   ♣ x

The effect of Ripstra, as compared with Landy, is to widen slightly the choices available to the partner of the overcaller. He may more comfortably pass with a weak hand and length in the suit overcalled, since the overcaller is known to have some support for that suit. It is, of course, possible that the sense of added security that this gives will be a false one, for sometimes the Ripstra bidder will have five cards in each major suit and no more than two in the minor suit he is forced to bid. Occasionally, he will have two minor suit singletons.

The use of the Ripstra convention deprives the partnership of the possibility of making a natural two diamond overcall. Considering the marginal advantage of this convention over the Landy convention, the loss of yet another natural overcall is probably too great a price.

ASTRO

The Astro convention over one notrump openings uses a two club overcall to show a two-suited hand in which one suit is hearts and the other suit is a minor. It uses a two diamond overcall to show a two-suited hand in which one suit is spades, and the other may be any of the three remaining suits.

The suit specifically shown by the Astro bidder is called the "anchor" suit. When the Astro bidder's partner has four or more cards in the anchor suit, or has three cards headed by an honor, he is expected to bid that suit. Holding three small cards or worse in the anchor suit, the partner of the Astro bidder will generally bid the cheapest suit. Although this cheapest suit is called the "neutral" suit, it may in fact be the Astro bidder's second suit.

An Astro auction might go as follows:

North	East	South	West
1 Notrump	2 ◇	Pass	2 ♡
Pass	Pass	Pass	

The two diamond bid by East showed spades and another suit. West's two heart bid said nothing about his heart suit; it was simply a neutral bid. East's pass showed that his second suit happened to be hearts.

The strength needed to make an Astro overcall is comparable to that needed for a Landy overcall. However, the responses to Astro may be somewhat different since the Astro bidder's partner does not know which is the Astro bidder's second suit.

If the partner of the Astro bidder has a hand strong enough to warrant a game try and he has a fit for the anchor suit, he may jump in the anchor suit. If he has a hand worth a game try and no fit for the anchor suit, he should bid two notrump.

PINPOINT ASTRO

Pinpoint Astro is a modification of the Astro convention that serves to identify most suit combinations precisely with one bid. The overcalls and the suits shown are as follows:

$$2 \clubsuit = \text{hearts and clubs}$$

$$2 \diamondsuit = \text{hearts and diamonds}$$

$$2 \heartsuit = \text{hearts and spades}$$

$$2 \spadesuit = \text{spades and a minor suit}$$

See also BROZEL.

For strength and distribution requirements, responses, etc., *see discussion under* LANDY.

ROTH-STONE ASTRO

The Roth Stone System uses a series of overcalls over one no-trump to show specific two-suit combinations as follows:

2 ♣ = clubs and spades

2 ◇ = diamonds and spades

3 ♣ = clubs and hearts

3 ◇ = diamonds and hearts

DBL = hearts and spades

However, if the opening notrump bid was a weak notrump, the double does not promise anything with respect to the major suits holdings, but instead shows at least 15 points.

For strength and distribution requirements for the over-calls, and responses, etc., *see discussion under* LANDY.

MODIFIED ASTRO

A modification of the Astro convention intended to facilitate description of a major suit two-suiter uses the overcalls as follows: a two club bid shows a long heart suit, and it may or may not be accompanied by a long minor suit. A two diamond bid shows spades and a minor suit. A two heart bid shows hearts and spades.

The responses to a two club overcall or a two diamond overcall are as they are for ASTRO. For example, the partner of the two club overcaller should bid hearts if he has four hearts or three hearts headed by an honor. Falling short of these holdings, he should bid two diamonds, the neutral suit. If the overcaller has a one-suited heart hand, he will bid two hearts. If he has hearts and diamonds, he will pass two diamonds. And if he has hearts and clubs, he will bid either two hearts or three clubs, depending on the strength of his hand and the relative strengths of his suits.

The responses to a two heart overcall, which shows specifically both major suits, are almost the same as for LANDY. The exception, of course, is that in order to take a simple preference for hearts, the partner of the overcaller need only pass.

BROZEL

Brozel is a very flexible convention that can allow the partnership to play in any suit at the two level over the opponent's one notrump opening. In exchange, it gives up the ability to double the opponents with a hand equivalent to a strong notrump opening.

Using the Brozel convention, a double shows a one-suited hand of at least average strength. However, this does not mean that a penalty cannot be inflicted; the partner of the doubler may pass with a smattering of values.

The doubler might have a hand such as

♠ A x   ♡ K Q J x x x   ◇ x x   ♣ Q x x

and his partner might have

♠ K J x x   ♡ x x   ◇ A J x x   ♣ J x x

If the partner of the Brozel doubler does not have the necessary values to allow him to pass the double, he must bid two clubs. This bid shows nothing about his club suit; it is merely a relay bid to allow the doubler to rebid his long suit, or to pass if his suit was clubs.

The Brozel double can be used either immediately over the opening notrump, or in the pass-out position. In addition the Brozel double can be used after the partner of the notrump opener has made a weak one-suited response:

North	East	South	West
1 Notrump	Pass	2 ♡	Double

455

West's double of two hearts is not intended either for penalties or for takeout, any more than the double of one notrump would have been. The double simply shows a one-suited hand. The partner of the doubler is again allowed to pass, so long as he holds a few values and good trumps. Otherwise he must bid the next ranking suit, which is a relay to allow the doubler to reveal his suit by passing or bidding.

Two-Suited Hands

Brozel also provides a system of bids to describe two suited hands. The system, which is similar to Pinpoint Astro, pivots principally around the heart suit:

2 ♣ = hearts and clubs

2 ♢ = hearts and diamonds

2 ♡ = hearts and spades

2 ♠ = spades and a minor suit

2 NT = both minor suits

If the auction has proceeded

North	East	South	West
1 Notrump	2 ♠	Pass	

West may pass two spades if he has support for spades; if he does not have support for spades he should bid two notrump asking the Brozel bidder to reveal his minor suit.

Two-suited hands may also be shown after the partner of the notrump bidder has made a weak one-suited response. The bid of any suit over the responder's bid shows that suit and the next higher unbid suit. Thus West would bid as follows:

North	East	South	West		
1 Notrump	Pass	2 ♡	2 ♠	=	♠ & ♣
			3 ♣	=	♣ & ◇
			3 ◇	=	◇ & ♠

If West should have a very strong hand in this situation, he may jump in the lower of his touching suits.

Three-Suited Hands

To show a three-suited hand that has good high card strength, the Brozel convention uses a jump to three of the short suit. This bid shows a relatively strong hand, such as

♠ A J 10 x   ♡ K Q x x   ◇ —   ♣ A J x x x

With this hand, the Brozel bidder would jump to three diamonds over one notrump. His partner is requested to set the final contract.

In order to show a three-suited hand after the partner of the notrump bidder has made a weak one-suited response, there are two bids available. A bid of two notrump shows a three-suited hand of moderate strength, and asks partner to choose among the three remaining suits. A cue-bid makes the same request, but shows a stronger hand.

TWO-WAY EXCLUSION BIDS

Some partnerships use what might be called two-way exclusion bids over the opponents' one notrump openings. An exclusion bid is the bid of a short suit, promising length in all of the other suits. Using two-way exclusion bids, a suit overcall has one of two meanings: either the overcaller has that suit, or he is very short in that suit and has the other three suits. Using this convention, West would overcall two hearts over one notrump with either of the following hands:

♠ x x ♡ K Q J x x x x ◇ A x ♣ x x

♠ K Q x x ♡ x ◇ A x x x ♣ K J x x

This convention has the advantage that one can make either a natural overcall, or can make the equivalent of a take-out double even though all four suits are still unbid. The disadvantage, of course, is that the bid is the epitome of ambiguity.

If the partner of the overcaller has fewer than three cards in the suit overcalled, he must assume that the overcaller has length in that suit. Normally the strength of his hand will be such that he is forced to pass. This may occasionally result in the partnership's playing in a 2–1 fit, but not doubled. If the overcall is doubled, either immediately or after the overcaller's partner has passed, the overcaller should redouble if he has bid his short suit rather than a real suit. This will allow the partnership to escape into a more reasonable spot. (*See also* s.o.s. RE-DOUBLES.) Conversely, if the opponents double the overcall of a real long suit, the overcaller must pass.

If the partner of the overcaller has great length in the suit overcalled he will infer that that is the overcaller's short suit. He may nevertheless pass if he has no side four card suit.

If the partner of the overcaller has three or more cards in the suit bid, he usually will not be able to tell whether that is his partner's long suit or his short suit. In these circumstances, the partner of the overcaller should bid his longest suit in case his partner's bid was the exclusion bid. If the overcaller rebids the suit in which he overcalled, he shows that his original bid was not an exclusion bid but a natural bid.

TWO CLUBS FOR MINORS,
TWO DIAMONDS FOR MAJORS

A convention similar to Landy and Ripstra uses only the two diamond overcall to show both major suits. It uses the two club overcall to show length in both minor suits. Use of this convention enables the partnership to play in any suit at the two level. The strength required is the same as that for a Landy bid.

UNUSUAL NOTRUMP AND MINORS OVER NOTRUMP

A part of the Lea System, this convention consists of three artificial overcalls over the notrump opening, each showing a different pair of suits. An overcall of two clubs shows diamonds and spades; an overcall of two diamonds shows hearts and spades; a two notrump overcall shows diamonds and hearts. Two-suited hands in which one of the long suits is clubs cannot be described using this convention.

For strength and distribution requirements, responses, etc., *see discussion under* LANDY.

NEGATIVE DOUBLES

When the partnership has agreed to use five-card major suit openings, the frequency of their opening the bidding in a minor suit is, of course, increased. One of the hazards of opening the bidding in a minor suit is that it is easier for the opponents to overcall. If the opponent overcalls a minor suit opening with one spade and the responder has a four card heart suit he was planning to bid, the overcall may prove embarrassing.

The Negative Double is a convention that copes with this situation. It is a double of an opponent's overcall for takeout rather than for penalties. The double tells the opener that the responder has some high-card values and support for at least one of the unbid suits, usually the unbid major suit. For example, if the bidding has started

South	West	North	East
1 ◇	1 ♠	Double	Pass

North's double shows at least four hearts, and at least enough strength for him to have responded to the one diamond opening bid had there been no interference. North might have a hand such as

[A] ♠ x x x   ♡ A x x x   ◇ x x   ♣ Q x x x
or
[B] ♠ x x x   ♡ K J x x   ◇ K x x x   ♣ x x

Responder hopes his partner will be able to bid two hearts. If instead he bids two clubs, responder will pass with Hand A, or will correct the contract to two diamonds with Hand B.

After the negative double the opener is expected to bid

the major suit shown by the responder if he has four-card support for that suit. If he has a minimum hand, he will bid just two of the responder's suit. If he has about a trick better than a minimum hand, he should jump in the responder's suit. For example, the opener might have

[C] ♠ K x   ♡ Q x x x   ◇ A J x x   ♣ A x x
or
[D] ♠ x x   ♡ A Q x x   ◇ A K x x   ♣ Q x x

After the auction has started

South	*West*	*North*	*East*
1 ◇	1 ♠	Double	Pass

the opener would bid two hearts with Hand C. With Hand D opener would jump to three hearts, just as he would have if the bidding had gone, without interference:

Opener	*Responder*
1 ◇	1 ♡
3 ♡	

Opener's jump to three hearts invites the responder to bid a game if he has extra values; however, it is not forcing. After the responder has made a negative double the only forcing bid available to the opener is a cue-bid of the suit in which the opponent overcalled.

The responder may have a very strong hand and still make a negative double if the overcall has made it difficult for him to bid his hand naturally. For example, responder might hold

♠ A x   ♡ K Q x x   ◇ Q x x x x   ♣ A x

If his partner has opened with one diamond and the next hand has overcalled with one spade, the responder has no convenient bid. Therefore he uses a negative double to find out whether or not his partner has four hearts, and plans to force at least to game thereafter.

Although the negative double was originally used primarily by partnerships which had agreed not to open four-card major suits, its use has spread, and it may be useful even if the opener was allowed to open the bidding in a four-card major. For example, using negative doubles, the responder can distinguish between four-card and five-card major suit responses. Suppose the bidding has started

South	West	North	East
1 ♣	1 ♡	1 ♠	

If the partnership is not using negative doubles, North's one spade response could be made on either a four-card suit or a five-card suit. If the partnership is using negative doubles, North's free bid of one spade in the above auction would guarantee a five-card suit since he could have shown a four-card suit by making a negative double.

Many partnerships limit the use of negative doubles to low levels of the bidding, and to auctions in which the responder has been prevented from showing his four-card major suit safely and naturally. However, there is no technical reason why this double cannot be used at quite high levels, and over any combination of openings and overcalls. Of course, the higher the level at which the negative double is made, the stronger the doubler's hand must be, and the more likely opener becomes to pass for penalties.

Suppose, for example, that the bidding goes

North	East	South	West
1 ♠	2 ♡		

and South has a hand such as

♠ K x   ♡ J x x   ◇ A x x x   ♣ K x x x

It is very useful for South to be able to use a negative double to describe his hand. His negative double in this situation shows at least a 10 point hand, since if opener is to bid one of responder's suits it must be at the three level. South also shows that he probably has no five-card suit since he chose to double rather than bidding a suit.

Passing for Penalties: Opener's Duty to Reopen

Use of the immediate double of an overcall as a negative or takeout double means that the responder cannot double the overcall for penalties. Therefore, if North has a hand such as

♠ x x   ♡ A x x   ◇ K J 10 9 x   ♣ Q x x

in an auction such as

South	West	North	East
1 ♠	2 ◇		

North must pass West's two diamond overcall.

The fact that the use of negative doubles may force the responder to pass when otherwise he would have made a penalty double places a heavy obligation on the opening bidder. The opener should make every reasonable effort to keep the bidding open if his lefthand opponent's overcall is passed around to him, especially if he is short in the overcaller's suit. Thus, if the auction goes

South	West	North	East
1 ♠	2 ◇	Pass	Pass

and South holds

[A]　♠ A Q x x x　♡ K x x　◇ x　♣ K x x x

South should reopen the bidding.

One guideline for the opener as to whether or not to reopen is his length in the suit of the overcall. The shorter he is in that suit the more he should strain to keep the bidding open. Conversely, the more cards he has in the overcaller's suit, the less likely it is that his partner has passed with the equivalent of a penalty double, and the more inclined the opener should be to pass. If responder did not pass because he wanted to make a penalty double, he passed because he was weak. In Hand A above, if opener's diamonds and hearts were reversed, he should pass the two diamond overcall.

Once South decides to reopen, he should reopen with a double on any hand with which, if the partnership had not been using negative doubles, he would have been willing to pass an immediate penalty double by his partner. If the opener has a hand with which he would have removed his partner's immediate penalty double, he should keep the bidding open by bidding a suit. In this way, if responder had a hand with which he hoped to penalize the overcaller, he will at least be given another opportunity to bid. Opener and responder might for example have these hands:

(Opener)
♠ A Q x x x x   ♡ x x   ◇ A 10 9 x   ♣ x

(Responder)
♠ J x   ♡ A Q 10 x   ◇ Q x x   ♣ K J x x

With responder precluded from making a penalty double of a
two club overcall, the auction might go

North	East	South	West
1 ♠	2 ♣	Pass	Pass
2 ◇	Pass	3 Notrump	

When the responder has made a negative double, the opening bidder has an option to pass for penalties if he has a suitable hand. For example, suppose the opener has a hand such as

♠ A x   ♡ K Q x x x   ◇ K Q 10 9   ♣ x x

and the bidding has gone

North	East	South	West
1 ♡	2 ◇	Double	Pass

The opener has a choice between bidding notrump and passing
for penalties.

Thus, a secondary advantage of using negative doubles is
that the overcaller may have a penalty inflicted on him from
either side. Further, when the opening bidder has the necessary
length in the overcaller's suit to allow him to pass the double
for penalties, the partner of the overcaller will have had to
commit himself before knowing that a penalty is to be sought.

Consider West's predicament in the following auction:

North	East	South	West
1 ♠	2 ♣	Double	

If North and South were not using negative doubles, West would know that the double is for penalties, and he might well try to escape into a better suit. However, if South's double is for take-out, West cannot be sure that North and South have any interest in penalizing the overcall. East might after all have such a long or solid suit that North would not have sufficient club length or strength to pass for penalties.

RESPONSIVE DOUBLES

When one's partner has doubled an opening bid for takeout and the responder has raised the opener's suit, one seldom wants to double for penalties. The partnership may find it desirable in this situation to use Responsive Doubles.

A Responsive Double is a takeout double in response to partner's takeout double. For example, in each of the following auctions

(A)	*South*	*West*	*North*	*East*
	1 ♠	Double	2 ♠	Double

(B)	*South*	*West*	*North*	*East*
	1 ◇	Double	3 ◇	Double

East's double of North's raise is a responsive double. The responsive double shows support for at least two of the unbid suits. The double normally denies a five card suit, and shows strength appropriate for play at least at the level to which the responsive doubler invites his partner to bid. For example, in Auction A, East might have a hand such as

♠ x   ♡ Q x x x   ◇ K x x x   ♣ Q x x x

For Auction B, East might have

♠ A J x x   ♡ K J x x   ◇ x x x   ♣ J x

While a cue-bid would describe East's hand pattern in each of the above auctions, it would show a hand stronger in high cards, and might well get the partnership overboard. The responsive double thus allows description on moderate, rather than game-forcing, values.

When the Opponents Have Bid Two Suits

Responsive doubles are usually limited to situations in which the opponents have bid and raised the same suit. However, the partnership may agree to extend the responsive double to a situation in which the responder has bid a new suit over the takeout double. For example:

North	East	South	West
1 ◇	Double	1 ♡	Double

If the partnership has agreed, West may make a responsive double to show spades and clubs. This use of the responsive double, however, makes it somewhat more difficult for East and West to expose a psychic response by South.

When Partner Has Overcalled

Responsive doubles may also be used when the responder has supported the opener's suit after partner has made an overcall. The responsive double over an overcall suggests that the doubler is short in the overcaller's suit, and has length in each of the unbid suits.

For example:

South	West	North	East
1 ♠	2 ♣	2 ♠	Double

East's double invites West to bid one of the unbid suits if he has as much as three-card support. East might have a hand such as

♠ x x ♡ K J x x x ◇ K 10 9 x x ♣ x

COOPERATIVE DOUBLES

A cooperative double is a double that gives the doubler's partner the choice of passing for penalties or bidding on. OPTIONAL DOUBLES and COMPETITIVE DOUBLES are special types of cooperative doubles.

Cooperative doubles are used principally at low levels of the auction. Without special partnership agreement they may be used in situations where the doubler's previous bidding has necessarily limited his hand so that he would not be able to guarantee a penalty. For example:

North	East	South	West
1 ◇	1 ♠	2 ◇	2 ♠
Pass	Pass	Double	

South's two diamond response after the one spade overcall limited his hand. His double of two spades cannot, therefore, be based on massive strength. It suggests to opener that two spades can be defeated if opener is interested in defending; otherwise opener should bid on.

Some partnerships agree, especially playing match point duplicate, that all of their low-level doubles are cooperative doubles. For example, in the auction

North	East	South	West
1 ◇	1 ♡	1 ♠	Pass
2 ◇	2 ♡	Double	

such a partnership would treat South's double as cooperative, and not to be left in by North unless he could contribute substantially to the defense.

A cooperative double may be made even when the partner of the doubler has never bid. For example

North	East	South	West
1 ◇	Pass	Pass	Double
1 ♠	2 ♡	Pass	Pass
Double			

Opener has limited his hand by his failure to redouble at his second turn. His double suggests that he has a very good hand with about 19 or 20 points, and is willing to have South pass with good hearts, or bid any other suit.

COMPETITIVE DOUBLES

From time to time the opponents' overcalls will interfere with the opener's try for game, rather than with the responder's bidding. A convention designed to remedy this situation is called the Competitive Double.

For example, suppose South had a hand such as

♠ K Q x x x   ♡ x   ◇ A Q x x   ♣ K J x

and his partner had raised his one spade opening bid to two. South could make a natural game try by bidding three diamonds; or if the partnership had agreed to use SHORT SUIT GAME TRIES, South could invite game by bidding three hearts.

Suppose, however, that the bidding has gone

(A)	*South*	*West*	*North*	*East*
	1 ♠	2 ♡	2 ♠	3 ♡

A bid of three spades by South would be merely competitive, and he is deprived of whatever game tries he might have used without competition.

It is in this situation that competitive doubles (also called "maximal overcall" doubles when the opponents have taken up the maximum amount of room with their overcalls) are most useful. However, competitive doubles can be used even when the opponents' bids have not used up all the room for a game try. For example:

(B)	*South*	*West*	*North*	*East*
	1 ♠	2 ◇	2 ♠	3 ◇

Although opener could still bid three hearts as a game try, if he has good defensive, as well as offensive, strength, he may as well make his game try by doubling. If his partner has an appropriate hand, such as

♠ J 10 x   ♡ x x   ◇ K Q 10 x   ♣ A x x x

he will pass the game-try double for penalties.

The partnership loses little by using the doubles in Auctions A and B as competitive doubles instead of penalty doubles. Opener will rarely have a hand with which to make either a unilateral penalty double, or a cooperative double that his partner is likely to leave in.

Competitive doubles may be made by the responder as well as the opener. Consider the following auction:

South	West	North	East
1 ♠	2 ◇	2 ♠	3 ◇
Pass	Pass		

If North has a hand with which he wants to compete to the three level, he can, of course, bid three spades. However, if he competes with a double he not only conveys this message, but also gives the opener a chance to pass his competitive double for penalties. The North and South hands might be:

(South)
♠ A 10 x x x   ♡ Q x   ◇ K J 10 9   ♣ K J

(North)
♠ J x x   ♡ K J x x   ◇ x x   ♣ A x x x

NEGATIVE SLAM DOUBLES

When the partnership has bid and raised a suit preemptively in a competitive situation, and the opponents have reached a slam, the partnership frequently would like to sacrifice if it cannot defeat the slam. For example:

South	West	North	East
1 ♢	1 ♠	3 ♡	4 ♠
Pass	Pass	5 ♢	Pass
6 ♢			

There are two methods available to help the partnership to determine whether or not it has the two tricks necessary to defeat the slam. They are called Negative Slam Doubles and Positive Slam Doubles. The use of either convention requires the partnership to forego the use of LIGHTNER SLAM DOUBLES in competitive situations such as these.

The Negative Slam double convention requires the person in the first potential sacrifice position ("First Hand"—West in the auction above) to double if he has no defensive tricks against the slam. If First Hand has one or two defensive tricks, he is required to pass. His partner ("Last Hand") now evaluates his defensive potential.

If First Hand has doubled showing no defensive tricks, Last Hand will sacrifice if he has no more than one trick. If Last hand has two tricks, he will pass his partner's double.

If First Hand has passed, showing one or two defensive tricks, Last Hand will pass also if he has one or more tricks. If Last Hand has no defensive tricks, he will double. After Last Hand has doubled, showing no defensive tricks, First Hand will pass if he has two defensive tricks, or will sacrifice if he has only one.

POSITIVE SLAM DOUBLES

When the opponents have reached a slam after an auction in which the defending partnership has bid and raised a suit (see discussion in NEGATIVE SLAM DOUBLES), the partnership may find it advantageous to use Positive Slam doubles in order to determine whether it should sacrifice or should instead try to set the slam.

Positive Slam Doubles are so called because, unlike NEGATIVE SLAM DOUBLES, doubles are made with hands containing one or more defensive tricks, rather than with hands containing no defensive tricks.

Using the Positive Slam Double convention, First Hand doubles if he has two tricks; if he has one or none, he passes. After First Hand has doubled, showing that he expects to defeat the slam in his own hand, Last Hand of course passes.

If First Hand has passed, showing one or no tricks, Last Hand will sacrifice if he has no tricks; he will pass if he has two tricks, and he will double if he has one defensive trick. After Last Hand's double, First Hand will pass if he too has a trick; with no trick First Hand will sacrifice over Last Hand's double.

The Positive Slam Double convention is somewhat simpler and more natural than the Negative Slam Double convention, and has the added advantage of forcing opponents to play their contract doubled more often when they are going down.

TWO NOTRUMP AS A LIMIT RAISE OVER OPPONENT'S TAKEOUT DOUBLE

When the bidding has been opened with one of a suit and the next hand has passed, the responder's jump to two notrump shows a balanced hand of 13 to 15 points. However, if the intervening hand has made a takeout double and the responder has a balanced 13 to 15 count, he will frequently want to try to penalize the opponents.

Over the takeout double, therefore, the responder will normally redouble with any strong hand. Consequently the jump to two notrump loses its natural meaning.

The most frequent use of the jump to two notrump over the opponent's takeout double is as a limit raise, showing about 9 or 10 points, with three or four card support for partner's suit. For example, after North has opened with one heart and East has made a takeout double, South would jump to two notrump with

♠ x x   ♡ K J x x   ◇ A J x x   ♣ x x x

Use of the jump to two notrump as a limit raise allows the jump raise to three of the opener's suit over the double to be used strictly preemptively. For example:

♠ x   ♡ K J x x x   ◇ J x x x   ♣ x x x

TWO NOTRUMP AS A PREEMPTIVE RAISE OVER DOUBLE OF MINOR SUIT OPENING

The jump to two notrump over the opponent's takeout double can be used to show a hand worth a limit raise of partner's suit when partner has opened the bidding with a minor. Thus responder could make preemptive jumps in opener's suit. However, some partnerships reverse the meanings of the two notrump response and the jump to three of partner's suit. Using this method, in the auction

North	East	South	West
1 ◇	Double	2 Notrump	

South's two notrump bid would show a preemptive raise in diamonds, a hand such as

♠ x x x   ♡ x   ◇ K J 10 x x x   ♣ Q x x

In the auction

North	East	South	West
1 ◇	Double	3 ◇	

South's three diamond bid would show a hand worth a limit raise in diamonds, such as

♠ x x x   ♡ K J x   ◇ K Q x x   ♣ Q x x

The rationale for the reversal of the meanings of these two bids is that when the responder has a limit raise of a minor suit, the partnership may very well belong in three notrump. Using three diamonds as the limit raise accomplishes two things. First, it allows the opener, who has the stronger of the two hands, to be the notrump declarer. And secondly, making opener the declarer will make the doubler, who will have the stronger of the two defensive hands, be the opening leader. His lead will often be made without his knowing which suit his partner prefers, and he will be leading away from strength, rather than toward it.

STAYMAN AFTER NOTRUMP OVERCALLS

The partner of a player who has overcalled one notrump over an opponent's opening bid sometimes wants to find out whether or not his side has a four-four major suit fit. The Stayman convention can be used in response to the notrump overcall. Assuming that the one notrump overcall shows the same strength as a one notrump opening, the partner of the overcaller should have the same strength he would need to use Stayman in response to an opening bid.

There are three ways in which the partnership could agree to use the Stayman convention after notrump overcalls. Standard practice is to use a cue-bid as the Stayman bid:

South	West	North	East
1 ♦	1 Notrump	Pass	2 ♦

East's two diamond bid asks West whether or not he has a four card major. If West has no four card major he rebids two notrump.

An alternative method is to use a two club bid as Stayman, regardless of what the opening bid was. This provides the partnership with somewhat greater offensive flexibility, since the Stayman bidder can proceed just as he would have using non-forcing Stayman in a non-competitive auction. For example, if East held a hand such as

♠ Q x x x x   ♡ x x x x   ♦ x x   ♣ x x x

he would like to use Stayman, and pass if his partner bids a four-card major suit. If the two diamond cue-bid must be used as the Stayman bid, West's rebid with no four-card major would be two notrump. With this hand, using only the cue-bid as Stayman, therefore, East would be forced just to bid two spades, giving up on finding a four-four heart fit.

However, if the partnership is using two clubs as Stayman, East can safely bid two clubs to try to find a fit in either major suit. If West does not have a four-card major, his rebid will be two diamonds, and over this East can bid two spades.

The disadvantage of this method is that it leaves the partner of the notrump overcaller one less suit into which he can escape.

A third method of using Stayman when the bidding has been opened with something other than one club, is to play Two-Way Stayman over the overcall. Using this method a two club bid by the partner of the notrump overcaller would be the equivalent of non-forcing Stayman, and a cue-bid of the opponent's suit would be forcing to game.

Having this agreement would give the partner of the overcaller a complete range of bids; he could force to game by cue-bidding; or he could invite game by bidding two clubs and the jumping to three of a five-card major suit; or he could rebid his five-card major suit at the two level with a hand with which he had little interest in game.

STAYMAN OVER OPPONENT'S
NOTRUMP OVERCALL

Although seldom adopted, it is possible to use a two club bid as a Stayman-type of convention over an opponent's one notrump overcall. This is most useful when the partnership is using five-card major suit openings and the opening bid has been one club or one diamond. Thus in the auctions

	North	East	South	West
(A)	1 ◇	1 Notrump	2 ♣	

	North	East	South	West
(B)	1 ♣	1 Notrump	2 ♣	

the partnership could agree to use South's two club bid as Stayman.

The use of two clubs as Stayman in these auctions is similar to using a negative double. It may be the only way South has to bid a hand such as

♠ Q x x x   ♡ K x x x   ◇ Q x x   ♣ x x

483

LEBENSOHL

When an opponent overcalls over a one notrump opening, the responder frequently has a difficult time bidding his hand appropriately. Many partnerships have not agreed what bids are forcing, or what the responder can do to compete.

The Lebensohl convention is a method for the responder to make competitive and forcing bids after an opponent has overcalled over the one notrump opening. The Lebensohl method uses different methods for overcalls at the two level and at the three-level.

Against One-Suited Overcalls

After a natural overcall at the three level the Lebensohl method is fairly simple. Bids of new suits are forcing to game. A double is negative and promises four cards in any unbid major suit. The double is not forcing to game.

After a natural overcall at the two level, the double by the responder is for penalties. A new suit bid at the two level is competitive and not forward going. A new suit bid at the three level is forcing to game. A cue-bid of the overcaller's suit is also forcing to game and suggests that the responder has no long suit to bid.

If the responder wants to compete, but not force to game, in a suit that ranks below the suit of the overcall, he cannot bid it directly over the overcall, because bidding a new suit at the three level is forcing to game. To play in his suit, the responder must first bid two notrump. The two notrump bid is a relay bid, forcing the opener to bid three clubs. The three club bid permits responder to pass if his long suit is clubs; or to bid another suit, which his partner is normally expected to pass. For example, suppose responder has

♠ K x   ♡ x x x   ◇ J 10 x x x x   ♣ K x

If the opponent overcalled two clubs as a natural bid over the one notrump opening, responder would simply bid two diamonds. If the overcall was two hearts (or two spades), however, the auction would go

North	East	South	West
1 Notrump	2 ♡	2 Notrump	Pass
3 ♣	Pass	3 ◇	Pass
Pass	Pass		

If the responder has a long suit that can be bid at the two level over the overcall, but he has a strong enough hand to invite game, responder can bid two notrump, forcing the opener to bid three clubs, and then bid his suit. The message to opener, since responder did not bid his suit directly over the overcall is that he wants to invite game.

Showing Stoppers

The availability of the two notrump bid as a relay gives the responder added flexibility with game-going hands. Responder has, in effect, two ways to suggest game in notrump, and two ways to look for a major suit fit. For example:

(A)	North	East	South	West
	1 Notrump	2 ♡	3 Notrump	

485

(B)	North	East	South	West
	1 Notrump	2 ♡	2 Notrump	Pass
	3 ♣	Pass	3 Notrump	

In both (a) and (b) responder is suggesting that the partnership play three notrump. He should use the two auctions to distinguish between his possible holdings in the overcaller's suit. Tactically it is preferable to use auction (a) to deny a stopper in the overcaller's suit, because it inhibits West from raising his partner's suit. If three notrump becomes the final contract, East will have to guess how good opener's holding is in the suit of the overcall. If responder temporized with a two notrump bid without a stopper, West could more easily raise his partner's suit, solving the lead problem. Auction (b), therefore, should promise a stopper.

The same distinctions can be drawn between the following auctions:

(C)	North	East	South	West
	1 Notrump	2 ♡	3 ♡	

(D)	North	East	South	West
	1 Notrump	2 ♡	2 Notrump	Pass
	3 ♣	Pass	3 ♡	

In both auctions (c) and (d) responder has cue-bid, showing four cards in the unbid major suit and suggested that he has no long suit of his own. Since his partner may not have a matching four card suit, responder should also use these two auctions to show whether or not he has a stopper, in case opener wants to consider notrump. For the sake of consistency, auction (c) should be used to deny a stopper in the overcaller's suit, while auction (d) should promise a stopper.

Against Two-Suited Overcalls

There are many conventional overcalls over one notrump that show two-suited hands. Some, such as Landy and Brozel, show precisely which two suits the overcaller has. Some, such as Astro, specify one suit but not the other. In most respects the Lebensohl convention operates the same way against both types of overcalls.

Against a two-suited overcall in which only one suit is pinpointed, a double is for penalties in that suit. Against a two-suited overcall in which both suits are specified, the double shows the ability to penalize at least one of the suits. For example, against a Landy two club bid, responder would double with

♠ K J x x   ♡ Q x   ◇ K x x x   ♣ x x x

Against either type of overcall, responder's bid of a "new" suit—i.e., not one of the overcaller's known suits—is not forcing if bid at the two level. The bid of a new suit at the three level is forcing to game.

If responder wants to make a non-forcing bid in a suit that cannot be shown at the two level he must first bid two notrump. The two notrump bid is a relay, forcing opener to bid three clubs. Responder can pass three clubs if clubs is his suit; or he can bid his suit over three clubs. For example, suppose the overcall is two diamonds, Ripstra, for the major suits, and responder had a hand such as

♠ K x   ♡ x x   ◇ x x   ♣ Q J x x x x

The auction could go

North	East	South	West
1 Notrump	2 ♢	2 Notrump	Pass
3 ♣	Pass	Pass	Pass

It is in making cue-bids of the opponent's suits that the Lebensohl convention distinguishes between the overcalls that specify the two suits held, and overcalls that identify only one suit. When both of the overcaller's suits are known, two cue bids are available to the responder. When both of the suits are known, and the overcall has been at the two level, the Lebensohl convention uses the cue-bid of the cheaper suit as a non-game-going, competitive bid. Responder should have a hand that is strong enough to play at the three level, but not strong enough to force to game. In the auction above, if responder had cue-bid two hearts, the cheaper of the suits shown by the Ripstra bid, instead of bidding two notrump, he might have had a hand such as

♠ x x　　♡ x　　♢ K J x x x　　♣ Q 10 x x x

The cue-bid of the higher ranking suit specified by the overcall is forcing to game, and shows support for the unbid suits. If responder had cue-bid two spades in the above auction, he might have had a hand such as

♠ x x　　♡ A　　♢ K Q x x x　　♣ K J x x x

When the overcall has identified only one of the overcaller's two suits, there is only one cue-bid available. This cue-bid is forcing to game, and shows supports for all of the other suits.

If the two-suited overcall is made at the three-level and the two suits are identified, e.g., Roth-Stone Astro, the double of the overcall is negative, showing support for the other two suits. The double is not forcing to game. New suit bids are still forcing, and a cue-bid is forcing to game.

TRANSFERS OVER DOUBLES OF
ONE NOTRUMP

When the bidding has been opened with one notrump and the next hand has doubled for penalties, it is standard practice to redouble with good general strength, to pass with either a smattering of values, or no suit to run to, and to bid a suit naturally if possible. It is, however, possible to use transfer bids over the double, or to use a system of artificial bids that give the opener a choice of suits.

The reason most partnerships do not use Jacoby Transfer-type bids over the double of one notrump is that at first glance, transfers seem to reduce the number of avenues of escape. For example, using Jacoby Transfers a two diamond bid would show a heart suit; therefore two diamonds could not be bid naturally.

One convention dealing with this situation uses four-suit two-level transfers. It accomplishes this by the simple expedient of using a redouble to transfer to clubs, a two club bid to transfer to diamonds, a two diamond bid to transfer to hearts, and a two heart bid to transfer to spades.

In addition, a Stayman-type sequence can be used. If the responder wants the opener to bid his better major suit, he first redoubles, transferring temporarily to two clubs. Over opener's bid of two clubs, however, responder will bid two diamonds, asking opener to bid his better major suit.

What the partnership gives up in exchange for these transfers is the ability to redouble for penalties—a small price for the ability to transfer declarership in any suit to the strong hand, and the ability to use Stayman.

REDOUBLES FOR TAKEOUT OVER ONE NOTRUMP DOUBLED

As an alternative to the standard practice of making "penalty" redoubles of doubles of one notrump openings, some partnerships use the redouble as part of a minor suit escape route. Using this method, a redouble asks the opener to bid his better minor suit. Responder promises at least nine cards in the minor suits. A two diamond bid over the double asks the opener to bid his better major suit. Bids of two hearts and two spades are natural, and have their standard meanings.

In addition, a bid of two clubs shows one long minor suit, but not necessarily clubs. If two clubs gets doubled and responder retreats to two diamonds, his suit was diamonds. Opener should not "correct" to three clubs.

DEFENSE AGAINST OPPONENTS'
TWO-SUITED CALLS

When the opponents have intervened with a cue-bid or overcall that shows a two-suited hand, the partnership should attempt to maximize its chances of extracting a penalty when such a penalty would be severe. The most effective strategy is for the responder to double with a good 9 points or better, and strength in one or both of the suits shown by the opponent.

For example, in the auction

South	West	North	East
1 �	2 ♥		

if West's cue-bid shows spades and clubs, North should double with a hand such as

♠ K Q x x   ♡ x x x   ◇ x x   ♣ K J x x

or

♠ Q x x   ♡ x x   ◇ A x x x   ♣ A Q x x

Holding less than the strength necessary to double, the responder can make a single raise of his partner's suit with any hand that would have been worth a free raise after a simple overcall. For example, for the auction

South	West	North	East
1 ◇	2 ◇	3 ◇	

North might hold

♠ K x x   ♡ x x   ◇ A x x x   ♣ x x x x

If responder has a strong offensive hand, the two-suited overcall or cue-bid gives him an excellent weapon, the cue-bid. The responder should make a cue-bid with either a good fit for opener's suit or a powerful suit of his own.

For example, if his partner has opened with one heart and the next hand has cue-bid two hearts, showing spades and diamonds, and North has a hand such as

♠ x x x   ♡ K Q x x   ◇ A x   ♣ A J x x

North may cue-bid three diamonds, the opponents' suit in which he has the greater control. If South had a hand such as

♠ x   ♡ A J x x x   ◇ K x x x   ♣ K Q x

the partnership could reach its slam, since opener would realize that responder has good heart support rather than a self-supporting suit. The entire auction might be

South	West	North	East
1 ♡	2 ♡	3 ◇	Pass
3 ♠	Pass	4 ♣	Pass
5 ♡	Pass	6 ♡	

Cue-bids are very useful tools against two-suited overcalls since there are two suits that may be cue-bid. This method works over any two-suited overcall, so long as the partnership knows which two suits the overcaller shows.

UNUSUAL-OVER-UNUSUAL

The methods described under DEFENSE AGAINST OPPONENTS' TWO-SUITED CALLS can be used over the opponent's jump to two notrump as the Unusual Notrump. An alternative method has been devised to assign precise meanings to the cue-bids of the suits shown by the Unusual Notrump, in an effort to define over-all strength as well as suit length. The meanings assigned are entirely artificial, hence the name "Unusual-over-Unusual".

The Unusual Notrump shows two suits, normally the minor suits, as in the auction

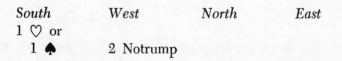

South	West	North	East
1 ♡ or			
1 ♠	2 Notrump		

Unusual-over-Unusual uses a cue-bid in the opponent's lower ranking suit, here clubs, to show a hand with length in the lower of the two suits not shown by the overcall; it uses a cue-bid in the opponent's higher suit to show a hand with length in the higher ranking of those two suits. Whenever the bidding has been opened with a major suit, a club cue-bid would show hearts, and a diamond cue-bid would show spades.

A cue-bid of the minor suit that shows length in the opener's suit promises a hand worth a limit raise or better. Thus in the auction

(A)	North	East	South	West
	1 ♠	2 Notrump	3 ◇	

South's three diamond bid shows at least a limit raise in spades. In the auction

(B)

North	East	South	West
1 ♡	2 Notrump	3 ♣	

South's three club bid shows at least a limit raise in hearts. In auctions (a) and (b), if North has a hand with which he wishes to be in game opposite as little as a limit raise, he should avoid rebidding his suit at the three level.

A cue-bid that shows the unbid suit—i.e.,

(C)

South	West	North	East
1 ♠	2 Notrump	3 ♣	

(D)

South	West	North	East
1 ♡	2 Notrump	3 ◇	

shows that responder has at least five cards in the unbid suit, and a hand worth an invitation to game, but not worth a game force. (Some partnerships instead use the cue-bid to show a game forcing hand, and would treat a simple bid of the suit as not forcing.)

For auction (d) above, North might have a hand such as

[E]   ♠ A Q J x x   ♡ x x   ◇ K x x   ♣ x x x

If opener wants to be in game opposite such a hand he should avoid bidding either his suit or the responder's suit at the three level.

Use of the cue-bids to show invitational hands frees the direct bids of the opener's suit and the unbid suit for other uses. A simple raise of opener's suit at the three level is merely competitive:

South	West	North	East
1 ♠	2 Notrump	3 ♠	

The free bid of the unbid suit at the three level is forcing to game:

South	West	North	East
1 ♠	2 Notrump	3 ♡	

or

South	West	North	East
1 ♡	2 Notrump	3 ♠	

Having methods to describe both invitational and game forcing hands solves the responder's problem with a hand such as (e) above.

If the bidding has been opened with a minor suit and the Unusual Notrump has been overcalled, promising the two lower unbid suits, the Unusual-over-Unusual convention operates in exactly the same way. For example,

South	West	North	East
1 ◇	2 Notrump	3 ♣	

Here the two notrump bid promises hearts and clubs. The three club cue-bid shows at least a limit raise in the lower suit, diamonds. A cue-bid of three hearts would show at least a five card spade suit and an invitational hand.

Some partnerships use the unusual notrump overcall always to show the minor suits. In this event if the bidding is opened with a minor and the unusual notrump overcall is made, responder should consider that the cue-bids show length in the major suits. The overcaller probably does not have length in either major, and the responder, after all, is hardly likely to want to play in opener's suit when one opponent has five of them. In these circumstances, a cue-bid of three clubs should show hearts, and a cue-bid of three diamonds should show spades.

HERBERT NEGATIVE RESPONSE TO A TAKEOUT DOUBLE OR ONE-BID

A Herbert Negative is a bid of the cheapest suit in response to partner's action. It may be used in responding to takeout doubles. For example:

South	*West*	*North*	*East*
1 ♡	Double	Pass	1 ♠

Using the Herbert Negative, East's one spade bid shows a very weak hand. The one spade bid shows nothing about East's spade suit; it simply shows a dearth of high cards.

Herbert Negatives may also be used over one-level opening bids. The ROMAN CLUB SYSTEM, for example, uses a response of the cheapest suit as a negative for all opening bids of one of a suit (all of which are forcing in the Roman system). The most advantageous use of the Herbert convention, however, is in responding to very strong opening bids, such as forcing two-bids and strong forcing artificial club bids. It is in this situation that the responder will presumably have least to say about his own suits, at least that his partner is interested in. In other situations, where the opening bid is not so powerful, the Herbert convention is less useful since its use may waste a round of bidding, or its inapplicability may waste a level of bidding.

S.O.S. REDOUBLES

An S.O.S. Redouble is a redouble that asks the redoubler's partner to select another denomination. A redouble is an S.O.S. only when it could not have any other meaning.

The S.O.S. redouble is most often made by the person whose bid has been doubled. For example

South	West	North	East
1 ♣	Double	Pass	Pass
Redouble			

South may have opened with a three-card club suit. His double asks North to choose another suit. However, in the auction

South	West	North	East
1 ♡ or 1 ♠	Double	Pass	Pass
Redouble			

South's redouble shows strength rather than requesting a rescue.

Sometimes a player may deliberately make a bid in a short suit in order to induce a double, so that he may make an S.O.S. redouble to tell his partner that he has the other suits. The most frequent example is a bid over the penalty double of a notrump opening bid:

North	East	South	West
1 Notrump	Double	2 ♣	Pass
Pass	Double	Redouble	

In this sequence, South's bid of two clubs showed a weak hand, one at any rate that was not strong enough to tolerate playing the hand in one notrump doubled. Having announced a weak hand he cannot logically be strong enough to make a penalty redouble of two clubs. Therefore, the North should conclude that the redouble was an S.O.S., asking him to take his choice of the other three suits. In choosing, North should bear in mind that South is likely to have length in diamonds and one major suit rather than in both major suits. If South had four cards in each of the majors, he could have bid two diamonds over the double, and redoubled to ask North to choose between the majors. *See also* TWO-WAY EXCLUSION BIDS.

On occasion the S.O.S. may be issued by the partner of the player who has made the doubled bid. For example

North	*East*	*South*	*West*
1 ♣	Pass	Pass	Double
Pass	Pass	Redouble	

Since South did not have sufficient strength to keep the bidding open, he is unlikely to want to redouble naturally. His redouble should be considered an S.O.S.

KOCK WERNER REDOUBLE

By special agreement the partnership may use S.O.S. redoubles of penalty doubles of overcalls. For example

North	East	South	West
1 ♣	1 ♡	Double	Redouble

Using Kock Werner redoubles, West's redouble asks South to bid any of the other three suits, including the suit bid by the opener.

TAKEOUT DOUBLES OF PREEMPTS

The most common device used against an opponent's preempt is the takeout double. The double asks partner to bid, even with a very weak hand. Of course, if most of partner's strength and his principal length are concentrated in the suit of the preempt, he may pass. (*See also* OPTIONAL DOUBLES.)

Unless the partnership has agreed on some other treatment, the double is for takeout whether it is made immediately over the preempt or in the balancing position. A takeout double may be made over any level of suit preempt through the level of four hearts. Doubles of four spades and higher preempts are normally considered to be for penalties. Over four spades, a four notrump bid is available for takeout.

The higher the preempt, the stronger the doubler's hand should be, to take into account the higher level at which his partner will have to bid. For example, a takeout double of a weak two bid in diamonds might be made with as few as 13 points, while a takeout double of a weak two spade bid promises about 15 points. A takeout double of a three-level preempt promises at least 15 or 16 points.

It is also true that the higher the preempt, the more likely it is that the double will be passed for penalties. This is because it becomes easier and easier to envision setting the contract, and the visions of a large penalty become clearer and clearer.

Balancing Doubles

Because of the somewhat high requirements for an immediate takeout double, the partner in the balancing position may make a takeout double with a somewhat lighter hand. For example, over a three level preempt, the balancing hand needs only about 12 points to make a takeout double.

OPTIONAL DOUBLES

Many players mistakenly call takeout doubles "optional doubles" because the partner of the doubler may opt to pass the double for penalties. This, however, is a misnomer that results from focusing attention on the partner of the doubler rather than on the doubler himself. Even the partner of a takeout doubler may opt to pass if he has an appropriate hand. The nature of an optional double is to be found in the strengths and pattern of the hand of the doubler.

A double of a preemptive bid is an optional double if it shows a good balanced hand that includes a measure of strength in the suit of the preempt. For example, over a three heart opening bid, the following hand is worth an optional double:

♠ A K x x   ♡ A J x   ◇ x x   ♣ A Q x x

The optional double is a type of cooperative double that invites the doubler's partner to pass for penalties. However, being balanced, it promises partner some support for his suit if he should need to remove the double. In general, however, the partner of the doubler is not expected to bid unless he has a good suit and a somewhat unbalanced hand.

Use of optional doubles, of course, precludes the partnership from using takeout doubles over preempts.

WEISS

The Weiss convention uses an optional double of preemptive bids, and a bid of the cheaper minor suit for takeout. *See* OPTIONAL DOUBLE.

The Weiss double invites the partner to pass for penalties. If partner has a long suit and does not wish to pass, the double promises support for his suit.

Using the Weiss convention and holding a hand such as

♠ A Q x x   ♡ x   ◇ K Q x x   ♣ A x x x

over a preemptive opening of three hearts by South, West could not make a takeout double. His proper action would be to bid four clubs for takeout.

The major disadvantage of the Weiss convention is that it precludes use of the takeout double. A second drawback is that when the preempt has been in diamonds or hearts, the use of the cheaper minor suit for takeout uses up valuable bidding room. A workable solution to avoid the loss of bidding space problem is for the partnership to agree to use the Weiss convention only over preempts in spades and clubs.

FISHBEIN

The Fishbein convention is a convention designed to allow the player sitting directly over the preemptive opener to make a penalty double. Thus, using Fishbein, West's double in the following auction would be for penalties:

South	West	North	East
3 ♠	Double		

The Fishbein convention allows the penalty double only by the player sitting over the preemptive bidder. Thus in the above auction, if West and North had both passed over South's preempt, East would not have been allowed to double for penalties. His double in that position would be for takeout.

To compensate for the loss of the use of the double as takeout, the Fishbein convention substitutes the cheapest bid over the preempt as a takeout bid. For example, in the auction

North	East	South	West
3 ♡	3 ♠		

East's three spade bid would not show a long spade suit, any more than a takeout double would have. The three spade bid simply asks West to bid. East might have a hand such as

    ♠ A x x x   ♡ x   ◇ A K x x   ♣ K Q x x

or

    ♠ Q x x   ♡ x   ◇ K Q x x x   ♣ A K x x

However, if East and South had passed in the above auction, a three spade bid by West would be natural.

The Fishbein convention has two principal flaws. The first is that it precludes the natural use of an overcall. The second problem is that the player sitting directly over the preempter must frequently make a decision without any help from his partner. His double would be a unilateral penalty double which his partner may not remove. And with a hand which is short in the suit of the preempt, he must bid to show length in the other suits, rather than doubling. This forecloses all possibility of penalizing the preemptor when the trump strength is not sitting directly over the preemptor.

CHEAPER MINOR TAKEOUT

A convention similar to the Fishbein convention uses a double by the player sitting directly over the preemptor as a penalty double, and uses the bid of the cheaper minor suit for takeout. The cheaper minor is, of course, clubs, unless the preempt has been made in clubs. The rationale for using the cheaper minor as the takeout suit is that frequently it will be desirable to make a natural overcall of three hearts over a three diamond preempt, or of three spades over a three heart preempt. For the strength requirements for the use of this convention, *see discussion under* TAKEOUT DOUBLES OF PREEMPTS.

CLUBS FOR TAKEOUT

A variation of the CHEAPER MINOR TAKEOUT convention is an agreement that the bid for takeout will always be made in clubs. This convention means that even when the preempt was in clubs, the next higher club bid would show a hand worth a takeout double. For the strength requirements for the use of this convention, *see discussion under* TAKEOUT DOUBLES OF PREEMPTS.

NOTRUMP FOR TAKEOUT

Another variation of the Fishbein convention uses the cheapest notrump bid for takeout. This suffers all of the disadvantages of the Fishbein convention. The notrump overcalls are useful as natural, descriptive bids, a two notrump bid showing about 16 to 18 points over a weak two bid, and a three notrump bid showing 18 or more points over a three-level preempt. For the strength requirements for the use of this convention, *see discussion under* TAKEOUT DOUBLES OF PREEMPTS.

TWO-SUITED TAKEOUTS OVER PREEMPTS

A convention designed to show a two-suited hand over a pre-emptive opening bid in a major suit uses a double for takeout, and a bid of four in a minor suit to show that minor suit and the unbid major suit.

For example, over an opening bid of three spades, a double would show tolerance for all unbid suits; a four club overcall would show hearts and clubs; a four diamond overcall would show hearts and diamonds. This convention can solve some difficult problems.

LEGHORN DIAMOND TAKEOUTS

The Leghorn Diamond system uses a double and a three no-trump bid to show two suited hands over a three-level pre-emptive opening. The double promises two suits of different rank; the notrump bid promises two suits of the same rank.

For example, over a three heart opening bid, a three no-trump overcall would show both minor suits. A double would show spades and an unspecified minor suit. Over a three club preempt, for example, the double would show both major suits, while the three notrump overcall would show diamonds and one of the major suits.

RIPSTRA AGAINST GAMBLING
THREE NOTRUMP

A double of a GAMBLING THREE NOTRUMP bid is strictly for penalties. Since the gambling three notrump bid is almost always based on a long minor suit, the defenders will usually have a large number of major suit cards. If they wish to compete over the three notrump opening, the most effective convention is probably Ripstra.

The Ripstra convention is a minor suit bid used as a take-out for the major suits. The Ripstra bid is made in whichever minor suit is better. For example, if South opens three notrump and West holds

♠ K Q x x x   ♡ K J x x   ♢ K Q   ♣ x x

West would bid four diamonds, Ripstra, asking his partner to bid a major suit.

Use of Ripstra can be quite advantageous on a hand such as this one, where the player sitting over the notrump bidder does not have an ace to lead, and thus may have only one chance to defeat the contract. The Ripstra convention gives the best choices in terms of taking out insurance against a fatal opening lead.

TAKEOUTS AGAINST FOUR-LEVEL PREEMPTS

Doubles of opening bids of four clubs, four diamonds and four hearts are takeout doubles. A double of a four spade preempt is a penalty double.

An overcall of four notrump after an opponent has opened the bidding with four of a major suit is a takeout bid. Standard practice is for the four notrump bid to be used as a minor suit takeout over four hearts since a takeout double could have been made to show spades. A four notrump bid over a four spade preempt would be a three-suited takeout bid. The four notrump bidder might have a hand such as

♠ x   ♡ A Q J x   ◇ A K J x   ♣ A K x x

A bid of four notrump over the opponent's preempt of four of a minor suit is generally considered not to be a takeout bid; it is considered to be either natural or Blackwood.

VI

Two- and Three-Suited Opening Bids

There are a number of conventions by which the opening bid shows that the opener does not have either a balanced hand or a one-suited hand. Some of these conventional openings show two-suited hands. See FLANNERY TWO DIAMONDS, FLANNERY TWO HEARTS, TWO DIAMONDS FOR MAJORS, TWO CLUBS FOR MINORS, TWO NOTRUMP FOR MINORS.

Hands containing three biddable suits are difficult to describe. Even if an opponent makes a bid in the short suit, a take-out double only suggests that the doubler has distribution approximating 4-4-4-1; he could easily have 4-4-3-2, or 5-4-3-1, or perhaps even 5-4-2-2 or 4-3-3-3. When the player who has three four-card suits, or two four-card suits and one five card suit, is the opening bidder, the job of describing his hand is formidable.

Some of the conventions described below use a conventional opening bid to show three-suited hands. Some of them can be used with hands that are either 4-4-4-1 or 5-4-4-0. See ROMAN TWO CLUBS, ROMAN TWO DIAMONDS. One, Neapolitan Two Diamonds, shows specifically 4-4-4-1 distribution. And one, Precision Two Diamonds, can be used even with a hand that is not always, strictly speaking, three suited, since it was devised to describe a type of hand that otherwise would be systemically impossible to open.

FLANNERY TWO DIAMONDS

The most widely used of the two-suited conventional opening bids is the Flannery convention. Flannery is designed to deal with the dilemma of which major suit to open when holding four spades and five hearts with less than the strength needed for a reverse. If the opening bid is one heart, the partnership might never bid the spade suit even if it is the partnership's best suit. If, for example, responder has three spades and one heart and a weak hand, he may respond one notrump to the one heart opening, and play the hand right there.

If the bidding is opened with one spade, however, and the responder has two or three cards in each major suit the partnership is not likely to end up in its best suit. For example, with three spades and three hearts and a modest hand, responder would raise opener's one spade bid to two, and the partnership would play in its four-three fit rather than its five-three fit. With two spades and two hearts, the responder might eventually take a preference to spades, leaving the partnership in its four-two fit.

The Flannery convention uses a two diamond opening to show a hand worth 11 to 15 high card points, with four spades and five hearts. The four minor suit cards may be distributed in any pattern.

With less than 10 points, responder signs off by bidding two hearts or two spades. If responder has no preference for a major but has a weak hand with six or more diamonds, he may pass the two diamond opening.

Responder may invite game by jumping to three hearts or three spades. In the alternative, responder may invite game by using a conventional two notrump response.

In order to learn more about opener's hand, responder may make the artificial bid of two notrump. This bid asks opener to

515

clarify his minor suit distribution. Opener rebids three clubs with a three-card club suit; he rebids three diamonds with a three-card diamond suit; he jumps to four clubs with a four-card club suit; he jumps to four diamonds with a four-card diamond suit.

If the opener has 4-5-2-2 distribution, he has three possible rebids. With 11 to 13 points, he rebids three hearts; with 14 to 15 points concentrated in the major suits he rebids three spades. With 14 to 15 points with his high cards concentrated largely in the minor suits opener may rebid three notrump.

Opener's rebids may help the partnership to assess game and slam prospects. For example, suppose responder held

♠ K Q x x   ♡ x   ◇ A K J x x   ♣ x x x

Responder would bid two notrump, hoping to hear opener bid three or four diamonds, showing by inference a singleton or a void in clubs. The responder could then use Blackwood to try for slam.

Some partnerships agree that if responder rebids three of a major after opener has shown his minor suit distribution, his bid invites game.

Responses of three of a minor suit ask the opener to rebid three notrump with one of the top three honors in the suit. Responder may use this bid to learn whether or not his own suit is solidified, or to learn whether or not the partnership has a stopper for notrump play. For example, responder could bid three clubs over two diamonds with either of the following hands:

[A] ♠ A x   ♡ x x   ◇ K x x   ♣ A K x x x x
or
[B] ♠ A x   ♡ x x   ◇ A K Q x x x   ♣ x x x

Responder may select a game in one of two ways. He may jump to four hearts or four spades. Or he may jump to four clubs or four diamonds. The latter bids are transfers. The four club bid requires the opener to rebid four hearts; the four diamond bid requires him to rebid four spades.

FLANNERY TWO HEARTS

The Flannery convention can be used with two hearts as the opening bids instead of two diamonds. The two heart opening would show four spades and five hearts.

If the responder has a weak hand and a preference for hearts he will pass the opening bid. Otherwise, all of the responses and rebids are the same as with Flannery Two Diamonds.

Using two hearts as the Flannery bid has three principal effects. First, it makes the Flannery bidder the declarer more often than when he uses the two diamond convention. Second, it frees the two diamond opening for some other use. Many partnerships which use Flannery Two Hearts use the two diamond opening to show three-suited hands. Finally, the use of the two heart bid as Flannery means that it cannot be used as a weak two heart bid.

TWO DIAMOND OPENING FOR MAJORS

As part of the Big Diamond system, a two diamond opening bid may be used to show a hand in the 14 to 16 point range with eight or nine cards in the major suits. The two diamond opening may be made with four-four in the majors, or with five of either major and four of the other. The distributions allowed are 4-4-3-2 and 5-4-2-2.

With a hand worth less than 10 points, responder may take minimum action. With a long diamond suit responder may pass. Responses of two hearts and two spades are preferences, and are not forcing. A response of three clubs shows a weak hand with a club suit; this bid is not forcing.

Responder may invite game with 10 or 11 points by bidding three diamonds, three hearts, or three spades. The jumps to three hearts and three spades show four card support. These are responder's only game invitational bids.

With 12 or more points, responder may force to game by bidding two notrump. This bid does not show a desire to play the hand in notrump; rather, it asks opener for further information about his distribution. Opener rebids as follows:

3 ♣ = three clubs, four-four in the majors

3 ♢ = three diamonds, four-four in the majors

3 ♡ = five hearts, two-two in the minors

3 ♠ = five spades, two-two in the minors

3 NT = good 16 points with 5-4-2-2 distribution; the five card suit could be either hearts or spades.

TWO CLUB OPENING FOR MINORS

In the Big Diamond system an opening bid of two clubs shows a 14 to 16 point hand with club and diamond suits. The distribution promised is 4-4-3-2 or 5-4-2-2. The two club opening is not forcing.

With a hand worth less than 10 or 11 points, responder will normally not look for game. He may pass if he has better clubs than diamonds; or he may bid two diamonds with better diamonds than clubs. If responder has a long major suit, he may make a non-forcing bid of two of his suit.

If responder has a hand with which he wants to invite game in a minor suit or notrump, he bids three clubs or three diamonds. If opener has a stopper in one of the major suits he will show it so that responder can decide whether or not the hand can be played in three notrump. This is responder's only way to invite game.

If responder has a game forcing hand with a long major suit, and he wants to know about the quality of opener's holding in that suit, he jumps to three of his suit. This bid is forcing and asks opener to describe his support in a series of steps as follows:

First   step = two small cards

Second step = three small cards

Third   step = two cards headed by the ace, king or queen

Fourth step = three cards headed by the ace, king or queen

If responder wants to force to game or to try for slam, he

can respond two notrump asking opener to clarify his strength and distribution. Opener's rebids are

3 ♣ = five clubs, two-two in the majors

3 ♢ = five diamonds, two-two in the majors

3 ♡ = three hearts, four-four in the minors

3 ♠ = three spades, four-four in the minors

3 NT = good 16 points, 5-4-2-2 distribution; the five-card suit could be either clubs or diamonds

TWO NOTRUMP OPENING FOR MINORS

The Two Notrump Minor Suit convention uses a two notrump opening bid to show a hand with at least five cards in each minor suit. Vulnerable, the two notrump opening shows 14 to 16 points; not vulnerable the opening may be made on 10 to 13 points.

The Two notrump opening promises that the opener's high cards are concentrated in the minor suits, and that the texture of the suits is good. For example

[A] ♠ x x   ♡ x   ◇ K J 10 x x   ♣ K Q J 10 x

[B] ♠ x   ♡ x x   ◇ A K 10 9 x   ♣ A K Q x x

[C] ♠ K x   ♡ x   ◇ K Q J x x   ♣ J 10 9 x x

[D] ♠ x   ♡ x x   ◇ A K x x x   ♣ A Q x x x

Hand A is the minimum hand that may be opened two notrump not vulnerable. Hand B is the maximum that may be opened with two notrump vulnerable. Hands C and D, however, are not appropriate for two notrump openings, Hand C because not all of the high cards are in the minor suits; and Hand D because the minor suits have poor texture.

Responses

If responder has a weak hand, his normal action is to take a preference between clubs and diamonds at the three level. If he has a weak hand with length in the major suits and no three-card or longer minor suit, he is allowed to pass the two notrump opening. If responder has one long major suit and a hand not worth game, he may bid three of his major suit. This bid is not forcing.

With four or more cards in one of the minor suits and a hand with which he wants either to preempt or to play game, responder may jump to four or five of the minor. His jump to the four level is preemptive rather than invitational.

If responder wants to explore for slam, his only recourse is Blackwood, four notrump.

ROMAN TWO DIAMONDS

A Roman Two diamond opening bid shows a hand worth 17 to 20 high card points. It promises either 4-4-4-1 or 5-4-4-0 distribution. The short suit is not identified until the opener rebids.

In order to try for game opposite a two diamond opening, responder needs about a 7 point hand. If responder has less than 7 points, he bids his best suit; if he has no real preference, he bids two hearts. If the suit bid by responder happens to be the opener's singleton, opener will bid the next higher suit, asking the responder to choose again.

If the suit bid by responder is one of opener's four card suits, opener will usually pass. However, if he has a maximum, he might well raise. For example:

♠ A K x x   ♡ A x x x   ◇ x   ♣ A K J x

After this hand is opened with two diamonds, if the responder bids a non-forcing two spades, opener will surely raise.

If responder has 7 or more points, he bids two notrump to make investigations toward game. The notrump response does not suggest that the hand should be played in notrump; it merely asks the opener to bid the suit in which he is short. For example:

Opener	Responder
2 ◇	2 Notrump
3 ♡	

Opener shows a singleton heart.

After learning which suit is opener's short suit, responder can invite a game by bidding one of opener's suits, or can place the hand in game. If the suit in which opener announced shortness is responder's only long suit, responder rebids three no-trump.

When the Opponents Interfere

If an opponent overcalls over the two diamond bid, the responder will pass with a weak hand unless he has some reason to believe he has a fit with one of the opener's suits. If, for example, responder had two suits of his own, at least one of them would fit with opener. In this situation responder may bid his cheaper suit freely.

If responder has a hand that is worth a game try, he should bid two notrump just as he would have had there been no over-call. Or if responder has strong trumps, he can double the overcall for penalties. Opener should not remove the double unless he is void in the overcaller's suit.

ROMAN TWO CLUBS

A Roman Two Club opening shows a hand worth 11 to 16 high card points, and either 4-4-4-1 or 5-4-4-0 distribution. The short suit is not disclosed until the opener rebids.

The responder needs about 10 or 11 points to try for a game. With less he simply tries to find a part-score resting place by bidding his best suit over two clubs. Lacking any substantial preference as among his suits, he bids the cheapest. If the suit he bids is one of opener's four card suits opener will usually pass, although he may raise if he has a maximum.

If responder has bid opener's short suit, opener will bid the next higher ranking suit, asking responder to bid his second choice. For example, suppose opener's and responder's hands were as follows:

(Opener)
♠ K J x x   ♡ A K x x   ◇ x   ♣ Q x x x

(Responder)
♠ Q x x   ♡ x x   ◇ A J x x x   ♣ x x x

The bidding would proceed

Opener	Responder
2 ♣	2 ◇
2 ♡	2 ♠
Pass	

Responder bid two diamonds, looking for a fit. Opener's two heart bid showed that diamonds was his short suit. Responder took a preference to spades. Had his spade and heart suits been reversed, he would have passed opener's two heart bid.

With a strong enough hand to try for a game, responder bids two notrump. This response does not signify a desire to play in notrump. It asks the opener to identify his short suit. Opener complies by bidding that suit.

If responder has four or more cards in one of opener's suits, he may either bid a game, or invite game by bidding three of that suit. For example:

Opener	Responder
2 ♣	2 Notrump
3 ♡	3 ♠

If responder's only suit is the opener's short suit, responder signs off with a bid of three notrump. Conceivably if responder has a very long and semi-solid suit he might simply pass opener's short suit bid. For example, if responder had a hand such as

♠ K x   ♡ x x   ◇ A Q J 9 x x   ♣ x x x

the bidding might go

Opener	Responder
2 ♣	2 Notrump
3 ◇	Pass

When the Opponents Interfere

If the opponent overcalls over the two club bid, responder generally passes with a weak balanced hand or a weak one-suited hand. If he has two long suits, he should bid naturally in order to compete, since he knows that opener has four-card support for at least one of his suits.

If responder has a hand worth a game try, he should bid two notrump just as he would have without the overcall. Alternatively, with strong trumps, responder can double the overcall for penalties. Opener should not remove the double unless he is void in the suit of the overcall.

TWO DIAMOND OPENING AS MINIMUM THREE-SUITER

The ROMAN CLUB SYSTEM is able to devote its two club opening bid to three-suited hands because, using the canape style of bidding, it does not have to open two clubs in order to show a long club suit. It can open any other suit and rebid clubs to show a long club suit. Partnerships not using the canape style usually cannot afford to spend their two club opening on three-suited hands. If the partnership is using a forcing one club opening, it needs a two club opening to show a club suit. If the partnership is not using a forcing one club opening but is using weak two-bids, it needs the two club opening to show a strong forcing hand.

Some of these partnerships, wanting to have a bid that promises a three-suited hand, use a two diamond opening to show a hand of average opening strength, with 5-4-4-0 or 4-4-4-1 distribution.

When two diamonds is used to show the three-suited hand in the 12 to 16 point range, the responder needs about 10 or 11 points in order to try for a game. With less he looks for a safe part score; with more, he forces to game. The mechanics of responding and rebidding are the same as for the ROMAN TWO CLUB and ROMAN TWO DIAMOND openings.

NEAPOLITAN TWO DIAMONDS

The Neapolitan Two Diamond opening, which is part of the Blue Team system, is made with a very strong three-suited hand. The two diamond bid shows 17 to 24 high card points, and its distribution is specifically 4-4-4-1, with the singleton temporarily undisclosed.

Once the two diamond opening has been made, the responder takes charge of the hand. He has a variety of alternatives open to him, depending on what type of hand he has. If he has a very weak hand, in the 0 to 5 point range, and has at least three spades, he bids two spades. The opener will pass if spades is not his singleton; if spades is his singleton, opener will bid two notrump, allowing the responder to choose a suit at the three level.

If the responder has a six-card suit, or has a hand with more than five points he has a choice of relay bids or descriptive bids to ask the opener to describe his hand further.

Responding with a Good Six-Card Suit

If the responder has a six-card suit headed by three honors, or by two of the top three honors, and a hand of about 6 or 7 points, his proper response is two notrump. The two notrump bid does not specify which is the responder's six-card suit, it simply states that he has one, and asks the opener to identify his singleton.

Opener shows his singleton by bidding the suit below the singleton. For example, with a singleton heart the opener would rebid three diamonds. With a singleton club, the opener would rebid three spades.

After opener has identified his singleton, responder bids the minimum number of his suit, with one exception. If the responder's suit is clubs and the opener has bid three spades showing a singleton club, the responder must bid three notrump. After the responder has disclosed his suit, both members of the partnership know whether or not the hand is a misfit.

If the opener's singleton is in the responder's suit, the opener has a choice of actions. If he has a minimum hand he should pass; if the suit in question is clubs and the responder has bid three notrump to show it, the opener may retreat to four clubs. If the opener has a strong hand for his two diamond opening, he may bid three notrump or game in the responder's suit. He uses his judgment as to which contract seems more attainable.

If the opener's singleton is not in the responder's suit, the partnership is committed to game, and may explore for slam. If the opener has a minimum hand and thinks slam is a poor prospect, he simply bids game in the responder's suit.

If the opener thinks that slam is a real possibility, he bids one of his side controls, asking the responder to bid a singleton if he has it. Lacking any singleton, the responder will return to his suit.

For example, suppose the opener has the following hand:

♠ x   ♡ K Q x x   ◇ A x x x   ♣ A K J x

If his partner responds with two notrump, showing a good six card suit, opener must rebid three hearts, showing that his singleton is in spades. If the responder now bids three spades, showing that spades is his six card suit, the opener will pass, since game is unlikely. The auction will have gone

Opener	Responder
2 ◇	2 Notrump
3 ♡	3 ♠
Pass	

If the responder has bid a suit other than spades, however, the opener will have visions of slam. Thus the auction might proceed:

Opener	Responder
2 ◇	2 Notrump
3 ♡	4 ♡
5 ♣	5 ◇
6 ♡	

Opener's five club bid showed the ace of clubs and indicated an interest in slam. It specifically asked the responder to bid a singleton if he had one. Responder's five diamond bid showed a singleton diamond, and opener was able to bid six hearts. If the responder had as little as the queen of clubs, or four spades, he should be able to bring home the slam.

Responding with a Fair Six-Card Suit

If the responder has a hand worth 5 to 6 points containing only a fair six-card suit (as compared with the more solid suit shown by the two notrump response), his proper action is to bid three of his suit. The responder might hold a hand such as

♠ K 10 x x x x   ♡ x x   ◇ Q x x x   ♣ x

If the responder's bid is in the suit in which the opener has a singleton, the opener will pass if he has a minimum for his two diamond opening. If he has a good maximum, such as

♠ Q   ♡ A K x x   ◇ A K x x   ♣ A Q J x

he may raise the responder to game despite the misfit.

If the opener has four-card support for responder's suit, the partnership is forced to game and opener should assess the prospects for slam. If slam seems out of the question, he should simply bid the game. For example, if the opener has a hand such as

♠ Q x x x   ♡ A K Q x   ◇ x   ♣ A K Q x

and the responder has bid three spades, opener will raise to four spades. Since the responder cannot have a hand with which the partnership is certain not to lose a trump trick, slam should not be bid.

If, however, slam is not out of the question, the opener cue-bids his singleton (not the suit below, this time). This cue-bid asks the responder to clarify his hand by showing whether he has the ace or king of trumps, or neither; and if he has the ace or king of trumps, he is asked to reveal whether or not he has a side singleton. The responder conveys this information in three steps, as follows:

First   step = no ace or king of trumps

Second   step = ace or king of trumps, but no side singleton

Third   step = ace or king of trumps and a side singleton

Suppose the opener holds

♠ K x x x ♡ A K x x ◇ x ♣ A K x x

Opener simply wants to know whether the responder has the ace of trumps, for if he has opener can virtually count twelve tricks. The auction might proceed

Opener	Responder
2 ◇	3 ♠
4 ◇	4 ♠ or 4 Notrump
6 ♠	

If responder had bid four hearts over the four diamond cue-bid, showing trumps no better than Q J x x x x, opener would have signed off in four spades. However, when responder shows the ace, opener can confidently bid the slam.

The Two Heart Relay Response

Most frequently in response to the two diamond opening, the responder will have neither a 0 to 5 point hand with spades, nor a 5 to 7 point hand with a fair-to-good six card suit. His proper course of action on all other hands, weak or strong, is to respond two hearts. The two heart response does not show anything about the responder's heart holding or about his strength; it is just a relay bid asking the opener for clarification. The opener's rebids show whether he has a minimum, i.e., 17 to 20 points, or a maximum, i.e., 21 to 24 points; with minor exceptions the opener bids the suit below his singleton.

The complete schedule of opener's rebids over the two heart response is as follows:

2 ♠ = singleton in either major suit, 17 to 20 points

2 NT = singleton club, 17 to 20 points

3 ♣ = singleton diamond, 17 to 20 points

3 ◇ = singleton heart, 21 to 24 points

3 ♡ = singleton spade, 21 to 24 points

3 ♠ = singleton club, 21 to 24 points

3 NT = singleton diamond, 21 to 24 points

If the opener's rebid has been two spades, showing a singleton in one of the major suits and a minimum hand, the responder may make a further relay bid of two notrump to obtain further information. Opener rebids three clubs with a singleton heart, or rebids three diamonds or three hearts with a singleton spade. Opener chooses the three diamond bid when he has 17 or 18 points and a singleton spade, and the three heart bid when he has 19 or 20 points and a singleton spade.

If opener has shown a singleton club or diamond and a minimum hand in response to the two heart relay, or if he has shown a singleton heart and a minimum hand by his responses to the two heart and two notrump relays, the responder can ask opener to narrow his point count range. Responder does this by bidding the suit in which the opener has shown a singleton. The first step by opener shows 17 or 18 points, and the second step shows 19 or 20 points. For example,

(A) *Opener*   *Responder*
    2 ◇   2 ♡
    2 Notrump   3 ♣
    3 ♡

(B) *Opener*
    2 ◇
    2 ♠
    3 ♣
    3 ♠

Responder
2 ♡
2 Notrump
3 ♡

In Auction A, the two notrump rebid by opener showed a singleton club and a hand worth 17 to 20 points in high cards. Responder's bid of three clubs, opener's singleton, asked whether opener had the top or the bottom of the range he had shown. Opener's three heart rebid, the second step, showed 19 to 20 points.

In Auction (B), the opener's two spade rebid said his singleton was in one of the major suits; his three club rebid over the two notrump relay said his singleton was in hearts. The three heart bid by responder asked opener about his point count; opener's three spade bid, the first step, showed 17 to 18 points.

Usually by this time, if not earlier, the responder can set the final contract. However, if he wants to explore further for a slam after opener has disclosed whether he has the top or the bottom of his 17 to 20 point range, responder can ask the opener precisely how many controls he has. Responder accomplishes this by again bidding the opener's known singleton. Notice that if opener has a singleton spade, he narrows his point range in the process of identifying his singleton. If responder wants to know about opener's controls after the latter has shown a singleton spade, he does so by cue-bidding the singleton spade immediately after it has been shown:

Opener
    2 ◇
    2 ♠
    3 ♡

Responder
2 ♡
2 Notrump
3 ♠

Since opener's three heart rebid has at once specified a singleton spade and 19 or 20 points, responder need not ask for further clarification of opener's point range. Responder's three spade bid asks about controls.

Counting each ace as two controls and each king as one, the opener shows his controls in a series of five steps. If the opener's first rebid has shown a hand in the 17 to 20 point range, the first step shows four controls:

First	step	=	four controls
Second	step	=	five controls
Third	step	=	six controls
Fourth	step	=	seven controls
Fifth	step	=	eight controls

For example, in the auction

Opener	Responder
2 ♦	2 ♡
2 ♠	2 Notrump
3 ♣	3 ♡
3 ♠	4 ♡
4 Notrump	

Opener's two spade bid showed 17 to 20 points, with a singleton in one of the major suits; his three club rebid said the singleton was a heart. Responder's three heart bid asked opener to narrow his range; opener's three spade bid showed 17 or 18 points. Responder's four heart bid asked about controls, and opener's four notrump bid, the second step, showed five controls. Opener's hand might be

♠ A K x x   ♡ x   ◇ K Q x x   ♣ K Q x x

If the opener's first response to two hearts has shown a hand in the 21 to 24 point range, the responder can ask about controls directly over the singleton-showing response without first asking for a narrowing of the point count range. Again, opener shows his controls in a series of five steps; this time, however, his first step will show six controls:

> First   step   =   six controls
>
> Second step   =   seven controls
>
> Third   step   =   eight controls
>
> Fourth step   =   nine controls
>
> Fifth   step   =   ten controls

For example, in the auction

Opener	*Responder*
2 ◇	2 ♡
3 ◇	3 ♡
3 ♠	

opener's three diamond rebid showed a singleton heart with 21 to 24 points. Responder's three heart bid, therefore, immediately asked about opener's controls. Opener's bid of three spades, the first step, showed six controls. He might have a hand such as

♠ A K Q x   ♡ x   ◇ K Q J x   ♣ A Q x x

After the opener has revealed how many controls he has, if the responder bids opener's singleton yet another time, he asks how many queens opener holds. Using the standard method, opener rebids the first step with no queens, the second step with one queen, the third step with two queens, and so forth. An alternative way of agreeing to show queens is for the opener to bid notrump if he holds no queens, or to bid a suit in which he has a queen; if he has two queens he will bid the less expensive queen.

Suppose the responder held the following hand in response to a two diamond opening:

♠ K Q x   ♡ A x x x x   ◇ A x x   ♣ x x

So long as opener does not have a singleton in one of the major suits, responder can visualize a slam easily, perhaps even a grand slam. His mission is to find out as much as possible about opener's hand. Suppose the auction proceeds:

Opener	Responder
2 ◇	2 ♡
3 ♣	3 ◇
3 ♡	4 ◇

Opener's rebids have shown a 17 to 18 point hand with a singleton diamond. The question now becomes how many controls opener has.

If opener has only four controls, a grand slam will be out of the question; if he has five or six, the grand slam will depend on the opener's holding in the heart suit. If the opener shows six controls, by bidding four notrump in the auction above, responder will know that opener's hand includes the ace of spades, the king of hearts, and the ace and king of clubs. If it also includes the queen of hearts, the grand slam should be laydown.

Using standard step responses to show queens, the complete auction could be

Opener	Responder
2 ◇	2 ♡
3 ♣	3 ◇
3 ♡	4 ◇
4 Notrump	5 ◇
5 ♡	6 ♡

When opener bids five hearts, the first step, to show no queens, responder places the final contract at six hearts.

If the opener had bid five spades in the above auction, showing one queen, responder still would have bid just six hearts, not knowing whether opener's queen was in clubs or hearts. (Use of the alternative queen-showing method would solve this problem, since opener would bid five hearts with the queen of hearts, or six clubs with the queen of clubs and no queen of hearts, or five notrump with no queens.) Over responder's bid of six hearts after opener had shown one queen, if opener's queen is the queen of hearts, opener should, for the first time in the entire auction, exercise his judgment and bid seven hearts, since responder was probing for a grand slam and must have been worried about the queen of trumps.

Notice that the responder has such complete control of the auction, that the opener does not know until responder sets the final contract, here at the six-level, which suit responder wants to play in.

PRECISION TWO DIAMONDS

Using the Precision Club system, the one club opening shows at least 16 points, and opening bids of one of a major suit show at least five cards. Most hands worth less than 16 points that contain no five-card major suit will therefore be opened with one notrump or one diamond; however, hands that are very short in the diamond suit are nearly impossible to bid naturally.

The Precision two diamond opening shows a hand worth 11 to 15 high card points with at most a singleton diamond, and no other suitable opening bid. The most common distributions for this opening are 4-4-1-4 and 4-4-0-5, although two diamonds may also be opened with a hand distributed 4-3-1-5 or 3-4-1-5 if the five card club suit is too weak for a two club opening. For example, opener might have either

[A] ♠ A K x x   ♥ A x x x   ⋄ x   ♣ A x x x

or

[B] ♠ A J x   ♥ A Q x x   ⋄ x   ♣ K x x x x

With Hand A and Hand B, the proper opening bid is two diamonds. However, with a hand such as

♠ A Q x x   ♥ x x x   ⋄ x   ♣ A K x x x

the club suit is strong enough for the hand to be opened two clubs.

Responses

The two diamond bid, even though it shows at most a singleton diamond, is not forcing. The responder is allowed to pass if he has ten points or less with at least six diamonds. If the responder has 0 to 7 points with fewer than six diamonds, he makes a minimum bid in another suit. This response is not forcing.

The only forcing response to a two diamond opening is two notrump. The two notrump response shows at least 8 high card points, but does not show a desire to play in notrump. Rather the two notrump response asks the opener to describe his hand further in terms of its distribution and point count.

Opener rebids over the two notrump response as follows:

3 ♣ shows three spades, four hearts, one diamond and five clubs

3 ◇ shows four spades, three hearts, one diamond and five clubs

3 ♡ shows 4-4-1-4 distribution with 11 to 13 high card points

3 ♠ shows 4-4-1-4 distribution with 14 to 15 high card points

3 Notrump shows 4-4-1-4 distribution with 14 to 15 high card points, including the singleton ace or king of diamonds

4 ♣ shows 4-4-0-5 distribution with 11 to 13 high card points

4 ◇ shows 4-4-0-5 distribution with 14 to 15 high card points

If the opener has rebid three clubs or three diamonds over the two notrump response, responder may bid the cheapest suit to ask opener to specify his point range. The opener's cheapest bid shows 11 to 13 points, and the next cheapest bid shows 14 to 15 points. For example, in the auction

Opener	Responder
2 ◇	2 Notrump
3 ◇	3 ♡
3 ♠	

Opener's three diamond rebid shows 4-3-1-5 distribution, and responder's three heart bid asks how strong opener's hand is. Opener's three spade bid, the cheapest bid, shows 11 to 13 points.

VII

Offensive Preemptive Conventions

Preempts may be made on hands widely varying in strength and distribution. Three of the five conventions described below are transfer preempts, designed to help the partner of the preemptor, when he has a strong hand, to know whether or not to try for slam. See FOUR CLUBS AND FOUR DIAMONDS AS STRONG TRANSFERS, FOUR CLUBS AND FOUR DIAMONDS AS WEAK TRANSFERS, FOUR NOTRUMP AS WEAK MINOR PREEMPT. Another convention is sometimes used in aid of the transfer preempts. See THREE NOTRUMP AS WEAK MINOR PREEMPT. The Gambling Three Notrump convention is just what its name implies.

FOUR CLUBS AND FOUR DIAMONDS
AS STRONG TRANSFERS

Using standard methods, preemptive openings of four of a major suit may be made on a wide variety of hands. For example, four spades might be opened with a hand such as

[A] ♠ A Q J x x x x x   ♡ x   ◇ x x   ♣ x x

Or, opposite a passed hand, four spades might be opened with a hand such as

[B] ♠ A K Q x x x x   ♡ x   ◇ A J x x   ♣ x

With Hand A a slam is a remote possibility. With Hand B, however, even opposite a partner who has passed, slam is possible if responder has either two aces and a doubleton diamond, or one ace and the king of diamonds.

To distinguish the strong major preempts from the weak ones, some partnerships use an opening bid of four clubs to transfer to four hearts, and an opening bid of four diamonds to transfer to four spades. As most frequently used, the openings of four clubs and four diamonds show stronger hands than the direct openings of four hearts and four spades.

After the four club or four diamond openings some partnerships allow the responder to decide which hand should be the declarer. If responder wants to be declarer, he simply bids four of the opener's true suit. If responder wants opener to be declarer, he bids four of the next ranking suit as a relay, transferring back to the opener.

For example, opposite a four diamond opening, showing a good four spade preempt, responder might have either of the following hands:

[C] ♠ x x   ♡ Q x x x   ◇ x x x   ♣ A x x x

[D] ♠ x   ♡ K x x x   ◇ K x x x   ♣ K x x x

With Hand C, responder has no tenaces to protect, so he makes the relay bid of four hearts, telling his partner to bid four spades. With Hand D, however, it is better for the lead to come up to responder's kings rather than through them. Therefore, with Hand D, responder bids four spades.

Although responder's relay, transferring back to opener, does not show slam interest, responder may try for slam over opener's rebid of his suit.

Asking Bid Responses

Some partnerships have agreed to regularize the four club and four diamond openings as much as possible in certain respects, and to use the relay bid (four diamonds over four clubs, or four hearts over four diamonds) as an asking bid rather than just a re-transfer.

Some partnerships agree that the four club and four diamond openings guarantee that the opener does not have two quick losers in more than one suit, and that he does have the king of his trump suit. For example:

[A] ♠ A Q J x x x x   ♡ K x   ◇ x x   ♣ K x

[B] ♠ A K Q J x x x   ♡ K x   ◇ x x   ♣ x x

[C] ♠ A K x x x x x   ♡ K x   ◇ x x x   ♣ x

Hand A is missing the king of trumps; using these methods this hand would be opened with one spade. Hand B has two quick losers in two suits; it too should be opened with one spade rather than four diamonds. Hand C meets all of the requirements for a four diamond opening.

Using these methods, a response in the relay suit asks the opener to identify the suit in which he has two quick losers. Thus, in the auction

Opener	Responder
4 ♣	4 ◇
4 ♠	

Opener shows that he has at least two losing spades.

If opener has no suit in which he has two quick losers he may rebid his suit. However, if his suit is solid, opener may capitalize on the fact that he does not have two quick losers by rebidding four notrump, which is Blackwood. For example, suppose opener's and responder's hands were as follows:

(Opener)
♠ x   ♡ A K Q x x x x x   ◇ K x x   ♣ x

(Responder)
♠ A x x x   ♡ x x   ◇ A x x   ♣ A K x x

The bidding could go

Opener	Responder
4 ♣	4 ◇
4 Notrump	5 ♠
5 Notrump	6 ◇
7 Notrump	

FOUR CLUBS AND FOUR DIAMONDS
AS WEAK TRANSFERS

Most partnerships which use four club and four diamond openings to show heart and spade preempts, use the four club and four diamond openings to show the stronger preempts. Their rationale is that the lower opening is more desirable with the type of hand that is more likely to produce a slam, leaving the partnership more room to explore, and that the higher opening is more desirable with the more preemptive type hand.

Some partnerships, however, prefer to use the four club and four diamond openings to show the weaker major suit preempts. Their reasoning is that transferring with the weaker hand ensures that the stronger hand will be the declarer. This may have value with respect to the opening lead, and may serve to conceal from the opponents the best line of defense.

GAMBLING THREE NOTRUMP

The Gambling Three Notrump convention is an opening bid of three notrump based on a long solid minor suit. The typical Gambling three notrump opening has at most one stopper outside of the running minor:

♠ x   ♡ Q x x   ◇ A K Q J x x x   ♣ x x

With scattered values, responder should pass. If responder is quite weak, however, or if three notrump is doubled and responder lacks stoppers, he may bid four clubs to escape. The four club bid shows nothing about responder's holding in clubs. If opener's suit is clubs he will pass; if his suit is diamonds, he will bid four diamonds.

If responder wants to play game in a minor suit rather than in notrump, he may jump to five clubs. Again, this club bid does not mean that responder has clubs; he expects opener to pass if clubs is his suit, or to bid five diamonds if diamonds is his suit. Similarly, if responder wants to play in a minor suit slam, he jumps to six clubs. Opener will pass if he has a club suit or bid six diamonds with a diamond suit.

A bid of four of a major suit by the responder is natural, showing a self-sufficient six-card or longer suit. Opener is required to pass.

Responses of four diamonds and four notrump are special responses. Four notrump may be used as Blackwood, with opener's ace-showing responses amended to take into account the fact that the ace of one suit has already been shown by his opening bid. Thus a response of five clubs would show no *additional* aces, and a response of five diamonds would show one additional ace.

A bid of four diamonds may be used to ask the opener to bid his better major suit. Thereafter any bid by responder would be a slam invitation.

A response of five notrump may be used to ask opener to bid a grand slam if he has anything extra—such as an eighth card in his suit, or a king or a queen on the side. Responder might have a hand such as

♠ A J x   ♡ A K x   ◇ x x   ♣ A K x x x

THREE NOTRUMP AS WEAK
MINOR PREEMPT

Some of the partnerships which use four club and four diamond opening bids to show major suit preempts use an opening bid of three notrump to replace the lost four club and four diamond openings. A typical hand might be

♠ x   ♡ x x   ◇ K Q J x x x x x   ♣ J x

In order to pass the three notrump opening, responder must have a relatively strong hand with a high card in each minor suit for safety. In order to retreat from three notrump, responder bids four clubs; opener will pass if his suit is clubs, or will bid four diamonds if diamonds is his suit.

Other responses except four notrump and five notrump may be used as they are over GAMBLING THREE NOTRUMP OPENINGS. Over the three notrump bid as a weak preempt, the four notrump Blackwood bid asks about aces in accordance with the normal schedule of responses. And a jump response to five notrump would be a normal GRAND SLAM FORCE bid, asking opener to bid seven with two of the top three honors in his suit.

FOUR NOTRUMP AS WEAK
MINOR PREEMPT

In order to distinguish a high level minor suit preempt that has a broken suit and no slam interest, from one that has solid values, some partnerships use an opening bid of four notrump as a minor suit preempt. Using this convention, the four notrump opening shows no slam interest, and the hand probably has fewer than five controls, counting aces as two and kings as one.

The four notrump opening might be made on a hand such as

♠ K x   ♡ x   ♢ K Q x x x x x x   ♣ x x

The responder is asked to bid five clubs over four notrump. If opener's suit is clubs he will pass; if his suit is diamonds he will bid five diamonds.

The use of the four notrump convention allows the opener to reserve the five club and five diamond openings for hands with solid values such as

♠ A x x   ♡ —   ♢ A K Q x x x x x   ♣ x x

VIII

Conventions for the Defenders

There are a number of conventions that are designed to help the side that has not bought, or clearly is not going to buy, the contract. These conventions fall into three general categories: (a) lead-directing doubles that ask the opening leader to start a particular suit; (b) opening lead conventions that lay down rules as to which card should usually be led from a given suit; and (c) signals after the opening lead has been made.

Specific opening lead problems fall into three general groupings. One question is which card should be led from two or more touching honors. See ACE FROM ACE-KING, RUSINOW, QUEEN FROM ACE-KING-QUEEN, JOURNALIST HONOR LEADS AGAINST NOTRUMP, JACK TEN OR NINE TO SHOW 0 OR 2 HIGHER HONORS. A second question is which card should be led from a suit headed by one honor or non-touching honors. See THIRD BEST LEADS, JOURNALIST SPOT CARD LEADS AGAINST SUIT CONTRACTS, JOURNALIST SPOT CARD LEADS AGAINST NOTRUMP CONTRACTS. A third question is which card should be led from a suit headed by no honors at all. See MUD, ROMAN MUD, JOURNALIST LEADS FROM HONORLESS SUITS.

After the opening lead has been made, a defender can attempt, by the order in which he plays his cards, to give his partner an idea of how the hand should be defended. He may try to encourage or discourage the lead of a certain suit. See ATTITUDE

SIGNALS, UPSIDE DOWN SIGNALS, ODD-EVEN SIGNALS. Or he may attempt to disclose how many cards he has in a certain suit, perhaps by inference giving his partner information about another suit. *See* COUNT SIGNALS, TRUMP ECHO, FOSTER ECHO, BECHGAARD SIGNALS. Or he may play a certain card in one suit to indicate that he wants a certain other suit led. *See* SUIT PREFERENCE SIGNALS, REVOLVING DISCARDS, ODD-EVEN DISCARDS.

LEAD-DIRECTING DOUBLES

When the opponents are en route to game or slam, they frequently choose to cue-bid suits in which they have some high card strength but not complete control, or to cue-bid short suits in which they have ruffing values but not high cards, or to make asking bids in suits in which they have neither top cards nor prompt ruffing values. And often an opponent may make an artificial response to a control-seeking inquiry, by chance bidding a suit in which he has less than full control.

When an opponent makes such a cue-bid or artificial response or asking bid, the next player may be able to double to suggest to his partner that the suit doubled would be an appropriate opening lead. Such a double is obviously not intended as a penalty double since the opponents are not expected to play the hand in their cue-bid or other artificial bid. However, the doubler should take care that the suit he doubles is one that the opponents cannot play in.

In addition to the information conveyed by the double of such a bid, information is gained when the partner of the opening leader has had an opportunity to make a double but has chosen not to do so. In this situation, the inference is that the suit of the cue-bid is not a lead that is clearly desirable from the point of view of the partner of the opening leader.

The conventional lead directing doubles described below are used after the opponents have arrived in their slam or game contracts. The prudent use of these doubles can be a gold mine. *See* LIGHTNER SLAM DOUBLES, DOUBLES OF THREE NOTRUMP, FISHER DOUBLES.

LIGHTNER SLAM DOUBLES

The double, by the player not on lead, of a slam voluntarily bid by the opponents with the expectation that it will be made rather than as a sacrifice, is not designed primarily to increase the penalty for setting the opponents. Since the opponents usually will not fail by more than one trick, the value of making a pure penalty double is marginal. The more lucrative use of the double is to call for a lead that is likely to set the contract. The Lightner Slam Double is such a double.

The Lightner slam double asks the partner of the doubler to make an aggressive but unusual lead. The opening leader is on no account to make the passive lead of a trump. Nor is he to make the routine lead of a suit bid by either himself or his partner.

The order of priorities usually assigned to the lead possibilities after a Lightner double are these:

(a) If a side suit has been bid by the dummy, the opening lead should be in that suit. If dummy has bid more than one side suit, the opening lead should be in the first side suit bid by dummy.

(b) If dummy has not bid a side suit but declarer has bid a side suit, the opening lead should be in declarer's side suit.

(c) If neither dummy nor declarer has bid a side suit, the opening lead should be in an unbid suit. Usually the opening leader's longest unbid suit is most appropriate, since the doubler generally has a void and wants to ruff the first round of the suit.

For example, in the auction

(A)

North	East	South	West
1 ♣	1 ♠	2 ♡	Pass
4 ♡	Pass	5 ◇	Pass
6 ♡	Double	Pass	Pass
Pass			

East's double forbids West to lead East's suit, spades. Instead, West should lead the side suit bid by the dummy, clubs. If the auction has gone,

(B)

North	East	South	West
1 ◇	1 ♡	2 ♡	Pass
3 ♠	Pass	4 Notrump	Pass
5 ♡	Pass	6 ♠	Double
Pass	Pass	Pass	

South, the dummy, has not bid a side suit. He has made a cue-bid showing strength, and probably length in both unbid suits. However, he has not actually bid a side suit. North, the declarer, has bid a side suit, diamonds, and West's double calls for a diamond lead.

Suppose that West holds

♠ x ♡ A K Q x x x ◇ x ♣ J x x x x

and the auction has gone

South	West	North	East
1 ♠	2 ♡	3 ♠	Pass
6 ♠	Pass	Pass	Double
Pass	Pass	Pass	

East's double calls for an unusual lead. West is not allowed to lead a heart, which would be a normal lead. Without the double, West might have thought of leading his singleton diamond, attempting to get a ruff. However, East's double cannot be based primarily on the ace of diamonds, because East cannot know that West has a singleton diamond. East's double suggests that he is void in a side suit other than the suit bid by West. Therefore, West should lead a club.

Using Lightner slam doubles places a burden on the partner of the opening leader not to double simply because he thinks he can beat the contract. He should not make a pure penalty double of the slam without considering the effect his double will have on his partner's lead. For example, suppose East has a hand such as

♠ x x　　♡ A K x x x x x　　◇ A x　　♣ x x

and the auction has gone

North	East	South	West
1 ♣	1 ♡	1 ♠	Pass
3 ♣	Pass	4 ♠	Pass
4 Notrump	5 ♡	5 ♠	Pass
6 ♠			

Since neither North nor South made a cue-bid in hearts and since North used Blackwood, East expects to be able to cash two aces to defeat the slam. However, if he doubles, West will lead a club, and the red aces are likely to disappear in a landslide of clubs. Thus, East must pass and forego the slight increase of penalty in order to insure that there is any penalty at all.

The partner of the opening leader must also consider

whether or not his Lightner Slam double may frighten the opponents out of the slam that can be beaten and into one that can be made. If the opponents realize that a ruff will defeat their slam they may be able to neutralize the void by playing in no-trump, or by playing an alternative suit contract from the other side of the table, putting the hand with the void on opening lead.

Further, some partnerships have agreed to restrict their use of Lightner doubles to situations in which they are not obviously considering a sacrifice. In an auction such as

North	*East*	*South*	*West*
1 ♣	2 ♠*	3 ♡	4 ♠
5 ♡	Pass	6 ♡	Pass
Pass	Double		

these partnerships prefer to use the double to help them decide whether or not to sacrifice. *See* NEGATIVE SLAM DOUBLES, POSITIVE SLAM DOUBLES.

Previous Action by the Doubler

When the partner of the opening leader makes a Lightner slam double, the opening leader must consider the meaning of the double in light of the entire previous auction. Suppose, for example, that West has

♠ Q x x   ♡ Q x x x x   ◇ x x x x   ♣ K

and the auction has gone

---

*Preemptive

South	West	North	East
1 ♠	Pass	3 ♠	Pass
4 Notrump	Pass	5 ♡	Pass
6 ♠	Pass	Pass	Double

East's double calls for an unusual lead, and West's longest suit is hearts; East might be void in hearts. However, West should not lead a heart, because East had an opportunity to double hearts for a heart lead; he did not do so. Therefore, he cannot want a heart lead. East is likely to be void in some suit, so West looks for his next longest suit, diamonds. The whole hand might be:

North
♠ J x x x
♡ A K
♢ x x x x
♣ A x x

West
♠ Q x x
♡ Q x x x x
♢ x x x x
♣ K

East
♠ x
♡ J x x x x
♢ —
♣ Q J x x x x x

South
♠ A K 10 9 x
♡ x
♢ A K Q J x
♣ x x

Unless West leads a diamond, he will get his trump trick and nothing more. A diamond lead, however, beats the spade slam.

If the partner of the opening leader has doubled the slam but has also doubled a cue-bid or other artificial bid during the course of the auction, a question is raised as to the meaning of the final double. For example, suppose that in the above auction East had doubled five hearts and then doubled the final contract of six spades. Some players would hold that the message in East's final double is mere emphasis that the slam is sure to be defeated if the suit previously doubled is led. However, the stakes are so much greater than the 50 or 100 point increase in the value of the penalty, that the better view is that the final double said, "Cancel previous message."

Indeed, when the partner of the opening leader has the opportunity to double twice it is sometimes possible for him to remove all guesswork for the opening leader as to which suit should be led. For example, if the bidding has gone

South	West	North	East
2 ♠*	Pass	2 Notrump*	Pass
3 ◇	Pass	4 ◇	Pass
4 ♡	Pass	4 ♠	Pass
4 Notrump	Pass	5 ♣	(?)
6 ◇	Pass	Pass	(?)

If East doubles only the final contract of six diamonds, his double clearly calls for a spade lead—the only obviously genuine side suit bid by the opponents. If East doubles five clubs and does not double the final contract of six diamonds, his double clearly calls for a club lead. Since East can convey either of those messages so unambiguously with one double, if he doubles both five clubs and six diamonds, his final double should ask for a heart lead.

Sometimes the player who will eventually be the opening leader doubles a cue-bid or other artificial bid knowing it can-

---

*Strong two-bid with negative response.

not affect the lead, but hoping that it will assist his partner in the defense. If the opponents have not bid a side suit and his partner doubles the final contract, it asks the opening leader to lead the suit he had doubled.

Lead Directing Doubles of Suit Game Contracts

Lightner doubles may be extended to game contracts bid in power auctions. For example:

North	East	South	West
1 ♠	Pass	3 ♠	Pass
4 ♠	Pass	Pass	Double

West's double is a Lightner double, calling for an unusual lead. But in an auction such as

North	East	South	West
1 ♣	Pass	1 ♡	Pass
1 ♠	Pass	2 ♠	Pass
3 ♠	Pass	4 ♠	Double

West's double suggests that the opponents have overreached and are going down. West probably has strength in dummy's side suit, hearts, but the double does not require an unusual lead.

Which Card to Lead

When leading from a suit that the Lightner doubler is expected to ruff, informing the doubler how many cards the leader holds in the suit is usually unimportant. The opening leader should attempt, therefore, to give his partner a SUIT PREFERENCE SIGNAL. He leads the lowest card he has in the suit to recommend that his partner return the lower ranking side suit; he leads a very high card to recommend the return of the higher ranking side suit; or he leads a middle card to deny any strong preference as between the two side suits.

When the lead directing double is more likely to have been made on power than on a void, and the lead is being made in a suit in which dummy has length, the opening leader should lead the highest card he has in the suit. For example, suppose West has

♠ x x   ♡ J 9 x   ◇ J x x x   ♣ J x x x

and the auction has been

South	West	North	East
1 ♣	Pass	1 ♡	Pass
1 ♠	Pass	2 ♠	Pass
3 ♠	Pass	4 ♠	Double

West should lead the jack of hearts. East may well have the ace and queen; if he has the ten as well and dummy has the king, the lead of the jack will allow West to hold the lead for another run-through.

DOUBLES OF THREE NOTRUMP

Doubles of three notrump contracts have a variety of meanings depending on the previous auction. These doubles normally do not call for unusual leads unless the previous auction has not tended to suggest which may be the partnership's best suit.

If the doubler has bid a suit, the double normally calls for the lead of his suit. For example:

North	East	South	West
1 ♢	1 ♡	1 Notrump	Pass
3 Notrump	Double		

East's double of three notrump requests a heart lead. East is likely to have a semi-solid suit and a diamond stopper.

If the doubler has not bid a suit but the opening leader has bid a suit, the double calls for the opening leader to lead his own suit. For example:

South	West	North	East
1 ♢	1 ♠	2 ♣	Pass
2 Notrump	Pass	3 Notrump	Double

East's double requests a spade lead. He is likely to have a filler for West's broken suit, plus some high cards that suggest to him that the declarer will not be able to make nine tricks if a spade is led.

If both the doubler and the opening leader have bid suits of their own, there is no logical way to tell definitively which suit the doubler wants led. The partnership should make explicit agreements as to which suit is called for.

If neither the doubler nor the opening leader has bid a suit but dummy has bid a suit, the double calls for the lead of the suit bid by dummy. For example:

North	East	South	West
1 ♡	Pass	1 Notrump	Pass
2 Notrump	Pass	3 Notrump	Pass
Pass	Double		

East's double calls for a heart lead. This principle, however, must not be applied willy nilly. For example if the dummy has rebid his suit, a double of three notrump more likely means that the doubler has a stopper in the suit, and a source of tricks elsewhere. For example if the bidding has gone

North	East	South	West
1 ♣	Pass	1 ♠	Pass
2 ♣	Pass	2 ♡	Pass
3 ♣	Pass	3 Notrump	Pass
Pass	Double		

East's double does not call for a club lead. He might have a hand such as

♠ x x x   ♡ A x x   ◇ K Q J x   ♣ K x x

If the defenders have not bid a suit and dummy has bid a suit by inference, the double should be interpreted to call for the lead of that suit. For example

South	West	North	East
1 Notrump	Pass	2 ♣	Pass
2 ♠	Pass	3 Notrump	Double

Having used two clubs as Stayman ostensibly to learn whether opener has a four card major suit, North appears to have four hearts, since he returned to notrump over South's two spade bid. East may double three notrump, therefore, to ask for a heart lead.

If no suit has been bid by any of the players, there are a variety of meanings that can be ascribed to the double. Most partnerships use the double to show a long running suit; the partner of the doubler is therefore required to lead his shortest and weakest suit. For example, if the auction has gone

South	West	North	East
1 Notrump	Pass	3 Notrump	Double

and West has

♠ Q J 10   ♡ x x   ♢ x x x x   ♣ J 10 9 x

West should lead a heart.

Some partnerships avoid having the opening leader guess which suit to lead by arbitrarily agreeing that the double calls for a specific suit. Some partnerships agree that the double calls for a spade lead; some agree that it calls for a club lead. *See also* FISHER DOUBLES.

FISHER DOUBLES

Fisher doubles assign precise meanings to the double of three notrump after the bidding has been opened one notrump. If the responder has not used a two-club Stayman bid, the double calls for a club lead. If the responder has used Stayman and the two club bid has not been doubled, the double calls for a diamond lead. For example

South	West	North	East
1 Notrump	Pass	2 ♣	Pass
2 ♠	Pass	3 Notrump	Double

Using Fisher doubles, East's double would call for a diamond lead.

ACE FROM ACE-KING

Standard practice is to lead the highest of all honor card sequences, with one exception. The exception is that the king is led from an ace-king combination. This exception creates an ambiguity in the lead of the king: assuming that no revealing cards are tabled in the dummy, the partner of the opening leader frequently does not know whether the king has been led from ace-king or from king-queen.

When the king is led and the third hand has the jack of that suit, he would like to signal encouragement if his partner has led from the king and queen, but not if his partner has led from the king and ace. When the king is led against a suit contract and third hand has a doubleton and the ability to ruff the third round of the suit, he would like to signal encouragement if his partner has led from the king and ace, but not if his partner has led from the king and queen. The ambiguity of the king lead is therefore a serious problem on many hands.

In order to eliminate the ambiguity of the king lead, some partnerships agree to lead the ace from a suit headed by the ace and king. Using this convention, the lead of the king is always from a suit headed by the king and queen (unless the leader has a doubleton).

The drawback to this arrangement is that, against a suit contract, it is frequently advantageous to lead an unsupported ace. Therefore, rather than eliminating all ambiguity, the ace-from-ace-king convention may simply transfer the ambiguity from the king lead to the ace lead. *See* RUSINOW LEADS.

RUSINOW LEADS

Rusinow leads, which are used only against suit contracts, not against notrump, remove the ambiguity of the standard king lead (*see discussion under* ACE FROM ACE-KING) by requiring that the second ranking of touching honors be led. With more than two honor cards in sequence, the second ranking is still led. Thus, from the A K or A K Q, the king would be led; from K Q or K Q J, the queen would be led; from Q J or Q J 10, the jack would be led; from J 10 or J 10 9, the ten would be led; and from 10 9 or 10 9 8, the nine would be led.

Rusinow leads are used only on opening lead, and only in a suit that the leader's partner has not introduced. After the opening lead has been made the highest of touching honors is led. Similarly, if the opening leader is fortunate enough to have touching honors in a suit introduced by his partner, his lead from that suit should be the highest of those honors.

If the honors to be led are doubleton, the order of leading is reversed. Thus, using Rusinow leads, the higher honor is led, followed by the lower in order to show a doubleton.

Rusinow leads are not used against notrump contracts. Against notrump it is more important to exchange information as to the length and general strength of the suit led, than to clarify the ambiguity created by standard king leads.

QUEEN FROM ACE-KING-QUEEN

Some partnerships agree that the queen will be led from suits headed by the ace, king and queen. This convention allows the partner of the leader to encourage when he has the jack in the suit. However, it does not give him sufficient information to allow him to encourage confidently with a doubleton.

JOURNALIST HONOR LEADS
AGAINST SUITS

See RUSINOW LEADS.

JOURNALIST HONOR LEADS
AGAINST NOTRUMP

Standard practice against notrump contracts is to lead the highest of touching honors from a complete, or nearly complete, three-card sequence. For example, the king is led from K Q J; the queen is led from Q J 10; the jack is led from J 10 9; the ten is led from 10 9 8.

If the third card in the suit to be led is one pip away from being in sequence with the two top touching honors, the top card is led. For example, the king is led from K Q 10; the queen is led from Q J 9; the jack is led from J 10 8; the 10 is led from 10 9 7.

When the top honor in a suit is one or more cards distant from a sequence headed by an honor, the sequence is called an interior sequence. For example, the jack heads the interior sequence in A J 10 x or K J 10 x. The ten heads the interior sequence in A 10 9 x, or K 10 9 x or Q 10 9 x. Standard practice when leading a suit containing an interior sequence is to lead the second highest card, i.e., the top of the interior sequence. Thus, the jack would be led from A J 10 x or K J 10 x; the ten would be led from A 10 9 x, or K 10 9 x or Q 10 9 x.

The practice of leading the highest of three-card sequences and leading the top of interior sequences creates ambiguities when the jack or the ten is led. Frequently the partner of the leader will have a holding in the suit with which he will wish to continue the suit if it is the top of an interior sequence, but shift to another suit if the jack or ten is the leader's highest card in the suit. For example, suppose the jack of clubs is led by West against a three notrump contract and the dummy and third hand are as follows:

North
♠ A K J x x
♡ A Q J x
◇ x x
♣ x x

Lead: ♣ J

East
♠ x x x
♡ x x x
◇ Q J 10 x
♣ A 9 x

If West has led from K J 10 x x of clubs, East should continue clubs in order to defeat three notrump. On the other hand, if the jack is West's highest club, East should shift to the queen of diamonds in hopes that West has the ace and that the partnership can take four diamond tricks to beat the contract.

Using Journalist methods, the opening lead of the jack denies possession of a higher honor in the suit; the lead of the ten promises possession of the ace, king or queen. In this way the Journalist system eliminates the ambiguity of the standard leads which use both jack and ten leads from interior sequences. In the hand above, in which West led the jack of clubs, a partnership using Journalist leads would have no trouble shifting to a diamond, because the lead of the jack cannot be made from a holding such as K J 10 x, but promises a holding such as J 10 9 x or J 10 8 x. From an interior sequence, such as A J 10 x, A 10 9 x, Q 10 9 x, etc., the ten is led.

In Journalist, the lead of the nine promises either the ten, or no higher honor, or at most a doubleton in the suit. The nine must be led from a holding such as 10 9 8 x or 10 9 7 x because the lead of the ten would promise one of the top three honors in the suit. From three cards headed by the nine, therefore, the nine may not be led; the middle card should be led instead.

The Journalist method of leading against notrump contracts deals not just with the ambiguous jack and ten leads, but assigns a specific message to each honor card lead. Each honor card meaning is designed to make it easier for the leader or his partner to know whether the suit led should be continued or abandoned.

The lead of the ace is usually from a holding such as A K J x x, or A K Q 10 x (x), or A K 10 9 x.

The partner of the leader is requested to unblock a high card in the suit; otherwise he should start a COUNT SIGNAL, playing his lowest card with an odd number of cards, or starting a high-low echo with an even number of cards. For example, if third hand has J x x, he should play the jack on the lead of the ace. If he has 4 3 2, he should play the two to give count. If he has the 10 9 8 x, he should play the 10, followed by the 8 and 9, in case the opening lead was from a suit such as A K Q 7 x.

Using Journalist methods, the lead of the king could be from a suit headed either by the ace and king or the king and queen. The lead of the king asks third hand whether or not he likes the suit. If he likes the suit he encourages by following with a high card; if he prefers another suit, he plays a low card. The opening leader might have length in the suit led, but he might also have just A K x or K Q x and be trying to find his partner's long suit.

The lead of the queen may be made from a suit headed by the Q J 10, or from a suit headed by the K Q 10 9. In the latter event, third hand is requested to play the jack under the queen if he has it. The use of the queen lead to ask partner to unblock the jack avoids the Bath coup situation, in which the declarer, holding A J x in the suit led, plays low on the standard lead of the king. In the standard situation, the opening leader frequently continues the suit into the declarer's ace-jack tenace; or the opening leader sometimes shifts to another suit not knowing that his partner has the jack. The Journalist queen lead solves this problem, because if the partner of the leader does not play the jack under the queen, he does not have it.

JACK, TEN OR NINE TO SHOW 0 OR 2
HIGHER HONORS

Some partnerships use a system of secondary honor card leads against notrump that reduces, but does not eliminate entirely, the ambiguity of the standard jack and ten leads. (*See discussion under* JOURNALIST HONOR LEADS AGAINST NOTRUMP.) They agree that the opening lead of the jack, ten or nine promises that the leader has either two honors higher than the card led, or no higher honors. For example, the jack would be led from A Q J 10 x; the 10 would be led from A J 10 x or K J 10 x; the nine would be led from A 10 9 x, or K 10 9 x, or Q 10 9 x.

While there is obviously an inherent ambiguity, usually the partner of the opening leader can determine whether the leader has two higher honors or none. For example, in the example given above, in which the opening lead was the jack of clubs and the partner of the leader had A 9 x of clubs, it would be clear that the jack was the highest honor held by West in that suit; since he obviously would not lead the jack from K Q J he must have no honors higher than the jack. If West had led the ten of clubs in that example, instead of the jack, and East again held the A 9 x, East could infer that West had led from the K J 10 x (x) of clubs; since West did not have the nine, the ten could not have been from the top of a sequence.

Since the partner of the opening leader will more often than not gain sufficient information from the auction and holdings in dummy and his own hand to infer whether his partner has two honors or no honor higher than the jack, ten or nine he has led, the ambiguity in this conventional system of leading is not a substantial drawback. And in return for the slight ambiguity for the defenders, the lead may make it more difficult for the declarer to determine just where the high cards in the suit led are located.

Some partnerships use these jack, ten and nine leads throughout the hand.

THIRD BEST LEADS

Standard practice is to lead the fourth best card from a suit headed by one honor or non-touching honors. From a three-card suit headed by an honor, it is also standard practice to lead the lowest card. Therefore, the lead of the deuce of a suit (either the actual deuce or the effective deuce, as when the lead is the 4 and third hand can see the 2 and 3 in his own hand or dummy) could be from either a four-card suit or a three-card suit. The difference may be crucial to the defense, as when third hand must decide whether to try to cash another trick in the suit led or to try another suit.

One method devised to help clarify the length of the suit in which a low card is led is to lead the third highest card in the suit. Using this method, and holding Q 8 6 2, for example, the six would be led rather than the two. It will be noted that, using this convention, the lead of a non-deuce does not reveal immediately to the partner of the leader whether the lead is from a three-card suit or a four-card suit. However, the lead of the deuce shows immediately that the lead is not from four cards.

Third-best leads are equally usable against notrump and suit contracts. With respect to fourth-best leads, the partner of the leader usually applies the Rule of Eleven in order to reconstruct the declarer's potential high card holding in the suit led. Using third-best leads, the partner of the leader should apply a Rule of Twelve. Thus, he would subtract the size of the card led from twelve rather than from eleven, to determine how many cards higher than the card led are in the hands other than that of the opening leader.

JOURNALIST SPOT CARD LEADS AGAINST SUIT CONTRACTS

Against suit contracts, Journalist methods distinguish between three-card suits and four-card suits in the same manner that THIRD-BEST leads do. The Journalist method is to lead the third best card from a four-card suit. However, leading the third best card from suits of all lengths would fail to help the partner of the leader to distinguish between four-card and five-card suits, or between five-card and six-card suits.

In order to provide maximum assistance, Journalist applies what it calls the "two-card difference principle". The theory, which is also a basis for using the lead of the JACK, TEN OR NINE TO SHOW ZERO OR TWO HIGHER HONORS, is that it is a great deal easier to fathom which of two holdings the lead is from when the possibilities are two cards apart than when they are one card apart.

Thus, Journalist methods require the lead of the third best card when the suit has an even number of cards in it. The partner of the leader should be able to determine whether the lead is from a doubleton, or a four-card suit or a six-card suit, or an eight-card suit. From suits containing an odd number of cards, Journalist methods use the lead of the lowest card: third best from three, fifth best from five, seventh best from seven.

While there are inherent ambiguities, these leads can be of valuable assistance to the partner of the leader. For example, suppose West leads the deuce of a suit in which North and East have the following holdings:

North
Q 8 x x

Lead: 2

East
A J 9 x

A low card is played from dummy. Using standard methods, East is tempted to play the ace for fear that declarer might have the singleton king. Using Journalist leads, however, West must have either three or five cards in the suit, having led the lowest. Therefore, if declarer has the king of the suit, he has at least one other card with it; East is safe in playing the ten (assuming there are not sufficient discards in other suits for declarer to rid himself of the rest of the suit).

In a similar situation the lead of the non-deuce can help to clarify matters for East. Suppose West leads the four of a suit in which North and East have the following holdings:

North
Q 8 7 5

Lead: 3

East
A J 9

Here again, the auction may lead East to fear that the declarer has a singleton king in the suit led. Using standard methods, West's three could be from a five-card suit. Using Journalist methods, however, if West has a five card suit, declarer's singleton must be the deuce.

When third hand believes that the opening leader has led his fifth best card, he can reconstruct the declarer's potential by applying the Rule of Ten. He subtracts the size of the card led from ten, and the remainder represents the number of cards in his own hand, dummy and declarer's hand that can beat the opening leader's card.

Some partnerships agree to use Journalist spot card leads not only on opening lead, but throughout the hand. These leads are tantamount to COUNT SIGNALS—a high lead from a suit with an even number of cards, and a low lead from a suit with an odd number of cards. Use of these leads during the course of the defense can be quite useful.

JOURNALIST SPOT CARD LEADS AGAINST NOTRUMP

The Journalist method of leading against suit contracts is not carried over into leads against notrump contracts. Against notrump the important goal is to recognize which is the best suit in general for the defense, rather than specifically how many cards the opening leader has in the suit.

Against notrump contracts, therefore, the Journalist method is to lead a low card from a suit that the opening leader wants returned. Usually this suit is headed by one or more honor cards. In general, the lower the card that is led, the more eager the leader is to have the suit returned. For example, from A 10 8 6 3, the correct lead would be the three.

Conversely, when the opening leader has little strength in the suit he starts, and wants some other suit returned, he should lead a high card. For example, against a contract of one notrump, with a hand such as

♠ K J x x   ♡ A Q x   ◇ 10 8 7 2   ♣ K x

the best lead is probably the eight of diamonds, in order to encourage partner to return another suit in which a tenace is held.

MUD LEADS

Perhaps the most troublesome of all specific leading questions is what to lead from three small cards. The difficulty is that it is impossible to formulate an unvarying rule as to whether it is better to clarify length than strength, or vice versa.

The traditional lead of the top three small cards has the virtue of relieving the leader's partner of any notion that the lead is from a suit headed by an honor. Unfortunately, it also relieves the declarer of any such notion, and, in addition, may deceive the partner of the leader into believing that it is the top of a doubleton.

The lead of a low card from three small cards avoids the confusion as to whether the opening leader has three cards or a doubleton. However, the price of this clarification is the suggestion to the leader's partner that the suit led might be headed by an honor.

One compromise that has been devised is to lead the middle card from a holding of three small cards. When next that suit is played the opening leader will play his highest, and lastly his lowest. This convention is called MUD, an acronym for the order in which the cards are played: Middle, Up, Down.

MUD leads are not used in a suit bid by the partner of the opening leader. In such a suit the opening leader should lead low from three small cards if he has not supported the suit. If he has supported the suit, however, his partner will infer that he has at least three card support, and in that circumstance he should lead his highest card to deny possession of an honor.

Like all compromises, MUD leads are a little bit fishy and a little bit fowl. A system that requires the lead of the same card from, e.g., K 7 3 or 9 7 3 or 7 3 does not give the partner of the leader a great deal of help.

ROMAN MUD

MUD methods may also be used when leading from four small cards. Using this extension, called Roman Mud, the opening leader leads the second highest from his four small cards, then he follows with the highest, then with the third highest and finally plays the lowest. For example, if the suit in which the opening lead is to be made is 8 5 3 2, the five would be led; at his next opportunities the opening leader would play the eight, then the three, then the two.

Roman Mud is easier on the partner of the opening leader than simple MUD is. On the two-card-difference principle, it is easier to recognize a lead as being from a doubleton when the alternative is that it is from four cards, than when the alternative is that it is from three cards. However, the partner of the leader will be at pains to guess whether the lead is from three small or four small cards.

JOURNALIST LEADS FROM
HONORLESS SUITS

Using Journalist leads, the lead of a small card tends to suggest that the suit is headed by an honor. From an honorless suit the opening leader using Journalist methods is allowed to use his judgment as to whether it is more important that his partner be apprised of the length or of the strength of the suit led.

If the leader wants to tell his partner that he has no honor in the suit, he leads the highest card he can afford. In Journalist this is never higher than the eight since the nine would imply possession of the ten.

In the leader wants instead to reveal his length in the suit led, he makes his normal Journalist lead of third best from an even number of cards and the lowest from an odd number of cards.

ATTITUDE SIGNALS

Traditionally, a defender shows interest in having a suit led or continued by playing a high card in that suit. He discourages by playing a low card. For example, if West leads the king of diamonds against a four spade contract and dummy has ◇ Q x x and East has ◇ 9 x, East will play the nine of diamonds if he wants the suit continued so that he may get an immediate ruff. If he does not want to ruff, or if he wants some other suit led first, he will play his lower diamond.

A defender may encourage the lead of a particular suit by playing discouraging cards in the other suits. For example, suppose West leads a club against a three notrump contract, and dummy and East have the following hands:

North
♠ K J
♡ K x x
◇ Q x x x
♣ A J x x

Lead: ♣ 8

East
♠ A Q 10 9
♡ x x x x
◇ x x x
♣ x x

After the lead, declarer cashes four rounds of clubs. East must discard on the third and fourth clubs. He plays his lowest heart and his lowest diamond, to encourage West, if he gets the lead, to play a spade.

If East had held instead

588

♠ A Q 10 9 8   ♡ x x x   ◇ x x   ♣ x x x

and had to make only one discard on the run of the clubs, he would have thrown the ten of spades to give West the same message.

When a defender plays a high card to encourage his partner to play that suit, he should take care not to be wasteful. For instance, in the above example, if East had ♠ A Q 10 3 2, he could not afford to signal with the ten, for South might have three spades headed by the nine, which would then become a stopper.

When to Show Attitude

In general a defender should signal encouragement or discouragement to his partner's lead of an honor card. The opening lead is the most difficult facet of bridge, and often the opening leader needs a sign from his partner as to whether or not his attack has hit pay dirt.

However, third hand need not encourage just because he has a doubleton, or just because he has a filling card in the suit led. He must consider the hand as a whole. For example, if West leads the king of a side suit of which dummy has Q x x and East has 9 2, East cannot determine whether he will signal encouragement without considering his other suits as well. If East has the J 10 9 8 of trumps, for instance, he is not normally interested in ruffing; he has a natural trump trick, which one ruff will not augment.

If dummy had Q x of the suit led and East had the 9 2, East would have to examine his own and dummy's trumps in order to know whether or not to encourage. If East has the 3 2 of trumps and dummy the 5 4, there is no point in encouraging, because East cannot overruff the dummy.

If East, rather than dummy, had the Q x of the suit led, he should not signal with the queen, because the play of that card has a specific meaning. *See* SIGNALS TO SHOW SPECIFIC HONOR CARDS.

Sometimes East will have a filling card for West's lead, but will want West to shift to another suit. Suppose West led the king of diamonds against a three spade contract in the following hand:

North
♠ K x x x
♡ K x x
♢ x x
♣ A K 10 x

Lead: ♢ K

East
♠ x x
♡ A Q J
♢ Q 8 5 2
♣ x x x x

East should play the two of diamonds at trick one to defeat the three spade contract. He wants West to shift to a heart while West still has the ace of diamonds as an entry for a second heart lead.

Occasionally against a slam contract, rather than encouraging or discouraging, East will want to tell his partner how many cards he holds in the suit led. For example, suppose West leads the king of hearts against a six spade contract, and dummy and East have the following hands:

North
♠ K Q x
♡ Q x x
♢ A Q J x
♣ A J x

Lead: ♡ K

East
♠ x x
♡ J 7 4 2
♢ K x x x
♣ x x x

East has no way of knowing whether a second heart can be cashed, or whether West should shift to a diamond. East should therefore play the seven of hearts to show an even number of hearts. West should recognize that East is giving count rather than attitude, and be able to determine whether or not the second heart can be cashed. From East's point of view declarer might have

♠ A J x x x   ♡ x x   ♢ x   ♣ K Q x x x

in which case a second round of hearts is required to prevent declarer's taking a ruffing finesse in diamonds and discarding his losing heart. Alternatively, declarer might have

♠ A J x x x   ♡ x   ♢ x x   ♣ K Q x x x

in which case a second round of hearts would allow South to discard his losing diamond on the queen of hearts. East's count signal will clarify for West which hand declarer holds.

After the initial stages of the hand, a defender may signal attitude by making a high or low discard in a suit other than the suit led. His first discard in any suit should indicate whether or not he is interested in having that suit led. Again, however, his interest is a relative matter; he should not discard a high card simply to show tolerance for a lead of that suit if he prefers the lead of another suit.

UPSIDE-DOWN SIGNALS

Upside Down signals are attitude signals that reverse the traditional method of showing interest and aversion. To encourage the lead or continuation of a suit using Upside Down signals, the defender plays a low card in the suit; to discourage he plays a high card.

This method has two benefits. First it minimizes the danger that a useful card will be wasted in signaling. Second, it reduces the declarer's ability to falsecard successfully. Suppose for example that West leads the jack of spades in defending against a three notrump contract, and the spade suit is distributed as follows:

North
♠ 10 7 6 3

West	*East*
♠ J 5	♠ K Q 9 2

South
♠ A 8 4

East cannot afford to encourage with the nine. Use of Upside Down signals allows him to encourage with a card he can spare.

Suppose West leads the king of hearts against a spade contract and dummy's and East's hearts are as follows:

North
♡ 9 8 7

Lead: ♡ K

East
♡ 6 5 3

Using standard signals East would play the three of hearts. If declarer has ♡ A J 4 2, he should play the four. West then would know whether East started with ♡ 6 5 3 or ♡ A 3 2 or ♡ J 3 2.

Using Upside Down signals, however, East would follow suit with the 6 from 6 5 3, which West would surely read as a high and discouraging card. If East had J 6 5 3 instead, he would play the three to encourage. It is true, of course, that the declarer could still play the four from ♡ A 4 2, attempting to persuade West that East's three is a high card. However, if East wants to discourage it is quite likely that he can afford a spot higher than the three.

ODD-EVEN SIGNALS

Odd-even signals, sometimes called Roman signals, are a method of encouraging or discouraging that depends on whether the number of the card played is odd or even, rather than on whether it is high, middle or low. A defender plays an odd numbered card to encourage, or an even numbered card to discourage.

In addition, when an even card is played, the size of the card tends to suggest which of the other suits the defender prefers. For example, if a defender holds ♡ 8 5 2 and wants to encourage the lead or continuation of the heart suit, he plays the five. If he wants to discourage, he has his choice between the eight and the two. He plays the eight if he wants his partner to lead the higher ranking non-trump suit, e.g., spades if clubs or diamonds are trumps; he plays the two if he wants his partner to lead the lower ranking non-trump suit, e.g., diamonds if clubs are trumps.

Just as problems arise with standard signals when "subtle" cards are held (e.g., Q 3 2 in a suit in which partner leads the king), sometimes it will occur that a defender does not have an odd card when he needs it, or an even card when he needs it. In the absence of an odd card with which to encourage, the Odd-Even practice is to play an even card that would call for the more improbable suit preference.

For example, suppose East has the 8 5 doubleton in diamonds against a spade contract, and his partner leads the king of diamonds, promising the ace. East would play the ◇ 5 to encourage continuation of diamonds. If East's doubleton were the ◇ 7 4, he would play the 7 to encourage. However, if East's doubleton were the ◇ 6 2, he would have a slight problem. In this situation, he examines dummy's side suit holdings,

clubs and hearts, and issues the more improbable suit preference signal. For example, if dummy has ♣ A K Q x and ♡ K x,
East would play the ◇ 2, technically calling for a club shift.
However, the club shift is so improbable that West should be
able to infer that East simply has no odd numbered cards, but
in fact wants to encourage West to continue.

If East has no even cards but wants to discourage, he should
tend to discard as he would have if he were not using odd-even
discards. Holding 7 5 3, for example, if the partnership is using
standard signals East would play the three. If the partnership is
using UPSIDE DOWN SIGNALS, East should play the seven.

SIGNALS TO SHOW SPECIFIC
HONOR CARDS

When a defender has two or more honors in a suit and can afford to discard one of them, it is standard practice for him to throw the higher honor if his honors are touching. If the top honor is out of sequence with the other(s), he should throw the second highest.

For example, when West leads the king of spades and East has ♠ Q J x, he should play the queen. The play of the queen promises that East has the jack, and enables West to underlead his ace of spades to put East on lead, either to clear the suit without further crashing of honors, or to lead another suit. If East had ♠ J 10 x, his proper play would be the jack, which would deny possession of the queen and promise the ten.

Because of the traditional meaning of the play of the queen under the king, East cannot signal high-low with a doubleton queen, because West will likely place East with the jack and underlead his ace at the second trick. Holding J x, however, East is allowed to throw the jack if he wants a ruff. The rationale is, first, that West is unlikely to have the A K Q of the suit, without which he could not underlead at the second trick, and second, that the Jack is not so valuable a card as the queen.

If West leads a low card against a notrump contract and East has three cards in the suit led headed by a pair of honors, which cannot beat the card played from the dummy, East should throw the higher honor if his honors are touching, and throw the second ranking honor if his honors are not touching. For example, suppose West leads a heart and the dummy's and East's holdings are as follows:

North
♡ A 8

Lead: ♡ 3

East
♡ Q J 4

When the ♡ A is played from the dummy it is standard for East to follow with the queen. This play is in part a signal that East has the jack but not the king, and in part an unblocking of partner's suit. If instead of ♡ Q J 4 East had K 10 4, his proper play would be the ten, which would promise either a higher honor not including the jack, or a sequence headed by the ten.

Similarly, when discarding honor cards on the run of another suit, the ace is played from A K Q, the king from K Q J, the queen from Q J 10, and so forth. If there is a gap in the sequence, the second highest honor is thrown. Thus, the queen is thrown from A Q J, the jack from A J 10 or K J 10, the ten from A 10 9, K 10 9 or Q 10 9.

For example, suppose South has opened the bidding with two notrump which is passed out, and East and dummy have the following hands:

North
♠ x x x x
♡ x x x
♢ Q x x
♣ x x x

Lead: ♠ J

East
♠ K Q 9 x
♡ Q x x
♢ A x x
♣ x x x

West has led the jack of spades, which South ducked once, and then won the second round with the ace. South played the king and jack of diamonds which East ducked, and then a third diamond which East won. When East cashed his third spade, West followed, but when the fourth spade was cashed West discarded the ten of hearts. The discard of the ten denied possession of the jack; therefore East knew that if declarer had the king of hearts he also had the jack, so that a heart lead would only give South a chance to guess the heart position. East therefore exited with a club to force declarer to play hearts from his hand.

See also JOURNALIST HONOR LEADS AGAINST NOTRUMP, *and* FOSTER ECHO.

COUNT SIGNALS

The traditional method of giving count in a suit is to play first a high card followed by a low card with an even number of cards in the suit, and to play a low card followed by a higher card to show an odd number of cards. The reverse method is standard in some countries; and some partnerships use a combination of methods, playing high-low with an even number when following to a suit led by partner, and playing high-low with an odd number of cards if the suit is being led by the declarer or if the suit is being discarded on the run of another suit.

Length signals usually may not be given at the same time that attitude signals are being given. However, count signals may be given after the defender's attitude toward a certain suit has already been shown, by showing the defender's present count. For example, if a defender discards from ♡ 9 8 7 5 4 2 on the run of a suit in which he is void, his first discard should be the two to show disinterest, rather than a higher card to start showing an even number of cards in the suit. Thereafter the defender may show the present number of cards he has in the suit by playing the four—his lowest from his five remaining cards—followed by a higher card. If the defender had started with ♡ 9 8 5 4 2, his first discard would be the two, but his next two discards would be in high-low order to show an even number of cards remaining after the attitude signal. *See also* BECHGAARD SIGNALS.

Count signals should rarely be given in following to the opening lead, when the opening leader more often needs to receive encouragement or discouragement. Similarly, when a new suit is led by a defender, it is frequently more helpful for the other defender to signal his attitude rather than his length, although there are circumstances when length should be shown.

When the declarer attacks a suit, however, it is usually more advantageous to show length than attitude. If it is really desirable for declarer to be playing the suit, it is unlikely that a defender will want to encourage the other defender to lead it. Count signals, however, should not be given when they would help the declarer more than the defense.

Length signals have their greatest utility when the declarer is attempting to establish a long suit in a dummy that has no outside-entries. When one defender has the ace of the suit and needs to hold up only long enough for declarer's supply to be exhausted, he depends on his partner to signal his own length in the suit. For example, suppose the diamond suit were distributed as follows:

North
◇ K Q J 10 7

West　　　　　　　　　　　　*East*
◇ A 4 2　　　　　　　　　　◇ 9 6 3

South
◇ 8 5

On the first lead of the suit East would play the three to show an odd number of cards. West would then know that he should win the second round of the suit, either because East has three and South has a doubleton, or because East has a singleton and West cannot exhaust South's supply. If, instead of 9 6 3, East had 6 3, he would play the six on the first round, followed by the three on the second round. West would therefore realize that declarer had three diamonds and could hold up until the third round of the suit.

TRUMP ECHO

In the trump suit, if one defender wants to show his partner how many trumps he has, he does so by playing high-low with an odd number of trumps, and low-high with an even number. The use of the trump echo may be important when the question is whether or not a ruff is available. In order not to give declarer too much information, the trump echo is best reserved for such ruffing situations.

FOSTER ECHO

The Foster Echo is a combination count signal and unblocking play against notrump contracts. When a lead is made, if the third hand either cannot top the card led or cannot top the card played from the dummy, the Foster Echo convention requires him to play his second-highest card in the suit. If third hand has three cards in the suit his next play in the suit will be the highest card; if he has four cards in the suit his next play will be his third highest, followed by his highest, then his lowest.

For example, suppose a heart is led against three notrump, and the dummy and East have the following cards in the suit:

North

♡ A 8

Lead: ♡ 5

East

♡ 9 7 3

When the ace is played from dummy, East must follow with the seven. When the suit is next played, East will play the nine, showing that he started with three hearts.

The same principle applies when East started with two honors in the suit led. If his honors are not touching, the effect of using Foster Echos is not different from standard practice. However, if East had ♡ J 10 3, for example, using the Foster Echo would require him to follow with the ten rather than the jack; this creates a potential ambiguity, since East would also have played the ten from Q 10 3.

BECHGAARD SIGNALS

Bechgaard Signals are a precise method of discarding from long suits to reveal the length held in those suits. These signals are used to help the other defender to know declarer's length in the various suits. Each requires at least three discards to complete the message.

From a five-card suit, cards are discarded in a delayed echo pattern: for example, first the three, then the four, then the two. From a six-card suit, three cards are discarded in descending order: for example, the four, then the three, then the two. From a seven-card suit, four cards are discarded in a double-echo pattern: for example, the three, then the two, then the five, then the four.

Bechgaard signals are strictly count signals. They should not be used if there is a possibility that attitude should be shown in the suit being discarded.

SUIT PREFERENCE SIGNALS

A suit preference signal is a signal that obviously asks the partner of the signaler to play a specific other suit at his first opportunity. The purpose of the suit preference signal is to eliminate the guesswork as to which suit should be played next. When properly used, suit preference signals do not conflict with attitude signals. Therefore, in order to make a suit preference signal, the defender must play an unusually high card to call for the lead of a higher ranking suit, and an unusually low card to call for the lead of the lower ranking suit.

The suit preference signal never asks for a trump lead, nor for a continuation of the suit led; the choice is strictly between the side suits. For example, on the lead of a diamond against a spade contract, a low suit preference signal would ask for a club lead; a high suit preference signal would ask for a heart lead.

Suit preference signals should not be given in situations in which it is probable that length signals would be more useful. For example, suppose the king of hearts is led against a six spade contract and dummy and East are as follows:

North
♠ K Q x
♡ Q x x
♢ A Q J x
♣ A J x

Lead: ♡ K

East
♠ x x
♡ J 7 6 5 2
♢ K x x
♣ x x x

605

Obviously the primary question for West is whether or not he can cash the heart ace. Since East has no way of knowing how many hearts West has, his first responsibility is to tell West how many hearts East has. With the above hand, therefore, East's proper play is the two of hearts; this card promises an odd number of hearts; it does not ask West to shift to a club.

To be a suit preference signal, it must be obvious that a mere continuation of the suit led is not being requested. For example, suppose the king of hearts is led against a six spade contract and the dummy and East hands are these:

North
♠ K Q x
♡ x
♢ K Q x x x
♣ x x x

Lead: ♡ K

East
♠ x
♡ Q 10 7 3 2
♢ A x x x
♣ x x x

On the lead of the king of hearts, East would play the queen, an unusually high card in order to induce West to shift to a diamond. However, if East played the seven instead of the queen, this would not be a suit preference signal, but merely an encouraging card asking West to continue the suit. Instead of the hand above, East might have a hand such as

♠ J x x x   ♡ Q 10 7 3 2   ♢ x x   ♣ x x

and want to force dummy to ruff so that his jack of spades cannot be finessed.

Suit preference signals also should not be given where the play of the suit preference card could be mistaken for a signal of a specific honor card holding. For example, West leads the king of diamonds against a three spade contract, and dummy and East have the following hands:

North
♠ A K J x
♡ K x x
◇ x x
♣ J x x x

Lead: ◇ K

East
♠ x x
♡ A Q J
◇ Q 8 5 2
♣ x x x x

East would like to have West shift to a heart at trick two, so that East can return a diamond and West can lead through dummy's ♡ K another time. However, East cannot play the queen of diamonds to ask for a heart shift, because if West does not have the jack of diamonds, he will interpret East's queen as promising the jack. Instead, East must content himself with playing a discouraging two of diamonds, and hoping West will figure out that a heart should be led.

Suit preference signals are most valuable in situations in which a defender is giving, or will give, his partner a ruff, and wants to show where his entry is. For example, suppose West leads a singleton heart against a spade contract, and East has

♠ x x   ♡ A 9 7 5 4 2   ◇ A K x   ♣ x x

East wins the ace of hearts, and should return the nine of hearts, his highest, to show that his re-entry is in the higher ranking of the two side suits.

East can also give a suit preference signal in the situation in which he lacks the ace of the suit of the singleton, but has an entry elsewhere. Suppose the auction has been

North	East	South	West
Pass	1 ♡	1 ♠	2 ♡
2 ♠	Pass	3 ♠	4 ♡
4 ♠	Pass	Pass	Pass

West leads the two of clubs and the dummy and East hands are as follows:

North
♠ 10 7 5
♡ 3 2
♢ 7 4 3
♣ A K Q J 4

Lead: ♣ 2

East
♠ 9 2
♡ K J 10 7 4
♢ A K
♣ 10 8 6 3

West's club deuce is clearly a singleton. If he has a trump entry he will try to reach East for a club ruff. East should attempt to show West that his fast entry is in diamonds by playing the three of clubs. If East had the ace of hearts rather than the ace of diamonds, his proper suit preference signal would be the ten of clubs. Since there can be no question of encouraging or discouraging West in the club suit, and since West cannot have any interest in how many clubs East has, both partners should recognize East's opportunity to make a suit preference signal at trick one.

Suit preference signals may also be used by a defender who is clearing a suit at a notrump contract, to indicate to his partner in which suit he has an entry to his established cards. For example, suppose West leads the four of spades against three notrump and the spade suit is distributed as follows:

North
♠ x x x

West　　　　　　　　　　　*East*
♠ Q 9 8 4 2　　　　　　♠ A x

South
♠ K J 10

East wins and returns a spade, on which South plays the jack, West winning with the queen. West now has a choice of the 9, the 8 or the 2 to return. These cards are equals since the two remaining spades will fall together. West can choose to play the card that best reflects his side entry. If his entry is in hearts, the highest ranking suit, he may lead the nine; if his entry is in clubs, he may lead his lowest spade, the two; if his entry is in diamonds, he may lead his middle card. West may, of course, choose to return a deceptive card in order not to help declarer decide how best to play the hand.

REVOLVING DISCARDS

Suit preference signals are useful in discarding as well as in leading or following suit, although the American Contract Bridge League has not approved the use of such discards—called Lavinthal signals—for tournament play.

There are two methods by which suit preference discarding signals may be given. The first is similar to the SUIT PREFERENCE SIGNALS described above, in which the rank of the card played corresponds with the rank of the suit the defender wants led. For example, suppose West leads the three of hearts against three notrump, and the dummy and East hands are as follows:

North
♠ K 8 5
♡ 6
♢ K 10 9 8 4
♣ Q 7 3 2

Lead: ♡ 3

East
♠ 10 7 3
♡ A Q 5
♢ 7 2
♣ J 10 8 6 4

East plays the queen of hearts in order to retain the ace and to lead through South at the crucial time. South leads out the queen, jack and another diamond, West holding up until the third round to try to learn where East's entry lies. Using suit preference discards, East throws the four of clubs on the third round of diamonds, indicating that West should lead the lower ranking of the remaining suits, i.e., hearts. If East held only four clubs, so that he could not afford to discard a club, he could instead have discarded the ten of spades, asking for the higher ranking of the other suits, i.e., hearts.

The other method of making suit preference discards treats the suits as a complete circle, with clubs ranking above spades. Using this method, the discard of a low card in a suit calls for the lead of the next lower ranking suit; the discard of a high card calls for the lead of the next higher ranking suit. Thus, in the hand given above, East would have discarded the ten of clubs to call for the next higher ranking suit (excluding the suit being played by the declarer), i.e., hearts. Again, if East had held only four clubs and therefore could not afford a club discard, he could have thrown the spade three, calling for the suit ranking below spades.

The principal value of these suit preference discards is that they allow a clear signal to be given with a single card, even if the defender cannot afford to release a high card in the suit he wants played. And since the lead of any given suit can be called for in two ways, it is almost always possible for the defender to issue the signal without wasting a card he cannot afford.

ODD-EVEN DISCARDS

The use of odd-even cards for suit preference increases the already considerable flexibility available with Lavinthal and RE-VOLVING DISCARDS. As discussed above (*see* ODD-EVEN SIGNALS), the play of an odd card encourages the lead or continuation of that suit; and the size of an even, discouraging, card indicates which of the side suits the defender prefers.

Therefore, using odd-even discards for suit preference, the defender has three ways in which he can ask for the lead of a specific suit: he can play an odd card in the suit he wants led; or he can play the appropriately high even card from one of the side suits to call for the suit he wants; or he can play the appropriately low even card from the other side suit to call for the suit he wants. If East has, for example, a hand such as

♠ 10 7 2   ♡ A Q 4 3   ◇ 7 3   ♣ K 8 5 2

against a diamond contract, and he wants a heart lead, he has three choices. He can discard the three of hearts. Or he can discard the ten of spades, calling for the higher of the remaining side suits. Or he can discard the two of clubs, calling for the lower of the remaining side suits.

Using "revolving" odd-even discards, in which preferences are shown for touching suits, East would still have three choices. He could still play the three of hearts; or he could play the two of spades to call for the next suit below spades; or he could play the eight of clubs, calling for the next higher suit above clubs.

Index